The Quiet Man ... and Beyond

The Quiet Man ... and Beyond

Reflections on a Classic Film, John Ford and Ireland

Edited by
Seán Crosson and Rod Stoneman

The Liffey Press

≋the
**liffey
press**

Published by
The Liffey Press
Ashbrook House, 10 Main Street
Raheny, Dublin 5, Ireland
www.theliffeypress.com

© 2009 Seán Crosson, Rod Stoneman and contributors

A catalogue record of this book is
available from the British Library.

ISBN 978-1-905785-56-8

This publication was grant-aided by the Publication Fund
of **National University of Ireland, Galway**

Photographs in the text courtesy of Des MacHale
unless otherwise indicated
Frontispiece photo © Grace Duncan

Printed in the United Kingdom by Athenaeum Press

Contents

II

Language, Style and the Visualised Nation

III

Landscape, Politics and Identity

IV

Gender, Ethnicity and Mary Kate

V

Final Reflections

Acknowledgements

Our first thanks must go to the indefatigable Des MacHale, maths lecturer from University College Cork and self-designated quiet maniac, who walked into the Huston School of Film & Digital Media and suggested holding a conference that became *New Perspectives on The Quiet Man* at the end of September 2005. We are indebted to all the participants at that event, many of whom became those most patient of essayists whose writings are contained in this volume. It is due to them, and the other contributors, and to the good offices of David Givens of The Liffey Press that we have arrived at this volume. Later in the narrative there was the crucial and sagacious advice from Jonathan Williams who guided the project to realisation.

We would also like to thank Des MacHale and Grace Duncan for providing some of the images used in this book, as well as the Lilly Library, Indiana University, Bloomington, Indiana for images used in Chapter 5, 'Echoes of *The Playboy*: *The Quiet Man* and the Abbey'.

About the Contributors

RUTH BARTON is Lecturer in Film Studies at Trinity College Dublin. Her publications include: *Jim Sheridan: Framing the Nation* (2002), *Irish National Cinema* (2004) and *Acting Irish in Hollywood* (2006). She is the editor of the forthcoming *Screening Irish-America* and is writing a critical biography of Hedy Lamarr.

JAMES P. BYRNE is adjunct assistant professor of English at Emerson College, Boston. He is the editor of *Ireland and the Americas: Culture, Politics, and History* (3 volumes, 2008), and has had his work published in a number of journals, including *MELUS* and *IJAS*. He is currently working on producing a comprehensive cultural theory of Irish American ethnicity.

FIDELMA FARLEY is the author of two short monographs and several essays on Irish cinema, the most recent of which is 'Breac Scannáin/ Speckled Films: Genre and Irish-language Filmmaking', in *Genre and Irish Cinema* (ed. Brian McIlroy, 2007). She is currently editing a collection of essays on New Scottish Cinema with Jonathan Murray and Rod Stoneman.

RODDY FLYNN is a lecturer at the School of Communications, Dublin City University where he chairs the Masters Programme in Film and Television Studies. He co-wrote (with Pat Brereton) the *Historical Dictionary of Irish Cinema* (2007) and has two other forthcoming books relating to Irish cinema: *Cinema and State: Irish Film Policy since 1922* and *John Huston: Another Look*, the latter edited with Tony Tracy.

ADRIAN FRAZIER is the Director of the MA in Drama and Theatre Studies and the MA in Writing in the English Department, National University of Ireland, Galway. He has published on Irish poetry, drama, and fiction of the 20th century and his previous works include *Yeats, Horniman, and the Struggle for the Abbey Theatre* (1990) and *George Moore 1852–1933* (2000).

LUKE GIBBONS is Keough Family Professor of Irish Studies, University of Notre Dame, Indiana. He is the author of *Gaelic Gothic: Race, Colonialism and Irish Culture* (2004), *Edmund Burke and Ireland: Aesthetics, Politics and the Colonial Sublime* (2003), *The Quiet Man* (2002), *Transformations in Irish Culture* (1996), and co-author (with John Hill and Kevin Rockett) of *Cinema and Ireland* (1987).

MICHAEL PATRICK GILLESPIE is the Louise Edna Goeden Professor of English at Marquette University. His latest book is *The Myth of an Irish Cinema* (2008). His ongoing project is breaking 100 on the golf course.

CONOR GROOME graduated from NUI Galway with a BA in Philosophy and Classical Civilisation and later completed his Masters in Film Studies at University College Dublin. He has contributed to conferences in Ireland, Britain and the United States on various topics including 'the window' in French Cinema, the sit-com *Scrubs*, and the novels of Douglas Coupland.

JOHN HILL is Professor of Media at Royal Holloway, University of London. He is the author of *Sex, Class and Realism: British Cinema 1956–63* (1986), *Cinema and Ireland* (1987) (with Kevin Rockett and Luke Gibbons), *British Cinema in the 1980s* (1999) and *Cinema and Northern Ireland* (2006).

DES MACHALE was born in Castlebar, County Mayo in 1946. He lives in Cork with his wife Anne and their five children. He is Associate Professor of Mathematics at University College Cork and has written over sixty books, including three books on *The Quiet Man: The Com-*

plete Guide to The Quiet Man (2000); *Picture The Quiet Man* (2004); and *A Quiet Man Miscellany* (2009).

BARRY MONAHAN lectures in the history and aesthetics of Irish and other national cinemas, and film theory, at University College Cork. His forthcoming monograph, *Ireland's Theatre on Film: Style, Stories and the National Stage on Screen*, considers the relationship between the Abbey Theatre and cinema from the beginning of the sound period until the 1960s.

BRIAN Ó CONCHUBHAIR is Assistant Professor in the Department of Irish Language & Literature at the University of Notre Dame, Indiana. He has edited *Gearrscéalta Ár Linne* (2006) and *Why Irish? Irish Language & Literature in Academia* (2008). He is currently finalising a monograph on the Irish language revival entitled *Fin de Siècle na Gaeilge: Charles Darwin, An Athbheochan agus Gluaiseacht Smaointeoireacht na hEorpa*.

DÍÓG O'CONNELL teaches film and media studies at the Institute of Art, Design & Technology, Dún Laoghaire. Her PhD thesis explores narrative techniques in contemporary Irish cinema, currently being updated and developed into a book for publication. She has contributed articles to many recent collections on Irish film.

CAITRÍONA Ó TORNA has a BA and a PhD in Modern Irish from NUI, Galway and is a translator with Rannóg an Aistriúcháin in the Houses of the Oireachtas. She is the author of *Cruthú na Gaeltachta 1893–1922* (2005) and has had articles published in *New Voices in Irish Criticism 3*, *Comhar* and *An Aimsir Óg*.

TOM PAULUS teaches film studies (with an emphasis on film history and film aesthetics) in the Department of Language and Literature, and is a member of the research group on visual poetics, at the University of Antwerp. His essays on pictorial style in the films of John Ford have been published in two other edited collections, *John Ford in Focus* (2007) and *Westerns: Movies from Hollywood and Paperback Westerns* (2007).

SEAN RYDER teaches English at NUI Galway. He has published on film and on nineteenth century writing, and is currently involved in the creation of digital and multimedia resources for the humanities, including the Thomas Moore Hypermedia Archive.

EAMONN SLATER is a Senior Lecturer in the Department of Sociology at the National University of Ireland, Maynooth. He has edited two books with his colleague Dr. Michel Peillon: *Encounters with Modern Ireland* (1998) and *Memories of the Present* (2000). He is currently researching Marx's ideas on colonialism of Ireland and its ecological impact on Irish agriculture in the nineteenth century.

About the Editors

SEÁN CROSSON is a lecturer on Irish and world cinema with the Huston School of Film & Digital Media at the National University of Ireland, Galway where he is Programme Coordinator of the MA in Film Studies. His book *"The Given Note": Traditional Music and Modern Irish Poetry* was published in 2008 and he is co-editor (with Nessa Cronin and John Eastlake) of *Anáil an Bhéil Bheo: Orality and Modern Irish Culture* (2009).

ROD STONEMAN is the Director of the Huston School of Film & Digital Media. Formerly Chief Executive with Bord Scannán na hÉireann/The Irish Film Board, he has made a number of documentaries for television and has written on film in various journals and books including *Screen, Sight and Sound, Kinema* and *Film Ireland*. His book *Chávez: The Revolution Will Not Be Televised* was published in 2008.

The Quiet Man ... and Beyond:
An Introduction

SEÁN CROSSON

'Consider what *The Quiet Man* and Maureen O'Hara did for Irish tourism. The film put the country on the international stage and opened doors that might not have been opened otherwise. We can be proud of that.' – Senator Michael McCarthy, Seanad Éireann, 13 December 2006[1]

In 1951, when John Ford came to Ireland to make *The Quiet Man*, few could have imagined the impact this ostensibly slight romantic comedy would have on the land of Ford's parents, as well as the film's lasting appeal. Irish-themed films had been a staple of American cinema since the silent era, but few films made in Ireland up to then had enjoyed more than modest success. *The Quiet Man*, however, would become Ford's greatest commercial success and set a template for Ireland's promotion of itself for over half a century.[2] While audiences have remained enthusiastic, the critical reception of *The Quiet Man* has been less assured. For many Irish filmmakers, *The Quiet Man* was responsible for a particular brand of whimsy which would be the target of much of their work, a development noted by Fidelma Farley and others in this collection.[3]

Nonetheless, particularly since the publication in 1987 of the influential Irish film studies text, *Cinema and Ireland* – including Luke Gibbons's seminal essay 'Romanticism, Realism and Irish Cinema' – the film has undergone considerable reassessment. Furthermore, the breadth of scholarship apparent in this collection reflects the continuing engagement with the film amongst the academic community, and few films have managed as successfully to maintain both the public's affection and critics' and academics' attentions. In 1996 the film topped an *Irish Times* poll for the best Irish film of all time.[4] Almost ten years later, in 2005, with many more Irish (and Irish-themed) films made, *The Quiet Man* still occupied number four in a poll of 10,000 people across Ireland organised by Jameson Irish Whiskey and the monthly magazine *The Dubliner*.[5] Arguably the film's impact is most apparent in the many subsequent films, some of which are mentioned in this collection, including *Waking Ned Devine* (1998) (discussed below by Michael Patrick Gillespie), which have attempted to recreate its style and content. There have even been rumours of a sequel of sorts to the film in recent years, though this has yet to materialise.[6]

Yet the impact of the film has gone beyond the landscape, cottages, whimsical storylines and characters found in subsequent film work. Irish fashion designer Paul Costello, for example, remarked controversially in 1998 that 'when we Irish think of style, we should be thinking of Maureen O'Hara in *The Quiet Man*'.[7] Indeed, the continuing public interest in O'Hara, who visited Ireland in July 2004 as special guest of the Galway Film Fleadh, owes more than a little to her iconic role in what Michael Dwyer, in an *Irish Times* interview at the time of her visit, called 'her most famous film and her personal favourite'.[8] In a testament to O'Hara's enduring popularity, the Samhlaíocht Kerry Film Festival inaugurated the Maureen O'Hara Award in November 2008 and included a screening of *The Quiet Man* in honour of O'Hara in its programme of events.[9]

The Quiet Man has even been invoked across the sectarian divide in Northern Ireland. In 2005 during a visit to a Protestant school on the Shankill Road in Belfast by the Republic's President Mary McAleese, the school's headmistress welcomed the President by recalling a scene from *The Quiet Man*:

'There's a lovely scene of John Wayne filmed in a bar where the men of Inishfree discover who he is. They say to him, "The men of Inishfree bid you welcome",' she said.

And she added: 'Then it comes to Squire Danaher, who is not a bit best pleased, who says: "There is one man in Inishfree, the best man in Inishfree, who doesn't." Well, let me tell you, we are the best of the Shankill, and we bid you welcome.'[10]

It appears that this reference to the *The Quiet Man* provided a means to articulate feelings often difficult to express given the sensitivities associated with relationships between Catholics and Protestants, Unionists and Nationalists in the North and that between the North and the South of the island.

Yet the film has not been without its critics. The remarks of then *Irish Times* columnist Kevin Myers in 2001 reflect continuing misgivings regarding the film:

> *The Quiet Man* is as utterly gruesome a misrepresentation of any country that I know of – it was, after all, set at the time when the nearby Letterfrack Industrial School was reaching prodigious heights of brutality and rapine. It prepared the way for further frolicsome grotesqueries such as *Finian's Rainbow* and *Far and Away*, and much other such rubbish.[11]

There is in Myers' remarks an implicit suggestion that film has a responsibility to represent reality, warts and all, though some contributors here – including Barry Monahan and Michael Patrick Gillespie – do suggest, in line with Luke Gibbons's seminal reading, that Ford's film is repeatedly raising questions about its own representation. However, the success of such an internal interrogation is challenged by others, including John Hill who raises 'doubts as to whether the ideological operations of the film are quite as complicated as recent writing has suggested' in a piece originally written for *Cinema and Ireland*, though published here for the first time. Sean Ryder is also keen to emphasise the limits of the political critique that others have recognised in Ford's work, while for Eamonn Slater, Ford's film achieves the remarkable distinction of making an English garden the most globally recognisable depiction of an Irish landscape. By including such criticisms of the film, we hope in this collection to offer some sense of the complexity of reactions Ford's work continues to evoke. Indeed, with regard to the character of Mary Kate Danaher, for example, this collection includes quite different and sometimes contradictory perspectives on her role and position within the film and its consequences for the representation of women more generally, evident in the chapters by John Hill and Díóg O'Connell's post-feminist analysis.

We have divided this collection into four sections, with a fifth 'Final Reflections' segment which includes contributions from the Chairman of *The Quiet Man* Fan Club, Des MacHale, and co-editor Rod Stoneman. MacHale, whose previous publications, including *The Complete Guide to The Quiet Man* (2000) and *Picture The Quiet Man* (2004), have contributed greatly to our understanding of *The Quiet Man*, considers his own personal fascination with the film, its role as a 'cult movie' and the emergence of the 'Quiet Maniacs'. Stoneman, meanwhile, while also reflecting on the film's continuing cult status, draws on his own experiences as Chief Executive of Bord Scannán na hÉireann/The Irish Film Board to consider the continuing popularity of the film with reference to representations of Ireland today and contemporary filmmaking practice.

The first section, entitled 'Ritual, Intertextuality and Style', features contributions which are concerned with, or touch upon, each or sometimes all these issues. It is appropriate that Luke Gibbons, whose pioneering work referred to repeatedly in this volume contributed significantly to the scholarship concerning this film, begins this collection with an examination of the role of ritual in Ford's work, prominent within *The Quiet Man* but apparent throughout the Irish-American director's *oeuvre*. The role of ritual is picked up elsewhere in this collection, including by Caitríona Ó Torna and Brian Ó Conchubhair who argue that the Irish language in Ford's film is intimately linked to ritual and rites of passage. While Gibbons begins with *The Quiet Man* and the prominence of ritual within that film, he moves from this to an examination of ritual, a significant part of Ford's Irish heritage, throughout the director's work and, indeed, its relevance in society for communicating and expressing what language and 'protocols of reason or instrumental action' find impossible to articulate.

Gibbons's chapter sets the tone for this collection as a whole in which, as our title suggests, contributions often use *The Quiet Man* as a taking off point for considering other or subsequent work, primarily by Ford but also by others, as well as the central point of study. This is a feature of James P. Byrne's following study which argues for *The Quiet Man* as a Western myth of Irish-American assimilation, placing the film in relation to contemporary political developments – including the Korean War – and the Western genre. In the process, Byrne moves from a consideration of the classic western genre to the representation of Irish America in Phil Joanou's *State of Grace* (1990), arguing that, while Joanou's film is suffused with western tropes, it questions and rewrites 'the simple mythology of American assimilation'.

Sean Ryder too is concerned with the Americanness of *The Quiet Man*, regarding it as a film whose depiction of Ireland is compromised considerably by its roots and focus, being centred ultimately in, and on, the United States. For Ryder, who examines *The Quiet Man* in relation to the more recent film adaptations *The Field* (Jim Sheridan, 1990) and *The Commitments* (Alan Parker, 1990), the local values and nuances of Maurice Walsh's original short story undergo an important readjustment in *The Quiet Man* in favour of a positioning of Ireland as 'some version of modernity's "Other", either in the form of "tradition" or of "postmodernity"'.

Adrian Frazier's contribution is also focused on the relation of *The Quiet Man* to Irish literature, though of the literary revival rather than the contemporary period. Frazier finds intriguing parallels between the literature of this formative period in Irish literary history and Ford's film, including with John Millington Synge's masterpiece *The Playboy of the Western World* (1907).

Fidelma Farley offers a comparative study of *The Quiet Man* and Vincent Minnelli's *Brigadoon* (1954), a film that John Hill also comments on and a work that occupies a comparable place in Scottish cinematic history to that of *The Quiet Man* in Ireland's. While recognising significant parallels in the manner in which Ireland and Scotland have been represented in film, Farley identifies important divergences in how scholarship concerning both countries' representations has interpreted such depictions.

Also drawing on scholarship of *The Quiet Man*, particularly the work of Luke Gibbons, Michael Patrick Gillespie's contribution offers a reconsideration of the much criticised *Waking Ned Devine*, a work Martin McLoone has described as representing the worst of what *The Quiet Man* encouraged.[12] However Gillespie argues for 'a narrative complexity that manipulates rather than panders to national stereotypes' within *Waking Ned Devine*, a provocative position that reflects the complex ways in which Ford's film has influenced subsequent readings of representations of Ireland and Irish people.

The second section, entitled 'Language, Style and the Visualised Nation', begins with Caitríona Ó Torna's and Brian Ó Conchubhair's examination of the place of the Irish language, rumour and myth in Ford's life and self-image in order to assess the function of the Irish language in *The Quiet Man*, as well as other films by Ford, including *The Informer* (1935) and *The Long Gray Line* (1955). For Ó Torna and Ó Conchubhair, language played an important role in Ford's work in allowing him to connect to, and speak on behalf of, other marginalised minorities within the United States.

Tom Paulus's contribution is concerned centrally with the language of film itself and provides a consideration of 'internal patterns of film-style and the filmmaker's craft' within *The Quiet Man*, looking in the process at Ford's style in previous and subsequent films, as well as other studio films produced contemporaneously. In a thought-provoking piece, Paulus considers the factors that bear upon, and the effects of, the style a director chooses in his film work, including the use of Technicolour in *The Quiet Man*, the first film depiction of Ireland to do so.

While Paulus is concerned with style in *The Quiet Man*, Barry Monahan contends that the film challenges the cinematic 'look'. By setting aural and visual cues against each other repeatedly, Barry argues that the film dramatises 'a particular mode of viewing the nation that is appropriate to the historical moment of its production', a transitional moment between the more inward-looking nationalism of de Valera and the outward-looking internationalism of Lemass marked by emigration and increasing tourism.

Section three, 'Landscape, Politics and Identity', begins with Eamon Slater's close study of the particular landscape represented in *The Quiet Man*, a landscape, Slater argues, atypical of the West of Ireland and actually closer to a traditional English garden. For Slater, studies of Irish landscape, including that depicted in *The Quiet Man*, are best focused on the construction of landscape as a cultural object, whether physically or ideologically.

Official concerns regarding the representation of the Irish landscape, and country as a whole, are the subject of Roddy Flynn's chapter, which examines the political machinations that surrounded the production of *The Quiet Man* in 1951 through a study of the government correspondences and records relating to the production of the film. Flynn charts the concerns expressed in government circles regarding the film's portrayal of Ireland and the efforts by the Department of External Affairs, which initially had acted as the interface between the film's producers and the government and went to considerable lengths to facilitate the production of the film, to subsequently assess, and frame, responses abroad in an attempt to shape international perceptions of the film and Ireland.

In the final chapter in this section, John Hill provides a useful review of the movement of critical study on *The Quiet Man* – and indeed Irish film studies more generally – in his contextualisation of his own contribution, originally written in 1983. Hill, in one of the more critical contributions on the film, which places *The Quiet Man* in relation to Ford's western films as a whole, examines its relationship with more general patterns of representing Ireland and contends that *The Quiet Man*'s portrayal conforms largely to a 'limited (and limiting) conception of Irish identity'.

The following section examines the role of Mary Kate, and Maureen O'Hara, whose continuing popularity reflects the centrality of the compelling character she plays within the film. Díóg O'Connell, through a formalist examination of the narrative function of some of the more controversial scenes within the film, attempts to account for how a film that ostensibly seems quite regressive in terms of its representation of women is still enjoyed by female viewers. O'Connell argues that the narrative complexity of *The Quiet Man* is such that it 'neither presents a story that can be appropriated for feminist ends, nor can it be simply boxed as another misrepresentation of women'.

Ruth Barton's study also looks at O'Hara's roles outside *The Quiet Man*, recognising in the process a 'peculiar combination of dominance and subordination' which for Barton 'is the key to O'Hara's characterisation in *The Quiet Man*' and which 'she brought with her to that role from her earliest screen performances'. For Barton, similarly to O'Connell, O'Hara's performances more generally often contested the 'male gaze', as articulated in Laura Mulvey's seminal essay.[13]

This section ends with Conor Groome's piece which contends that, given her independence and relationship with the elements in *The Quiet Man*, in any other Ford film Mary Kate might well have been classified as a 'whore' but for the unique ethnic situation of being Irish. By being Irish, Groome argues, Mary Kate 'traverses the gender and racial demarcations' one might usually associate with the characters she depicts.

As this outline of our contributions suggests, *The Quiet Man ... and Beyond* brings together a diverse and eclectic range of perspectives on *The Quiet Man*, from both established academics and emerging scholars. While their views may occasionally be at odds, their engagement with the film and Ford's work attests to the continuing relevance of both to Irish and international film and cultural studies. When this project was first mooted, prior to a conference held in the Huston School of Film & Digital Media in September 2005, one senior academic asked of one of the editors, in an unguarded moment, 'is there anything else to say about *The Quiet Man*?' As this collection indicates, there most certainly is more to say, and we hope these stimulating and sometimes provocative contributions will ensure that this conversation continues for some years to come.

Endnotes

[1] Seanad Éireann, Volume 185, 13 December, 2006. Irish Film Board (Amendment) Bill 2006: Order for Second Stage. Bill entitled an Act to amend and extend

the Irish Film Board Act 1980. Debate available at http://www.oireachtas-debates.gov.ie.

[2] For more on this, see S. Meaney and J. Robb, 'Shooting Ireland: The American tourism market and promotional film', *Irish Geography*, 39.1 (2007), 129–42.

[3] See also Luke Gibbons, *The Quiet Man* (Cork: Cork University Press, 2002), p. 3.

[4] Michael Dwyer, 'The Top Ten: taken as read', *The Irish Times*, 21 February 1996, p. 42.

[5] Michael Dwyer, 'Why boy couldn't eat girl at fleadh', The Ticket. *The Irish Times*, 1 August 2006.

[6] Anonymous, '"Quiet Man" to have a comedy offshoot', *The Irish Times*, 24 August 2000.

[7] Quoted in Brendan Glacken, 'Paul, Gene, Roddy and Style', *The Irish Times*, 8 October 1998.

[8] Michael Dwyer, 'Not such a quiet woman', *The Irish Times*, 10 July 2004.

[9] See Anne Lucey, 'Fricker to receive Maureen O'Hara award', *The Irish Times*, 28 October 2008. The first recipient of the award was Oscar-winning actress Brenda Fricker.

[10] Gerry Moriarty, 'Visit lifted by a welcome and cheerful event – *that* winning goal', *The Irish Times*, 9 September 2005.

[11] Kevin Myers, 'An Irishman's Diary', *The Irish Times*, 27 April 2001.

[12] See Martin McLoone, *Irish Film: The Emergence of a Contemporary Cinema* (London: British Film Institute, 2000), p. 59. Also Harvey O'Brien, 'Waking Ned', *Harvey's Movie Reviews*, 1999, http://homepage.eircom.net/~obrienh/wn.htm.

[13] Laura Mulvey, "Visual Pleasure and Narrative Cinema", *Film Theory and Criticism*, edited by Leo Braudy and Marshall Cohen (New York: Oxford University Press, 1999), pp. 833–44.

I

Ritual, Myth and Intertextuality

2

From Innisfree to Monument Valley: Irishness and Ritual in John Ford's Westerns

Luke Gibbons

One Fourth of July, early in the twentieth century, young John Ford and his father stood in the main street of Portland, Maine, to watch the parade. The name in those days was not Ford but Feeney. 'When the flag passes,' the father said, 'take off your cap.' But the boy was not wearing one. 'Then cross yourself, damn it!' – Thomas Flanagan[1]

In Ray Lawrence's film *Jindabyne* (2006), Gabriel Byrne plays an Irish exile in Australia, Stewart Kane, who finds himself at the centre of a bitter conflict between a white small town community and local Aboriginal peoples. The cultural breakdown is caused by the defilement of the body of a murdered Aboriginal woman found in a river in the mountains during a hunting trip. Kane tethers the body of the young woman with wire to the riverbank to stop it floating down the rapids downstream, but the local Aboriginal peoples take this as an unconscionable act of desecration. As the crisis escalates, owing to the apparent callousness of the hunter's treatment of the body, Kane's life falls apart. In one scene, a disagreement with his wife ensues in their home over the use of a St Brigid's Cross to commemorate the first of spring – a remnant of a ritual from his own discarded past in Ireland. It is this gesture that proves the turning point in the film, for, without any psychological motivation or plotting, Kane resolves to bring the friends from the hunting trip together to visit the communal mourning rituals of the local Aborigines. There is no real comprehension of the strange waking rituals: what matters is the show of solidarity, a sympathy with the plight of excluded others derived from the memory of one's own submerged past.

The implication here is that ritual – participation in communal practices, the sharing of symbolic behaviour – often picks up where intellect leaves off, acting as a crucial means of cultural crossings without the mediation of Western protocols of reason or instrumental action. Writing about a world in which the work ethic ensures that even enjoyment is measured in terms of efficiency, Friedrich Nietzsche observed that truth is also reduced to instrumental action, to what is direct, unmediated and economical:

> Just as all forms are visibly perishing by the haste of the workers, the feeling for form itself, the ear and eye for the melody of movements are also perishing. The proof of this may be found in the universal demand for gross obviousness in all those situations in which human beings wish to be honest with one another [...] One no longer has time or energy for ceremonies, for being obliging in an indirect way, for esprit in conversation, and for any otium at all.[2]

One such worker reduced to 'gross obviousness', his energies consumed in the steel furnaces of Pittsburgh 'so hot a man forgets his fear of Hell', is Sean Thornton (John Wayne) in *The Quiet Man* (1952), who comes back to Ireland looking for instant results in reclaiming his Irishness and, indeed, in affairs of the heart. 'I don't get this', he complains to Michaeleen Oge (Barry Fitzgerald) when he has to suffer the indignity of a chaperone during his courting of Mary Kate Danaher (Maureen O'Hara): 'Why do we have to have you along? Back in the States, I'd drive up, honk the horn, and a gal would come running.' This inability to grasp both the communal and sensory language of ritual is linked by Michaeleen Oge to a killjoy mentality of the kind excoriated by Nietzsche: 'America', he remarks scornfully: 'Pro-hib-ition'.[3]

In John Ford's *The Searchers* (1956), this incomprehension or short-circuiting of ritual acquires a more sombre cast in the scene where Ethan Edwards (John Wayne) disrupts the funeral of his brother Aaron and his family after their massacre by the Indians. As people stand around the grave intoning one of Ford's elegiac anthems, 'Shall we Gather by the River?', Ethan is at odds with the grieving rituals of the community. 'Put an amen to it', he says, as he storms away from the mourners, giving full rein to the compulsions of revenge and violence. For Ford, the breakdown of ritual leads not to freedom and individualism but to a world in which even the dead are not safe, as Walter Benjamin warned of the gravediggers of Nazi Germany. The defilement of the dead is an abiding theme in Ford from his earliest movies, signalled by the scene in *The Iron Horse* (1924) where the mourners at the untended grave of Ruby, the saloon girl, are left behind by the venality of the carpetbaggers following the building of the railroad. This violation of the past reaches its nadir in *The Searchers* when Ethan and the search party come across an improvised grave for a Comanche Indian, which leads one of the group, whose family has been murdered in an Indian attack, to attempt to smash his skull in a fit of rage. At this point, Ethan wheels around on his horse and, in an apparently senseless act, fires two bullets into the eyes of the corpse. 'What did you do that for?' asks the leader of the posse, the Reverend Clayton (Ward Bond). 'Ain't got no eyes', Ethan retorts, 'he can't enter the spirit land, has to wander forever between the winds.' In the ultimate act of desecration, Ethan uses his own (suspiciously intimate) knowledge of ritual to violate the afterlife of Indians.

Reclaiming the Wilderness

Though Ford's preoccupation with ritual is regularly glossed in the critical literature, few commentators relate it to questions of ethnicity and solidarity, still less to the sensitivities of cross-cultural communication in an increasingly diversified America.[4] J.A. Place, in her pioneering *The Western Films of John Ford*, notes its centrality in Ford's films but in keeping with critical trends of the period that looked to archetypal and mythic patterns in literature, sees ritual as the point where westerns, for all their quintessential 'Americanness', make contact with the universal themes of human experience:

> Rituals are formal, sometimes stylized re-enactments of very
> basic patterns for dealing with fearful or awesome human ex-
> periences. In his films, Ford establishes personal patterns of
> these experiences – dances, weddings, births, funerals, honor,
> and above all, sacrifice [...] The western, then, is defined by its
> relation to myth, through its use of ritual and dream, its cul-
> turally shared background of the American dream, and by its
> form and conventions. It repeats and re-affirms cultural and
> universal experience.[5]

Ritual may indeed be a point of contact with something outside American experience: but it is with the world of Ford's Irishness and Catholicism exemplified by *The Quiet Man*, not the eternal verities of the human condition. Nowhere in her account of ritual in Ford does Place allude to the possibility that this may have been part of the cul-tural baggage brought by the O'Feeney family (Ford's emigrant par-ents) from Connemara to the new world. If there is one trait more than any other which attests to Ford's disruption of the American Dream in the very act of celebrating it, it is the inscription of ritual on the wilderness, a landscape de-territorialized of all traces of habita-tion and memory in the American romantic imagination. Place's link-ing of ritual with myth has important narrative implications for it becomes a mode of reconciliation, magically re-enacting generic and symbolic resolutions in the killing fields of the wilderness:

> We respond to these rituals with emotion, and from the emo-
> tional experiences we take gratification. Even when story lines
> are clichéd and predictable, the working out of insoluble ten-
> sions and frustrations through fantasy helps to relieve similar
> tensions in our lives.[6]

While there is no doubt that ritual acts as a mode of reconciliation in Ford, it also operates as a site of contestation, a conflict zone exposing fault-lines between clashing cultures along the ever-receding frontier. In a telling aside, Place mentions that, for all Ford's identification with the abiding myths of the Western, there is a dissenting note: 'On the artistic level, however, the dream is subject to reinterpretation and change, even to fundamental questioning of the dream while still affirming the cultural values inherent in it'.[7] Hence customs prevail in *The Quiet Man* but in the context of a modernising society through which they retain their collective character but are no longer 'second nature', encumbered by unthinking conformity and the force of habit. Sean Thornton is both native and stranger, a fast (or slow?) learner who does not imbibe tradition so much as work through it, even in the very act of questioning its authority. 'It's your custom, not mine', he exclaims, handing Mary Kate back to Red Will by throwing her at his feet when he refuses to pay her dowry: 'No fortune, no marriage, we call it quits.' The reflexive element of ritual, its capacity to strike a chord with related practices in other cultures, enables this critical engagement, as Ford in his westerns draws on a cultural memory of what it is like to be on the other side of coercive civility and conquest.

The pervasiveness of ritual in Irish culture, the expressive codes and somatic spaces through which communities make sense of their lives, establishes affinities with Indian ways of life, a mode of cultural empathy that draws the opprobrium of the military academy in Ford's *Fort Apache* (1948). When young Lieutenant Michael O'Rourke (John Agar) has the misfortune to encounter the remains of an Apache massacre on his ride through the desert with Philadelphia (Shirley Temple), the daughter of his superior Colonel Thursday (Henry Fonda), it brings the wrath of his imperious commanding officer on his head. On handing his report of the incident to the irate Colonel, Michael receives the barbed compliment that somehow his Irish background gives him an inside track on Indian savagery:

Colonel Thursday: My compliments on the completeness of this report. It speaks knowledge of the savage Indian which I'm sure you did not acquire in the military academy. I call it to your attention that in taking my daughter without beseeching my permission, you have been guilty of behaviour more con-

sistent with an uncivilized Indian than an officer and a gen-
tleman. If I have not made myself sufficiently clear, Mister, I
will tell you this: You will not ride again with my daughter,
and for reasons which I feel it unnecessary to go into, you will
avoid her company in the future.

Ford had already signalled this tragic symmetry between native peoples and their 'Celtic' counterparts in his first sound feature, *The
Black Watch* (1929), depicting another conflict with other native Indians, this time on the Eastern Asian frontier. Scottish bonding rituals
of song, costume and military drilling are juxtaposed with similar
Muslim rituals among the native Pashtu anti-colonial movement, as
one of the Scots, King (Victor McLaglen), infiltrates the native tribe to
seduce their 'Joan of Arc' war leader, Yasmini (Myrna Loy). As Tag
Gallagher notes, this film reveals the capacity of ritual to induce excesses of collective behaviour, such as the unquestioning acceptance
of certain values, to the point of laying down one's life for a cause.[8]
Yet in the film this is given a twist as sacrificial logic is shown to be
the preserve not just of 'primitive' peoples but also of militaristic ap-
propriations of patriotism in the West. Militarism may produce heroes, but not always in the leaders who preside over such feats – at
the end of *Fort Apache*, Colonel Thursday's warmongering against the
Apaches brings out the heroism of his men, while revealing his own
reckless disregard for their lives.

    In *Fort Apache*, ritual becomes one of the lifelines enabling cross-
cultural contact with Indians, or, indeed, between immigrant peoples
themselves on the American frontier – an exercise in cultural exchange brought out eloquently in the peace negotiations between
Captain York (John Wayne), Sergeant Beaufort (Pedro Armendariz)
and Cochise (Miguel Inclan), framed against the mesas of Monument
Valley. In so doing, ritual also provides a means of contesting the
boundaries and proprieties of the official public sphere, with its
barely concealed grounding in WASP rectitude and decorum. The
eviction of ritual, custom and gesture from the public sphere was
part of a wider pattern in American culture, noted by commentators
as early as Tocqueville and continued down to the present day in the
work of historians such as T.J. Jackson Lears and sociologists such as

Robert Bellah,[9] which evinces a profound distrust of emplotting the expressive body in social space. The loss of ritual at critical junctures in American society is nowhere more evident than in 'rites of passage' or coming of age – an absence so marked that the conditions of the classic bildungsroman may not have been possible in a culture of prolonged adolescence: Huck Finn forever drifting on the river of life.[10] As Ford's cavalry films testify, the military – boot camp, national service, the draft – stepped in historically to help fill this void, but, in a not totally unrelated fashion, the generation gap and teenage angst movies of the 1950s also registered this vacuum, with the often psychotic consequences prefigured in Ford's westerns. Symbolic expressions of 'social death' in traditional rites of passage are taken in a literal-minded society to mean dicing with death itself, as in the kamikaze car race in Nicholas Ray's *Rebel without a Cause* (1955) or, no less drastically, the sadistic hazing and confraternity rituals that lead to death or homicidal rage in films such as Stanley Kubrick's *Full Metal Jacket* (1987). The futile heroics of self-sacrifice delineated in many of Ford's films may testify not so much to the binding force of rituals but to their absence, to the lack of truly participative structures enabling the individual to assume a larger social identity without the risk of self-extinction.

It is not, though, as if ritual has disappeared from American society, for what is decanted from the rhythms of everyday life in the interests of efficient action is distilled in a more pure form in the protocols of the state – and particularly the regimentation and mystique of the military. The state enjoys not only a monopoly on violence: it also aspires to a monopoly of ritual, drawing it away from its amorphous, performative expressions at street level to regimented, strictly regulated forms of activity. As Paul Gilroy has described this process:

> At its worst, citizenship degenerates into soldiery and the political imagination is entirely militarized. The exaltation of war and spontaneity, the cults of fraternity, youth, and violence, the explicitly anti-modern sacralization of the public sphere, and its colonization by civil religion involving uniforms, flags, and mass spectacle, all underline that these [...] are fundamentally military phenomena.[11]

Under this dispensation, ritual is a rule-driven, and not just rule-governed, activity, as performative and participative energies are regulated by 'rational' surveillance, hierarchical grids, and the disempowerment of spectacle. It is this tension between discipline and improvisation that Ford explores repeatedly in his cavalry and war films, as the unruly and disorderly bodies of the 'Fighting Irish' come up against the strict regimes of their 'social betters' in the military. This is often posed in Ford's movies as a contrast between dance and drill, the embodied eloquence of the dance floor – with its basis in music and the carnivalesque – bringing recalcitrant bodies into a collective unison at odds with the mechanised routines of the military body. In its most memorable expression, the choreography of the frontier is captured in the famous church celebration sequence of *My Darling Clementine*, when Wyatt Earp's (Henry Fonda) cowboy mind-set preoccupied with wandering and revenge is divested of its rebarbative elements on the open-air dance floor, his awkward body acquiring a new fluency as he is put through his paces with Clementine (Cathy Downs).

The contrast between official and vernacular ritual is related to another trend in Ford's movies which construes home as a barrier against the totalising designs of the military on the individual (exemplified in the tendency to define citizenship itself in terms of the right to own a gun). This might seem to be a simple opposition of private versus public sphere, the home acting as a haven for the individual, Hollywood style, from the collective pressures of the outside world. But in fact it is individualism itself that is called into question, since home is no less social than the barrack square, informed by mores drawn from ethnicity and the homeland rather than from the domestic sphere, narrowly conceived. In Ford's *The Long Gray Line* (1955), Marty Maher's (Tyrone Power) wife, Mary (Maureen O'Hara), counters his proposal to leave Westpoint and open a pub in Tipperary by installing a corner of Ireland in their home in America, in the form of his transplanted father and his brother, who proceed accordingly to dedicate the house in the Irish language to 'the grand country that offers us hope'. In *Fort Apache*, Colonel Thursday's resolve to prevent his daughter's romance with Lieutenant O'Rourke prompts him to barge into the home of the young officer's father, Sergeant O'Rourke (Ward Bond), who issues a stiff reprimand to his superior: 'This is my home, Colonel Owen Thursday, and in my home I will say who is to get out and who is to stay.' As Michael Coyne observes of this scene: 'This is the precise moment when Irish Catholicism becomes the dominant culture of *Fort Apache*' because 'Thursday, undoubtedly WASP, negates his status as natural patriarch of the fort's family–community by totally alienating his subordinates' affection and respect.'[12]

As against Partha Chatterjee's argument that in such circumstances cultural diversity is sequestered within the domestic arena,[13] Ford extends these alternative cultural codes into society at large, whether by means of the dance floor, the public bar, the meeting house square, weddings, funerals or other sites of collective assembly. Rituals of food and drink are central to this process, their importance in festivals, rites and other key events on the cultural calendar testifying to their key role in mediating the public and private, and in establishing ethnic markers. Thus in *Fort Apache*, Thursday's violation of the home is replicated in his almost compulsive tendency to intrude on the dance floor, most dramatically in his interruption of the non-commissioned officer's ball – in effect, the social space of the O'Rourkes and other cultural minorities. This indifference to anything not regulated by orders and regulations acquires an ominous dimension when Thursday uses the disruption of the dance occasion to announce that he is abolishing the Indian's claim to culture and humanity as well. Publicly revoking the undertakings given by Captain York and Sergeant Beaufort to Cochise, he seals the tragic fate of his regiment by declaring that there can be 'no question of honour between an American officer' and 'a breach-clothed savage, an illiterate uncivilized murderer and treaty-breaker'.

Ford's determination to (re)insert ethnic and Indian rituals in the public sphere can be seen, in effect, as a recreation of the American wilderness in the image of the culturally saturated world of *The Quiet Man*. In placing densely layered performative spaces between the individual and the State, 'Nature' or, indeed, other cultures, Ford sought to forestall the civic fundamentalism that closes the gap be-

tween rules and their applications, reducing everything, even the re-
cesses of everyday life, to rule of law. Taken to its unquestioning extreme, this form of closure culminates in the kind of mass ritual that,
in Mabel Berezin's words, 'attempts to obliterate the distinction between self and other, i.e. nation and state, private and public'.[14] The
suturing of inner and outer lives in mass ritual rules out any form of
reflexive critique, but it is at odds with the performative energies
Ford attaches to ritual, particularly in its colloquial guises. By virtue
of its opacity and somatic density, ritual renders problematic the
whole question of inner allegiance – grounded in 'sincerity' and 'authenticity' – in hierarchical societies, for no matter how meticulously
observed (or policed), ritual may reveal nothing about the mind behind it. As Rachel Moore notes of the role of the 'public intimacy' of
magical rites, which trade precisely on a lack of psychological conviction required in therapeutic narratives:

> Ritual cures work in [a] kind of public intimate way. Unlike,
> say, psychoanalytic healing, there is no mumbo-jumbo about
> one's innermost feelings, no bond with the healer. You show
> up, pay money or offer a gift of some kind, and partake in the
> ritual, often as part of a group of people you may or may not
> know.[15]

Moore draws on Marcel Mauss's distinction between religious rites
on the one hand and vernacular or magical rites on the other, according to which the former 'are always predictable, prescribed and official', whereas the latter involve a kind of secret intimacy, even if performed in the open: hence their 'unauthorized, abnormal and, at the
very least, not very estimable' status.

     It is in this sense that ritual allows for the possibility of critique,
for a reflexive, dissenting element that steps back from the ruling order under the very guise of conformity. As colonial regimes found
out to their cost, whether in Ireland, India or Algeria, the opacity of
vernacular culture often acted as a formidable obstacle to the inter-
nalisation of the ruling order – an affront to legibility which both colonial anthropology and the regional novel were determined to set
out to decipher, as if hoping to relay the gaze of the authorities into

the innermost layers of the self. At stake here, as Dipesh Chakrabarty suggests in the different context of Gandhian reworkings of the public sphere in India, are alternative routes to modernity that refuse metropolitan European narratives of interiority:

> The European modern is born in this condition – that the private be narratable – and, in that sense, the private self of the European exceeds or transcends the body [...] The Gandhian private is nonarratable and nonrepresentable. Not that it does not exist, but it is beyond representation, and dies with the body itself [...] It does not fulfill the condition of interiority that the discourse of rights both produces and guarantees for the modern state.[16]

Such a procedure not only opens a gap between the public and the private but also contests the very distinction itself, undermining the conformity that often passes for consent, or the civic codes that conceal hidden protocols of power. As Jay Clayton observes in relation to American society, drawing on the anthropological writings of Renato Rosaldo:

> Ritual may have a subversive or even a revolutionary tendency when performed in cross-cultural contexts [...] Classical norms portray ritual as static, timeless, a storehouse of collective wisdom [but] ritual is anything but static. It is dialogic, agonistic, impure, partial, changing, and improvisational. Instead of always reducing conflict, it sometimes becomes a place where grievances are aired, struggles staged. Instead of always stabilizing the community, it sometimes becomes a vehicle of social change.[17]

Resistance through Rituals

The civic animus towards vernacular ritual, particularly in its more desultory, everyday forms, is motivated by the fear of ungovernable cultural spaces, since outward conformity may belie inner dissent. This dissent need not result in a powerless Nietzschean resentment, the likely outcome if hostility is stripped of all public expression and interiorized in the psychological realm. For the avant-garde filmmaker Maya Deren, it was precisely the capacity of ritual to enlarge the personality beyond the psychological to the social, and, in the process, opening horizons onto different cultures, that made it a critical component of modernity.[18] Activated in the modern public sphere, the inherent ambivalence of ritual offers other social spaces, rendering endangered cultural ties and attachments impervious to decoding or surveillance. As Mabel Berezin relates of even the most regimented of state rituals:

> Ritual eliminates indeterminacy in social space through the carefully staged crowding of bodies in public spaces. But this does not presume that ritual eliminates indeterminacy as to meaning. Ritual, by acting out emotion, includes indeterminacy. Public political ritual, as [Claude] Lefort argued with respect to democracy, is a double-edged sword as it creates an open interpretive space. Solidarities and memories – the identities of subjects who have gathered under similar circumstances – may be extremely fluid. Emotion may obliterate the old self, but there is no guarantee as to what form the new self or identity might assume.[19]

Such reservations about ritual recall the ambivalence of Ford's challenging of American values, noted by J.A. Place above – a 'fundamental questioning', she writes, which yet 'affirm[s] the cultural values' – and acts as a rejoinder to the often voiced criticism of ritual that, by virtue of its attachment to tradition, repetition and communalism, it is inherently conformist and conservative. Can there be, as the title of an influential publication on subcultures once described it, resistance through rituals?[20] In his influential analysis of ceremony and ritual, Roy Rappaport notes:

> At the heart of some rituals [lies] not order, but hilarity, confusion, aggression, and chaos, expressed in clowning, transvestism, attacks upon initiates, self-mortification, sexual license, blasphemy, and otherwise indecorous actions seem to reign. Such behaviour may challenge, tacitly or explicitly, the very canons that ordain it.[21]

Some of the terms here would not be out of place in the burlesque scenes with Irish characters in Ford's cavalry movies, but as with the carnivalesque in Bakhtin, inversion of social values is not always the same as subversion. Further elaborating on the critical component of ritual, Rappaport suggests that its very formality and visibility 'lead[s] people to "think twice" before acting'[22] – and perhaps during action itself. Crucially, participation in, and acceptance of, ritual does not require belief:

> [B]elief is a second order process [...] an inward state, knowable subjectively if at all, and it would certainly be entirely unwarranted either for us or participants or witnesses to assume that participation in a ritual would necessarily induce such a state. Acceptance, in contrast, is not a private state, but a public act, visible both to witnesses and to performers themselves. People may accept because they believe, but acceptance not only is not itself belief; it doesn't even imply belief [...] [T]he private processes of individuals may often be persuaded by their ritual participation to come into conformity with their public acts, but this is not always the case.[23]

It is for this reason that ritual is often depicted as being 'visible [but] not very profound', involving 'nothing more than empty and even hypocritical formalism', but in fact, it is precisely this gap between outer and inner that leaves room for the modes of doubt and dissent that civic forms of fundamentalism seek to close:

> One can accept publicly not only that which one doubts but that which one privately despises and secretly denies [...] Acceptance, then, can be unconvinced and 'insincere', but insincerity does not nullify acceptance. In what appears to be a flaw of sufficient seriousness to vitiate its meaningfulness lies the very virtue of acceptance through liturgical performance. Its social efficacy lies in its very lack of profundity, in the possibility of disparity between the outward act and the inward state.[24]

In Ford, the crisis in inner faith opened by the gap between profession and conviction is explored in films like *The Informer* (1935) and

The Fugitive (1947), but this is not only a split between outer and inner worlds, between the social and the psychological. In cultural terms, it comes across as a rent in the social fabric itself, according to which certain practices – e.g. waking the dead, communal dancing, bar-room revelry – elicit very different responses, or indeed are anathema from the outset. Hence the capacity of ritual to pick up where comprehension leaves off, allowing the negotiation of cultural differences or, indeed, liminal spaces in which meaning collapses within a culture. In her recent elegiac memoir, *The Year of Magical Thinking*, Joan Didion describes the plunge into grief following the sudden death of her husband, and her slow recovery as ritual allowed her to enact what her mind still had not grasped: that her husband was dead. Everything else in her life rested on the assumption that he might come back: as she was attempting to throw out clothes, she became abruptly aware of his shoes:

> I stopped at the door to the room. I could not give away the
> rest of his shoes. I stood there for a moment, then realized
> why: he would need shoes if he was to return. The recognition
> of this thought by no means eradicated the thought.

Having gone through the public rituals of mourning, she found herself months later at a dinner table with various people, among them a theologian, when 'someone at the table raised a question about faith':

> The theologian spoke of ritual itself being a form of faith. My
> reaction was unexpressed, but negative, vehement, excessive
> even to me. Later I realized that my immediate thought had
> been: But I did the ritual. I did it all [...] And it still didn't bring
> him back. 'Bringing him back' had been through those months
> my hidden focus, my magic trick. By late Summer I was be-
> ginning to see this clearly. Seeing it clearly did not yet allow
> me to give away the clothes he would need.[25]

It is difficult not to think of such incongruities between objects and emotions when recalling the sequence in *The Searchers* when Martha (Dorothy Jordan), the wife of Ethan's brother Aaron, is caught through the peripheral vision of the Reverend Samuel Clayton (Ward

Bond) folding and caressing the great-coat of her nomadic brother-in-law. Ethan's reciprocal gesture, the quiet repetition of a kiss on Martha's forehead, also relays the undischarged emotion of ritual, and at the end of the film it is this capacity of the body to release the pent-up emotions lodged within it that defuses his pathological racism. When Ethan finally discovers the site of Debbie's captivity among the Indians, he vents his fury on the Commanche chief Scar (Henry Brandon) by scalping in his moment of triumph. As in Ford's later movies, it is not clear on which side true savagery lies, and as Ethan finally hunts down the renegade Debbie (Natalie Wood), we expect him to visit a similar barbaric fate on her. No sooner has he lifted her up to dash her in a frenzy off the rocks than his body recalls a similar act, over a decade earlier, in which he lifted her up as a small child on his 'homecoming' to the Edwards' homestead. In this earlier gesture, depicted at the beginning of the film, Ethan mistakes Debbie for her older sister Lucy, as if time had stood still and Lucy remained the same age she was when he left to fight in the Civil War. This lapse itself testifies to the different tempos of emotional time, and at the end of the film, the unconscious remembrance of ritual leads Ethan's body to act in ways at odds with his conscious racist beliefs, as he takes his niece in his arms: 'Let's go home, Debbie'. The gesture here recalls Ethan's own homecoming at the beginning of the film, and his unacknowledged love for Martha, embodied in repeated actions that acquire a life of their own. The additional irony here, picked up in one of the anecdotes relating to the making of *The Searchers*, is that Wayne's famous gesture of clasping his right elbow with his left arm as he walked out the door in the final shot is itself a recapitulation, an involuntary gesture recalling a mannerism of the actor Harry Carey in one of Ford's earliest films. The fact that Wayne at that moment was facing Olive Carey, Harry Carey's widow, who played Mrs Jorgenson, only adds to an understanding of how ritual acts as a repository of memories whose time has yet to come.

Endnotes

---

[1] Thomas Flanagan, 'John Ford's West', in *There You Are: Writings on Irish and American Literature and History* (New York: New York Review Books, 2004), p. 3.

[2] Friedrich Nietzsche, *The Gay Science*, trans. Walter Kaufmann (New York: Vintage, 1974), p. 259.

[3] I discuss these aspects at greater length in *The Quiet Man* (Cork: Cork University Press, 2003).

[4] Among the few commentators, other than J.A. Place discussed below, to do justice to its pervasive role in Ford's films are Joseph McBride, *Searching for John Ford* (New York: St Martin's Press, 2001); Tag Gallagher, *John Ford: The Man and his Films* (Berkeley: University of California Press, 1986); and John Baxter, *The Cinema of John Ford* (London: Zwemmer, 1971).

[5] J.A. Place, *The Western Films of John Ford* (Secaucus, NJ: The Citadel Press, 1974), p. 5.

[6] Place, *The Western Films of John Ford*, p. 5.

[7] Ibid., p. 5.

[8] Gallagher, *John Ford*, p. 61.

[9] See T.J. Jackson Lears, *No Place from Grace: Antimodernism and the Transformation of American Culture: 1880–1920* (Chicago: University of Chicago Press, 1994); Robert Bellah et al, *Habits of the Heart: Individualism and Commitment in American Life* (New York: Harper and Row, 1985).

[10] For the exclusion of the American novel from the classic bildungsroman, see Franco Moretti, *Way of the World: The Bildungsroman in European Culture* (London: Verso,1988), p. 229. Moretti points to the persistence of 'Nature' and the presence of the '"alien" – usually an Indian or a black' (229) – as the forces against which the individual has to struggle: in contrast to the social structures of European society.

[11] Paul Gilroy, *Against Race: Imagining Political Culture Beyond the Colour Line* (Cambridge, Mass: Harvard University Press, 2000), p. 82.

[12] Michael Coyne, *The Crowded Prairie: American National Identity in the Hollywood Western* (London: I.B. Tauris, 1999), p. 60.

[13] Partha Chatterjee, *The Nation and its Fragments: Colonial and Postcolonial Histories* (Princeton: Princeton University Press, 1993).

[14] Mabel Berezin, 'Emotions and Political Identity: Mobilizing Affection for the Polity,' in *Passionate Politics: Emotions and Social Movements*, ed. by Jeff Goodwin, James M. Jasper and Francesca Polletta (Chicago: University of Chicago Press, 2001), p. 88.

[15] Rachael O. Moore, *Savage Theory: Cinema as Modern Magic* (Durham, NC: Duke University Press, 2000), p. 5.

[16] Dipeah Chakrabarty, '*Khadi* and the Political Man', in *Habitations of Modernity: Essays in the Wake of Subaltern Studies* (Delhi: Permanent Black, 2002), p. 62.

[17] Jay Clayton, *The Pleasures of Babel: Contemporary American Literature and Theory* (Oxford: Oxford University Press, 1993), pp. 113, 119.

[18] On these aspects of Deren, see Moore, *Savage Theory*, pp. 6, 17.

[19] Berezin, 'Emotions and Political Theory', p. 94.

[20] Stuart Hall and Tony Jefferson, *Resistance through Rituals: Youth Culture in Post-War Britain* (London: Hutchinson, 1977).

[21] Roy A. Rappaport, *Ritual and Religion in the Making of Humanity* (Cambridge: Cambridge University Press, 1999). p. 381.

[22] Roy A. Rappaport, 'Enactments of Meaning', in Michael Lambek (ed.), *A Reader in the Anthropology of Religion* (Oxford: Blackwell, 2002), p. 451.

[23] Ibid., p. 454.

[24] Ibid., p. 455.

[25] Joan Didion, *The Year of Magical Thinking* (London: Fourth Estate, 2005), p. 43.

3

Ethnic Revenge: A Structural Analysis of the Western Tropes of Twentieth Century Irish-American Assimilation

JAMES P. BYRNE

For such a popular, even populist, film, *The Quiet Man* has proven to be fertile soil for critical enquiry. Simply conceived – the romantic remaking of Maurice Walsh's 1933 tale – it has, since its cinematic release in 1952, become the site of colonial, nationalist, gender and even trauma criticism.[1] This chapter investigates the possibility of its accommodation of one more reading: a structuralist reading of the film as a western myth of Irish-American assimilation.

This argument does not come from a reading of the film as we witness it now, but rather from a reading of the implicit understanding contracted between the film and its 1950s' Cold War, Irish-American audience – an understanding based on America's new-found standing as champion of democracy in the outer reaches of civilization, and Irish-America's contribution and commitment, both physically and emotionally, to this mission. To paraphrase Jameson, this chapter strives to read the absent history back into the text.[2] It seeks to investigate the response orchestrated by the superficial structure of this film for a typical Irish-American audience weaned on stereotypes and seeking to become the archetypal assimilated American community.

Utilising Will Wright's structuralist study of the Western, *Sixguns and Society*, this chapter investigates the western myth of Irish-American assimilation which *The Quiet Man* presented to, and its makers wanted accepted by, its audience. Following this, it argues that a more recent Irish-American audience – witnessing the earlier generation's complicity in figures and fairytales of easy assimilation – is bent on inverting the tropes and re-inventing itself as identifiably ethnic, is, in western terms, bent on ethnic revenge.

Although the film was released in 1952, Ford's fascination with *The Quiet Man* had begun much earlier, with the publication of Walsh's short story in the *Saturday Evening Post*, in 1933. Between his purchase of the film rights, in 1936, and his eventual contract to direct the film with Republic, in 1950, Ford's desire to make *The Quiet Man* grew from obsession to compulsion.[3] So much so, in fact, that not only did he agree to a three-movie contract with Republic – a largely B-movie studio – but he also agreed to first direct a standard Western in order to generate box-office returns for the struggling studio. This western, *Rio Grande* (1950) – using John Wayne, Maureen O'Hara and much of the ensemble cast chosen for *The Quiet Man* – not only helped achieve the 'greenlighting' of the production of *The Quiet Man*, it also left certain genetic traces in the later film.

In his biography *Searching for John Ford*, Joseph McBride argues: '*Rio Grande* can be read as Ford's early-warning allegory of the Korean War, which broke out ten days after it began filming'.[4] This allegory is subsequently inverted and further developed in Ford's next production – *This Is Korea!* (1951) – a jingoistic war documentary, shot in Korea for the US Navy. In this documentary, the US Cavalry of *Rio Grande* become the Navy's US Marines, come to rid the land of the native savages and drive them back across the border and into communist China. Ford's next production, *The Quiet Man*, would continue to develop this allegory, with the west of Ireland becoming the western landscape in which the American civilising mission could be played out as benevolent and naturally beneficial.

Thematically as well as stylistically, *The Quiet Man* inherited certain genetic traces from *Rio Grande*. The critic Richard Slotkin sees Ford's *Rio Grande* as a key example of what he has called the 'Cold

War Western'.[5] According to Slotkin, this was a post-war development in the Western genre which functioned 'to interpret forms of
industrial and ethnic strife and to rationalise the development of the
republican nation-state into an imperial Great Power'.[6] *The Quiet
Man*, 'a Western made in Ireland', as Lord Killanin characterised it,
continued this post-war tradition, disguising its implicit sanctioning
of American imperial ambitions in pastoral images of a nostalgic return to home.[7]

The year 1952 was a significant one for US imperial ambitions:
with the Cold War struggle with the Soviet Union beginning to take
shape in foreign theatres, such as Korea, America had begun testing a
new weapon of mass destruction, the hydrogen bomb. On the domestic front, it also appeared to be an ambitious year for the Irish-
American struggle for recognition of its first-class citizenship. With the
ominous and infamous words, 'I have here in my hand...', Joseph
McCarthy, a small-town, second-generation Irish-American, began
making anti-communism the badge of American identity and, by de-
fault, began announcing the arrival of Irish-Americanness as the exemplary paradigm of national American identity.

While McCarthyism struck fear and suspicion into the large majority of Americans, for an Irish-American community whose identity
was still uncertain, it registered pride and signified recognition of
their American status. Here was an ethnic group who, as Andrew
Greeley has testified, had certainly 'made it' by this time, but a
group, nonetheless, who were still being denied any stable category
of identification or allegiance – being seen as American by other ethnicities, but as distinctly ethnic by Anglo-Americans. McCarthy's
Irish Catholicism, being both an implicit and inherent part of his
American anti-communist stance, heralded the post-war Irish-
American community as the archetype of an Americanism which not
only defined nationalist ideology but further became the pretext for
American imperial actions in Asia.[8]

What better place for an Irish-American audience to play out its
fantasies about benevolent American incursion than in the Hibernian
reaches of the western isles, where there languished an island – their
ancestral homeland – still recovering from the blight of an unjust,

colonial rule. And what better structure to play out this dynamic of belated liberation and repatriation than the Western, which had made Hollywood a commercial success through its mythic retelling of the scenic frontier land saved from tyrannical lawlessness through the intervention of a benevolent outsider, one who in defeating the 'villains of democracy' would himself become an honoured member of lawful market society.

In the opening sequence of *The Quiet Man*, the archetypal Western hero – John Wayne – steps off the train at Castletown, to look for the mythic world of his mother's, and Yeats', imagination, Innisfree. The train here not only symbolises the arrival of modernsation to this rural land – the indication of the promise of advancing civilization implicit in the character of Thornton's (played by John Wayne) return – but also conjures up images of the American war-machine which Wayne has stepped off of so many times, to save so many 'helpless natives'.

In this opening sequence, our first view of these indigenous natives certainly conjures up images of exotic primitives coming to greet the symbol of western civilization: they stand a good foot smaller than Thornton (his physical dominance alluding to his superior civilization), and speak in a linguistic code unknown to him, even though it is supposedly the same language. The train's symbolic significance here – bringing civilization and order to a garden wilderness – marks these people as an indigenous group akin to native Indians of Ford's earlier Westerns. (In speaking once of how his sympathies lie with the Indians, Ford compared their oppression to that of the Irish in Ireland.[9]) It seems Ford's portrayal of these people, his father's people, was to be a pastoral idyll to the Celtic mysticism of Yeats' dream of rural, Irish peasantry.

In discussing this, Luke Gibbons, in his book *The Quiet Man*, talks of how 'the revival of the pastoral genre in the eighteenth century, with its notion of a "rural retreat" and the recreation of a primitive lifestyle, was itself a product of the very modernity from which it sought to escape'.[10] And this is exactly the irony captured in Ford's portrayal of twentieth century Ireland. It is a land of primitive lifestyle to which the very people who once sought to escape from it now seek to escape to it, but (and this is imperative in Ford's re-working of this pastoral myth), only if they can return to it touched by the modernity which they have embraced and questing to bring this modernity, or at least a display of it (as in the 'sleeping bag', which Michaeleen produces as evidence of Thornton's status as 'millionaire... Yank...') to the primitive people of this 'rural retreat'. For Ford, this land is both the mythic land of nostalgic remembering – captured in Sean Thornton's vision of his mother's cottage – and the primitive lifestyle to which Thornton brings the social benefits of modern civilization, in a quest to end the feudalism of a land ruled by a new breed of rack-renting landlords – the plague of 'Red' Will Danaher (the name symbolically evoking, for an Irish-American audience, not just the stereotypical Irish hair colouring but, more significantly, the scourge of communism against which they were to remain ever vigilant).

Although geographically distant, the Irish landscape's intimate physical and emotional connection to the American people, and its significant part in the making of American history, tie it psychologically to American identity. It has become annexed into the private and public psyche of American selfhood, a hyphenate linking the Irish and American spheres of Irish-Americanism. It is the mythical wilderness of a civilized people, the Wild West of their imagination.

Ford plays off this identification, in part his own, by readapting the symbolic signifiers of Hollywood's Western genre to reconstitute the mythology of the Western garden in this idyllic land. Through his casting, characterisation, and setting – with Wayne and O'Hara playing the Western hero and heroine whose struggle embodies the struggle between civilization and the wilderness – Ford creates a tale which uniformly adheres to Wright's recognition of the structural signifiers of the classical Western plot.

This plot, as Wright sees it, 'tells the story of a hero who is somehow estranged from his society but on whose ability rests the fate of that society. The villains threaten the society until the hero acts to protect and save it.'[11] It is less than subtly implied in *The Quiet Man* that without the aid of Thornton, the mythical village of Innisfree would fall victim to the villain's – 'Red' Will's – desire for personal gain at the expense of communal harmony. The symbolism of this action would not be lost on an American audience involved in a 'police action' in Korea to stop the communist movement from gaining control of a lawful market society. The mythic Western landscape of Ford's film works figuratively to resolve conflicts which, in reality, are both too distant and too complicated to be entertained or entertaining.

Wright's further argument – that 'the [Western] myth asks how we can maintain our independence and still be part of society, a problem faced by most of us almost constantly'[12] – is especially relevant to a 1950s' Irish-American community struggling to find an acceptable niche in the American social strata. Just as McCarthy had become a national paradigm for Irish-American citizenship, so Wayne, in his portrayal of an Irishman who has accepted and embraced American civilization, offered Irish-Americans the ethnic solution to their public dilemma: embrace your traditional beginnings but extol your American identity as an advancement in moral and social civilization. In the darkening theatre of 1950s' American nationalism, Thornton represented the iconic ideal of American and Irish-American identity; or rather the mythic idea of the Irish-American as the ideal American identity.

But the Irish-American community had linked itself to ideologies and icons which were already fading even as they were fêted, and, in the coming decades, its ties to these relics of unenlightened nationalism would ultimately thwart the rediscovery of its status as an ethnic minority in the age of civil rights and pro-minority discourse. What they would be left with is a spatial psychology of ethnic identification which would continue to register their nostalgia for an imaginary homeland without ever forcing them to deal with the reality of a modernising Ireland; Ireland to them would remain the frontier wilderness captured in Ford's film. The Western would allow them to embrace and endorse the Celtic mysticism of Yeats' Innisfree as the Irish homeland which still awaited their return; it would also condemn them to popular representation as the continuing 'outlaws' of an ever-progressive and newly inclusive multicultural America.

A lot would befall the American people between the 1952 box office success of *The Quiet Man* and Warner's release of *State of Grace* in 1990, not least the Vietnam War. In this time, a series of gaps would occur in the American psyche which would inflict permanent damage on the nation's jingoistic portrayal of and belief in Americanism: a generation gap, between those who blindly believed in the American Dream and those who actively turned away from it; a credibility gap, between what the government told the people and what they discovered to be true; and, most significantly, during the years of 'Reaganomics', an ever-widening economic gap, between those who had 'made it' and those who had not.

This economic gap was recognised by the Governor of New York, Mario Cuomo, in his keynote address to the 1984 Democratic National Convention. Improvising on Reagan's earlier announcement of America as 'a shining city on a hill', Cuomo spoke of the current state of the nation as 'a tale of two cities'. He went on to elaborate:

> A shining city is perhaps all the president sees from the porch of the White House and the veranda of his ranch, where everyone seems to be doing well.
>
> But there's another city, another part to the shining city; the part where some people can't pay their mortgages and most young people can't afford one, where students can't afford the education they need and middle-class parents watch the dreams they hold for their children evaporate.
>
> In this part of the city there are more poor than ever, more families in trouble, more and more people who need help but can't find it.
>
> Even worse: there are elderly people who tremble in the basements of the houses there.
>
> There are people who sleep in the city's streets, in the gutter, where the glitter doesn't show.
> There are ghettos where thousands of young people, without education or a job, give their lives away to drug dealers every day.[13]

This 'other city' was Hell's Kitchen – an ethnic American community abandoned to its fate of corruption, crime, drugs, suicide and gentrification by a state and a public which refused to recognise its minority status and need for economic and social benefit.

Phil Joanou's *State of Grace*, loosely based on T.J. English's account of the reign of a notorious 1970s' Hell's Kitchen mob, the Westies, tells the story of this disenchanted and dispossessed ethnic American community whose only loyalty is to outdated, parochial traditions of Irish solidarity. Sean Penn plays Terry Noonan, a cop and former Hell's Kitchen local, who, after spending years trying to escape the lawless frontier town of his past, finally returns to the old neighbourhood in the hopes of bringing American justice to this wilderness of anarchic tradition and feudal loyalty.

The film is set in the desolate landscape of a failing tradition which is slowly and finally succumbing to the civilizing process of economic gentrification (driven by the capitalist values of Reaganomics). Here Joanou recasts the spatial trope of western identification conceived as Ireland in Ford's film, as the American outpost of an abused and abusing ethnicity – the west and its western outlaws have come home, like Malcolm X's chickens, to roost in the heart of American civilization, New York.

Of course, the physical and psychological landscape of Hell's Kitchen in the 1970s was ideally set for this identification – a wasteland of old tenements being torn down and remodelled as upscale apartments left a landscape of empty lots and boarded-up buildings as the backdrop to an economically poor, hard-drinking, hard-living culture, where violence was frequently used to settle arguments or disputes. What comes through in Joanou's film, however, is not only the sense of Hell's Kitchen as an isolated outpost of feudal traditions in an age of corporate civilization, but, more significantly, the sense of this community's spatial identification of Irishness with its western landscape and psychology. Noonan returns as the civilizing hero – the modern sheriff – to this lawless frontierland, only to finally succumb to its alluring power of individual accountability and undying loyalty – public standards of a disenchanted Irish-American ethnicity.

This western identification is further emphasized by Joanou's suffusing the story with western signifiers and playing out the action against the backdrop of a western mise-en-scène. The signifiers are everywhere to see: from the lawlessness of Joanou's wilderness – Hell's Kitchen – to the romanticised code-of-honour of the Irish-American mob, putting fealty and fidelity to community over greed and economic gain. The western mise-en-scène comes through in Joanou's long-shots of the New York skyscrapers which symbolically evoke Ford's Monument Valley landscape, and his substitution of the old horse-trading towns of the west with the deserted streets of Hell's Kitchen – a New York neighbourhood has never looked so desolate as Joanou's West Side. To support this identification and truly evoke for the audience a modern-day western mythology, Joanou uses many of the shots pioneered by Ford which are synonymous with a western-style gaze. The most pronounced of these is the over-extended cross-cutting shot of Noonan and the St. Patrick's Day Parade, used both to build tension for the climatic shoot-out and as an indexical sign of the resurgence of Noonan's Irish ethnicity as stereotypically demonstrative and violent.

In this scene, Noonan's route to the classic western dénouement – the gunfight – takes him across town from Grand Central Station to Hell's Kitchen. As he crosses town on this, the one day of the year where 'everyone gets to be Irish', his journey is seen in counterpoint with and in contrast to the St. Patrick's Day parade's sanctioned celebration of Irishness *as* Americanness. At one point, as the camera follows him, he passes over the parade, the Virgilian hero (in contrast to Michaeleen's 'Homeric' perspective of Thornton in *The Quiet Man*) abandoning his life to fate and heading, literally, into the underworld of the ethnic Other, the hell of the Kitchen. The Irish mob – a paradigm of an anarchic tradition of demonstrative anti-citizenship – is cut off from the parade's conferral of acceptable ethnic citizenship by its distance, both physically and psychologically, from the whitening power of the event; they watch it on television, while getting drunk in an otherwise empty saloon. Terry Noonan, coming from the heart of this accepted, and acceptable, Irish-American identity, crosses over the publicly sanctioned display of ethnicity and into their world, a world physically and psychologically beyond the pale of American citizenship.

Moving between Wright's characterisation of the vengeance and professional variations on the classical Western plot, *State of Grace* most closely resembles the transition stage Wright constructed as a bridge between them.[14] (The film Wright uses as a structural paradigm for the transition stage is Fred Zinneman's *High Noon* (1952); released in the same year as *The Quiet Man*, it stands as patriarch to so much of what happens in *State of Grace*.) However, any simple association of *State of Grace* to Wright's transitional structural analysis is complicated here by the question of spatial ethnic identification and its relationship to American national citizenship – a theme explored but never fully real-ised in many of Ford's westerns. For Joanou, this seems to work itself out in (to paraphrase Cuomo) a tale of two societies, each of which the hero must respond to, and against which he must work out his indi-vidual identity.

These two societies – inherently the same but irredeemably differ-ent – are the natural offspring of a century of endured assimilation. One has accepted and progressed in American values and citizenship; the other has, if anything, regressed, associating itself with the tribal culture of an earlier ancestry. Terry Noonan and Kathleen Flannery exist on the cusp of these societies, like trickster figures *passing* with seeming ease amongst and between both. However, as the narrative reveals, passing between worlds comes at a very heavy personal cost, since both are ultimately forced to sacrifice what is most precious to them – love and life – in order to live up to the masquerade they have adopted.

Although it might be argued that these dual societies initiate a structural break from the western mythology envisioned by Wright, in fact what we are witnessing here is the natural progression of Wright's western mythology and Ford's western landscape. The ethnic pioneers of Ford's early Westerns have developed to become mainstream soci-ety, indistinguishable from the Anglo-Americans against which they were earlier seen in stark contrast. However, a significant minority have split from this identification to identify themselves, instead, as closer to the tribal communities negatively referenced in the earlier invocations of Hollywood's western mythology. In short, the ever-present cultural dynamic of cowboys and Indians has been recast and replayed as the transnational dynamic of ethnic identity. Shepherded on to this western reservation of Hell's Kitchen, these tribal-Irish people use archaic notions of communal identity, feudal loyalty and instinctual violence to defend their ever-decreasing territory against the inevitable encroachment of American capitalism and the absolute evisceration of their traditional heritage.

From Wright's structuralist vision of a western mythology trying to make sense of the struggle between social market and managed economy, we have advanced to a western mythology trying to resolve the struggle between socially economic and traditionally ethnic identity: a mythology conceived for a nation struggling with the dual notions of economic and cultural identity. With the release of Joanou's *State of Grace* would come a new western mythology: one which by recasting the spatial and cultural tropes of the classic Hollywood Western found in *The Quiet Man* would question and rewrite the simple mythology of American assimilation as the contrapuntal narrative of transnational ethnicities struggling to locate liveable identities.

Endnotes

[1] For a comprehensive look at the criticism surrounding *The Quiet Man*, see Luke Gibbons's *The Quiet Man* (Cork: Cork University Press, 2002) from the *Ireland into Film* series. For other interesting articles which develop or engage with the range of criticism, see James MacKillop's 'The Quiet Man Speaks' in *Contemporary Irish Cinema: From The Quiet Man to Dancing at Lughnasa* (New York: Syracuse University Press, 1999), and Gael Sweeney's 'A Good Stick to Beat the Lovely Lady: Violence and Equality in John Ford's *The Quiet Man*'.

[2] For more on this, see Fredric Jameson's *The Political Unconscious: Narrative as a Socially Symbolic Act* (Ithaca, NY: Cornell University Press, 1981).

[3] Ford's son, Dan, recalls in his biography of his father: '*The Quiet Man* was John Ford's most cherished personal project, his most beloved film' (Ford, p. 240). For more on Ford's struggle to get *The Quiet Man* produced, see Dan Ford's *Pappy: The Life of John Ford* (New York: Da Capo Press, 1998), James MacKillop's 'The Quiet Man Speaks' in *Contemporary Irish Cinema: From The Quiet Man to Dancing at Lughnasa* (James MacKillop (ed.), New York: Syracuse University Press, 1999), and Joseph McBride's *Searching for John Ford: A Life* (New York: St. Martin's Griffin, 2001).

[4] Joseph McBride, *Searching for John Ford: A Life* (New York: St. Martin's Griffin, 2001), p. 504.

[5] Quoted in McBride, *Searching for John Ford: A Life,* p. 504.

[6] Ibid.

[7] Lord Killanin, Ford's location adviser, has famously said of *The Quiet Man*: 'I've always said the film was a Western made in Ireland rather than an Irish film' (Quoted in McBride, *Searching for John Ford: A Life,* p. 515).

[8] In 'What "Americanism" Means', Theodore Roosevelt, in describing 'Americanism', has said: 'We shall never be successful, nor reach the lofty ideal which the founders and preservers of our mighty Federal Republic have set before us, unless we are Americans in heart and soul, in spirit and purpose, keenly alive to the responsibility implied in the very name American, and proud beyond measure of the glorious privilege of bearing it.' Theodore Roosevelt, 'What "Americanism" Means', *Forum* (April 1894): 198 (196–206).

[9] In speaking once of how his sympathies lie with the Indians, Ford said: 'My sympathy was always with the Indians. Do you consider the invasion of the Black and Tan [*sic*] into Ireland a blot on English history? It's the same thing, all countries do the same thing' (Quoted in Tag Gallagher, *John Ford: The Man and His Films* (Berkeley; London: University of California Press, 1986), p. 254).

[10] Luke Gibbons, *The Quiet Man* (Cork: Cork University Press, 2002), p. 10.

[11] Will Wright, *Sixguns and Society: A Structural Study of the Western* (Berkeley: University of California Press, 1975), p. 40.

[12] Ibid., p. 137.

[13] Richard D. Heffner, *A Documentary History of the United States* (New York: New American Library, 2002), p. 489.

[14] For more on these stages, see Will Wright's *Sixguns and Society: A Structural Study of the Western* (Berkeley: University of California Press, 1975), pp. 59–85.

4

Modernity's Other: *The Quiet Man, The Field* and *The Commitments*

SEAN RYDER

'Hey, is that real? She couldn't be ...' – so the unmistakable voice of John Wayne's 'Quiet Man' is inspired to ask, having stumbled upon an idyllic vision of Maureen O'Hara herding her sheep through a sunlit glade in John Ford's 1952 film. To his astonished eyes, the romantic and the real seem for a moment to coincide in Innisfree. The subsequent events in the film somewhat temper the Quiet Man's rosy-spectacled view of Ireland, but his early question is one that is central to the viewer's experience of this film and indeed many films about Ireland. The question of how one distinguishes the 'romantic' from the 'real' in the representation of Ireland has been central to debates about Irish cinema from its beginnings, just as it has been central to debates about Irish literature since the nineteenth century. In a way, of course, this question itself is misleading, since it presumes that the 'real' and the 'romantic' are fundamentally distinguishable. In fact any representation is by its nature a fabrication: it selects particular details rather than others, it presents them in a particular order, it privileges certain meanings and discourages others. 'Realism' is as much a construction as 'romanticism'; both offer different kinds of truth perhaps, but neither represents absolute and unmediated 'truth'. Thus, rather than simply asking which representation is true and which is false, the more interesting and useful question to ask is *why* certain meanings are considered true or realistic, while others are considered false or romanticised. Representation is a complicated process in which meanings are made, circulated and powerfully deployed with actual effects, regardless of their status as 'real' or 'romantic'.

Examining some of these problems in the specific context of cinematic versions of Irish literary texts, this chapter looks at certain patterns of 'translation' which have tended to occur when such literary works have been adapted for mainstream (Hollywood-style) cinema, and to ask why this may be so. In particular, it argues that in such film adaptations certain local and historical meanings produced by the literary texts tend to be replaced in the film versions by supposedly ahistorical, universal meanings which in fact reflect the quite specific and historical values of a US-dominated, transnational capitalist film industry. The problem is not simply one of 'realism' versus 'romanticism'; the meanings which the literary texts represent are not simply 'the truth' as opposed to Hollywood's falsehoods. Rather, the problem is a matter of the way alternate – and what might riskily be called 'native' – ways of understanding Ireland are entirely obscured by these films in the interest of making Ireland fit comfortably into a specific narrative and symbolic system associated with the culture of modern trans-national culture. More specifically, it seems that Ireland is almost inevitably translated into some version of modernity's 'Other', either in the form of 'tradition' or of 'postmodernity'. In both cases, the 'meaning' of Ireland is measured reductively by its difference to mainstream modernity.

By comparing Ford's film to two other films based on Irish literary texts from later in the century, *The Field* (1990) and *The Commitments* (1991), I hope to show that this tendency is not isolated, nor confined to an earlier generation of filmmakers. Significantly, perhaps, the literary texts on which these three films are based owed little to the modernist, experimental style of internationally known Irish writers like Joyce or Beckett. The authors of these three works – Maurice Walsh, John B. Keane and Roddy Doyle – were instead working within more populist traditions of twentieth century Irish fiction, which may help to explain why filmmakers have found it necessary to alter them for international consumption. Some of their local, communal, historically specific meanings, appealing to an Irish readership, refuse to be assimilated smoothly into the conventions of the international Hollywood film and its determination to fit Ireland into a simple binary scheme of (progressive) modernity and (regressive) otherness.

The Quiet Man

'The Quiet Man' was first published as a short story by Kerry-born writer Maurice Walsh in the popular American magazine the *Saturday Evening Post*, in February 1933 – even its first incarnation was thus addressed to an American readership. Walsh slightly expanded and revised the story when he included it in the book *Green Rushes*, published in London in 1935. In the story, the protagonist Paddy Bawn Enright (named 'Shawn Kelvin' in the first version) had left Ireland 'to seek his fortune' at the age of seventeen, working in the steel mills of Pittsburgh and becoming a professional boxer. Returning home to north Kerry after fifteen years, he buys a farm and attempts to forget his unhappy memories of America. After some five years, a marriage is arranged between himself and a woman named Ellen O'Danaher, whose unsavoury guardian and elder brother, Red Will, had underhandedly purchased the Enright lands while Paddy Bawn had been in America. True to his bullying character, Red Will delays the payment of her dowry and seeks to humiliate Paddy Bawn. Although he is initially unconcerned with the dowry, and is reluctant to engage Red Will in spite of public taunts, Paddy Bawn is eventually goaded into action by Ellen. In a dramatic gesture he returns Ellen to Red Will on the basis that the marriage bargain has not been honoured. The latter, stunned and publicly embarrassed, reluctantly hands over the money. Paddy Bawn and Ellen immediately burn the dowry in front of him, precipitating a fistfight between the two men, from which Paddy Bawn emerges as victor, having at last proved his manliness, won the respect of his wife, and confirmed his honour among the community.

When John Ford and his scriptwriter Frank Nugent came to adapt Walsh's story to film, some very significant alterations were made. For one thing, the film transformed the nature of the romantic relationship between Paddy Bawn and Ellen. In Walsh's story, Paddy Bawn had retired to his hillside cottage after the War of Independence in search of 'quiet'. According to the story, 'not once did he think of bringing a wife into the place, though often enough, his friends, half in fun, half in earnest, hinted his needs and obligations'.[1] It is only after some months that he becomes quietly attracted to Ellen, whom he sees at Mass every Sunday. The demure Ellen is initially unaware of his attentions, but her brother Red Will senses them and arranges a marriage between the couple, though he does so purely from a selfish motive, hoping that it will facilitate a marriage which he himself wants to make to a local widow. Ellen is thus merely a pawn between two men who dislike each other intensely, a fact that enables the story's narrator to comment on the sordid nature of 'bargained' marriages – 'the Irish way' as he cynically puts it. Fortunately, in this case, the bride does come to admire and even to love her new husband, but only after a period of several months. In fact it is her growing admiration for him which causes her to worry about his honour, and to urge him to demand the dowry which Red Will has been deliberately withholding.

As well as Walsh's commentary on matchmaking, his reference to the communal and religious 'obligations' of marriage highlights the complex social and economic dimension to marriage and sexuality in rural Ireland. Ford redefines the relationship as a tempestuous romance between Sean Thornton (as Paddy Bawn is renamed) and the feisty Mary Kate, who bears little resemblance to the faintly sketched Ellen of Walsh's story. Theirs is a very physical and erotically charged relationship, powerful and compelling, the centrepiece of the narrative. It is a disruptive force to the community and to the communally directed customs of rural Catholic society.

In this way, the film manages to assimilate the story's centrepiece – the love story – into a narrative structure based on the conflict between the 'modern' and the 'traditional'. The modernity/ tradition dynamic is evident elsewhere in the film. The love of Sean

for Mary Kate, for instance, is bound up with his romantic emigrant's search for home, an aspect absent from Walsh's narrative.
Ford's Sean Thornton, unlike Walsh's Paddy Bawn, is actually a
product of the culture of modernity, having been brought up in the
United States. His sense of 'home' is thus radically divided between
two opposite worlds: an imagined Ireland, the supposed source of
traditional and humanist values, and an actual Pittsburgh, where
individuals are dehumanised and reduced to the status of mere ex-
change-value. The film crucially depends on the fact that Sean is an
alien in both places; a representative of the disaffected modern individual suspended between opposing poles. This transformation
from Paddy Bawn to Sean Thornton also involves a major de-
historicisation of Walsh's narrative. In *Green Rushes*, the story of
Ellen and Paddy Bawn is merely one part of a web of stories concerning a common set of characters and events in north Kerry during the Irish War of Independence (1919–21).[2] In *Green Rushes* the
reader meets Paddy Bawn in other tales, where his character takes
on additional attributes that have nothing to do with either his marriage or his return from the United States. Most often, for instance,
he appears as the taciturn but stalwart member of an IRA guerrilla
band – in fact Walsh describes him at the start of the book as 'an ex
prize-fighter, known as "the Quiet Man" because he hoped to end
his days "in a quiet, small little place on a hillside", and was more
likely to end them in a Black-and-Tan ambush'.[3] Such political and
historical aspects of Paddy's identity of course severely complicate
the modernity/tradition structure upon which Ford wishes to hang
his character – and are dispensed with in the film. The psychical
and morally therapeutic dimension to Sean's return to Ireland is
absent from Walsh's story.

Some of these changes may be related to Ford's own complicated relationship with America. Himself the son of Irish emigrants,
Ford tended to see mainstream America from a certain critical distance, which enabled him to analyse rather than merely reproduce
standard versions of, for example, the myth of the American West.
Explaining his unorthodox sympathy for the Indian in movies like
The Searchers, for instance, Ford remarked: 'Perhaps it's my Irish

atavism, my sense of reality, of the beauty of clans, in contrast to the modern world, the masses, the collective irresponsibility'.[4] The irony is that the de-historicised, anti-modern values which he then locates in Ireland – the values of the atavistic clannish community of Innisfree – are themselves implicated in the very system Ford is trying to criticise. The specific polarisation of these values – the tendency to think in a binary way about the so-called modern and traditional – itself betrays Ford's 'complicity' with the perspective of modernity. Indeed the idealistic appeals to generalised family values, to community life, to traditions, are, as we know, a central feature of capitalist ideology, especially mobilised in times of crisis. Capitalism actually idealises and mythologises these values at the very same time as it makes their realisation impossible. After all, the alienating, modernising and commodifying forces of the capitalist economy depend on the values of exchangeability rather than permanence, mobility rather than rootedness, and individualism rather than communalism.

Thus a film like *The Quiet Man* remains at a deep level firmly dependent on the value system of modernity, even though its 'soft primitivism' simultaneously offers a critique of those values.[5] While Luke Gibbons argues persuasively that Ford's work in general offers significant elements of political critique, it is also important to draw attention to the limits of that critique. In *The Quiet Man*, Sean Thornton is reconstructed as a prototypical alienated modern hero, made guilty by capitalist modernity (he has killed a boxer in a prize fight); in search of a personal fulfilment that will be at once an expiation of his sin and a reunification with a pre-modern traditional society. An important readjustment of the social and cultural values found in Walsh's story has occurred whereby narrative motivation which is strongly attached to the social values and codes of a historical rural community has been replaced by one driven by the values of modern 'romantic love' and individualistic personal redemption. As recent theories about the relation between modernity and imperialism have argued, this kind of narrative is basic to modernised cultures like the United States, but has not been as fundamental or appropriate to postcolonial cultures such as Ireland, in which narratives of modernity and progress seem less sustainable and convincing, and where other kinds of narrative remain powerful.[6] For Ford, Ireland is partly a scenario for the idealised redemption of the modern individual: it is a place where such a disaffected subject can be rewarded, having paid his dues to capitalism.

The Field

Like Maurice Walsh, John B. Keane was born in north Kerry. His plays and comic prose have been enormously popular in Ireland since the 1960s, though little known outside the country. His play *The Field*[7] has always been a favourite with Irish amateur dramatic societies, though latterly Keane's work has also found recognition among professional critics, and in the national professional theatre. Like all Keane's work, *The Field* describes and speaks to a rural Ireland of farmers, shopkeepers, publicans, priests and politicians. The play describes a conflict over a small field which has been rented by 'The Bull' McCabe and his son Tadhg for several years. When the field's owner, a local widow, puts the field up for sale Bull feels that he has a certain right to it, having improved the land, but he is outbid at auction by an outsider, William Dee (an Irishman living in England), who wishes to set up a concrete block factory on the site. Intending merely to frighten Dee, Bull and Tadhg end up beating him to death the night before the auction. Sworn to secrecy, the village auctioneer, his family, and a local character, Bird O'Donnell, all maintain silence in the face of church and police inquiries, though everyone suspects that the McCabes are guilty. McCabe successfully purchases the field at the subsequent auction. The play particularly focuses on Bull's rationalisation of his crime, and on the effects of complicity on the family of the auctioneer.

Keane's play is a subtle exploration of the social as well as individual significance of murder, and attempts to analyse with sympathy the competing claims of commerce, custom, family loyalty, state law and church law. Keane's characters are not merely discrete individuals, but individuals constrained by relations with family, community, church and state – relations that are both enabling and disabling in various ways. A character like Leamy Flanagan, the auctioneer's son, for example, is torn between the moral demands of church and state, and the loyalty he owes to his family, who have agreed to remain silent about the crime. They themselves are shown to be torn between horror at the crime of murder, and sympathy for the McCabe's moral right to the land. Jim Sheridan's film of the play, on the other hand, forgoes subtlety for passion and spectacle, and substitutes an investigation of extreme psychological struggle for Keane's analysis of communal behaviour. In ways which link it to *The Quiet Man*, it constructs an Ireland that is distinctly mythic and pre-modern, though in a much more negative and disturbing way than Ford's film.

Among the many alterations that exemplify this shift, the reshaping of the main characters is perhaps most interesting. Sheridan's Ireland, unlike Keane's, is populated by the bizarre and extreme: dysfunctional families, sullen townspeople, an inexplicably obtuse foreigner, and, in Richard Harris's Bull McCabe, a kind of postcolonial King Lear. Tadhg is transformed from a clever, shifty boy in Keane's play to a cartoon psychotic in Sheridan's film. The Bird O'Donnell is alarmingly transformed from a subtle and interesting eccentric into a 'village idiot', straight from the traditions of stage Irishry. In fact, in its treatment of Bird and the other villagers, Sheridan's movie resembles Keane's play less than it does the stereotypes found in British director David Lean's Irish film *Ryan's Daughter* (1970). Lean's romantic vision of Ireland in that movie is predicated upon a view of Ireland as essentially pre-modern, with this pre-modernity alternatively taking shape as a backward, benighted rural ignorance or, more attractively but equally destructively, as wild, emotional, tragic excess.

Sheridan shares both this vision of benighted community and, in the character of Bull himself, the vision of excess. The cinematic Bull is no longer the bullying, but very human and vulnerable character of Keane's play; for Sheridan (assisted by Richard Harris's powerful acting) he becomes a figure of heroic proportions, even a symbol of a fundamental and unresolved psychic struggle within Ireland itself. The film's final image of Bull McCabe raging fruitlessly against the waves recalls Yeats's mythic figure of Cúchulainn fighting with the sea. It makes for powerful spectacle, which, in the global symbolic order, it is evidently Ireland's role to provide.

The outsider who bids against Bull is also remodelled by Sheridan. By changing him from an Irishman into an American, Sheridan is able to hire an American film star (Tom Berenger) and to elaborate a conflict between the profit-hunger of American capitalism and the atavistic land hunger of the postcolonial Irish peasant, which ends up stereotyping both Irish and American values. The narrative becomes centred on the struggle between two individual wills. The two antagonists are equally stubborn in their land-hunger: Bull McCabe out of ancestral passion, the Yank for more financial motives. And although an audience's sympathies with Bull may encourage viewers to value Bull's passionate obsession over the Yank's relative heartlessness, the very extremity of Bull's rage and violence, and the revelation of the dark secret of his son's suicide (an element absent from the play), mean that he becomes more like a tragic figure, and one viewed with fear as well as understanding.

In its narrative construction, Sheridan's film, like his other films (he directed *In the Name of the Father* and wrote *Into the West*), is especially concerned with the relations between fathers and sons. In his version of *The Field*, this obsession enables him to transform Keane's story into the stuff of Greek myth. Bull McCabe as father-tyrant has disrupted the natural order by effectively killing his son, and with tragic irony kills another son in an effort to atone for the death of the first. This mythic scenario is far removed from Keane's attempt to display the confusion, desperation, banality and pathos of murder, and to demonstrate the social meaning of individual action by displaying the culpability of the entire community in the murder of William Dee. Sheridan's mythologising allows him to reproduce the generalising modernity/tradition dichotomy which pits the individual against the communal, the forces of reason and enlightenment against superstition and emotion, and tragic passion against calculating avarice. Though Sheridan evaluates these qualities in somewhat different ways to Ford, he nevertheless accepts the basic validity of these binary oppositions as a means of understanding Irish culture. Keane's play avoids such polarisations: his William Dee, for instance, unlike Sheridan's 'Yank', cannot be read simply as a representative of a cold foreign modernity – his wife's family came from the locality, and he himself is an Irishman from Galway. In an important sense, Keane's play is written from *within* the community life he dramatises, with a feeling for its nuances and complications; Sheridan, on the other hand, sees that same life from the schematic and often uncomprehending eye of the modern cosmopolitan.

The Commitments

Roddy Doyle published his first novel, *The Commitments*, in 1988. The novel drew upon his experience as a schoolteacher in the northside Dublin suburb of Kilbarrack, an area of relative poverty, high unemployment and attendant social problems. Doyle's novel is written almost entirely in dialogue, which facilitated its adaptation to cinema, and Alan Parker's film version proved immensely popular with Irish audiences as well as American ones on its release in 1991. Both film and novel describe the brief rise and fall of a soul band from the northside of Dublin. Although apparently depicting an urban identity, usually a sign of modernity as opposed to the rural world of tradition and conservativism, this film, like many others of an urban Irish mould, turns out to rely on much the same myths and stereotypes as pervade the cinema of rural Irish life.

On the surface, however, the film frequently seems to depict Ireland as a place where stereotypes and fixed cultural identities no longer apply. One of the most memorable sequences in the film shows the teenage band manager Jimmy Rabbitte auditioning prospective band members. A long series of musicians and groups shows up at the door of Jimmy's house, all representing different musical styles and traditions. All the aspiring musicians are Irish, yet their musical identities are a kaleidoscope of multinational popular traditions, from the sublime to the ridiculous: they include traditional Irish music and dance, American blues, South African gospel, Cajun music, Bob Dylan and Joan Baez, Barry Manilow, heavy metal, British punk, new romantics, The Smiths. Contemporary Irish musical identity seemingly crosses national boundaries and time periods. Jimmy's father even offers to sing Elvis numbers: 'Elvis is God,' he announces, and appropriately we see Elvis's picture hanging beside the Pope's on the kitchen wall.

In one way the sequence illustrates the new and mould-breaking hybridity of late twentieth century Irish identity. It implies that modern Irish culture is plural and open to influence, a place where various unrelated cultural forms happily sit side by side in a new culture of mutual enrichment. In other words, Ireland seems to have become a quintessentially 'postmodern' culture – released from the old, narrow and single-minded definitions of 'tradition' which were stultifying and oppressive, but having also managed to avoid the destructiveness of that single-minded modernity which sweeps away the past altogether, dispensing with much that is valuable. Ireland from this perspective might seem to represent an interesting and non-combative commerce between the old and the new, the native and the foreign – a postmodern transcendence of the 'modernity versus tradition' dialectic.

But, as some critics of the postmodern condition have argued, the supposed pluralism of the postmodern can also be understood in a more alarming way as merely an unprecedented intensification of transnational capitalism. Under this economy, everything is ultimately reduced to the level of commodity and exchange value – even images and musical styles. At a notable moment in the film version of *The Commitments*, when the band are having their publicity photographs taken, Jimmy demands that the photographer produce images of 'urban decay' rather than 'picture postcards' – a deft but typically postmodern translation of politics into a matter of style options, whereby urban decay is essentially a marketing device for selling records. A similar translation occurs at meta-filmic level, too – the original video packaging for the movie had a photograph on its cover of the band giving a 'two-fingers' gesture to the camera (and by extension, the viewer). What has happened is that a normally aggressive gesture has become merely a kind of designer cheekiness, with the usual venom of such a gesture for Irish people completely diffused by its absorption into the conventions of the publicity poster, and by being incongruously juxtaposed with the band's exuberant, gleeful facial expressions.

From a critical perspective, cultural hybridity seems less a liberation than merely a by-product of global capitalism, which has commodified everything as styles, and created new global markets in which to exchange them. Detached from their original contexts, these commodified styles, like the two-fingers gesture, actually signify a kind of absence of meaning. By the logic of such unproblematic pluralism anyone can 'be' a Cajun or a soul singer simply by imitating the gestures, miming the role, wearing the style. The fact that styles and traditions carry historical and cultural baggage is hardly acknowledged.

Interestingly, Doyle's novel seems to illustrate a different possibility for creative hybridity, in which a more genuine exchange of cultural value takes place. For instance, even though Jimmy exhorts the band not to sing in their Dublin accents, it is clearly the band's ability to adapt American soul music to their local identity that makes them successful – when Deco starts singing out Dublin place-names instead of American cities in James Brown's 'Night Train', the local audience goes wild. But this element is entirely cut from the film. A genuinely productive process whereby Dubliners appropriate and transform American soul to speak to their own conditions and in their own language is not of interest to Parker. His cinematic Commitments are purely imitative; they illustrate less a liberatory postmodernism than an imperialist modernism at its most powerful and hegemonic.

Visually, the representation of Dublin as an actual place in the film does not extend much beyond cheerful and traditional images of the hordes of happy-go-lucky children, horses and bicycles, set unproblematically against images of modernist urban decay, accompanied by a thumping upbeat soundtrack. Even Dublin's contemporary drug scourge is merely the occasion for a joke. Thus Ireland is, yet again, a quaint, amusing, exuberant culture that somehow retains the values of family, imagination and tradition even in a modern urban setting. Where, in *The Quiet Man*, Ireland is a place where modernity hasn't fully arrived, in *The Commitments* modernity has indeed arrived, but just hasn't worked properly. In both cases, Ireland ends up as modernity's 'Other'.

As with the other films, the 'internationalisation' of the adaptation works at a more fundamental level in relation to the narrative itself. Here too the film significantly departs from the novel. At the end of Doyle's book, the Commitments have broken up because of personal jealousies and immaturity, just on the night when Jimmy has secured them their first recording deal. In the final scene of the book, a slimmed down but undeterred cohort of Jimmy, Derek, Outspan and Mickah are planning to have another try at the music business, this time as a 'Dublin country' band called The Brassers!

But this wry ending is entirely altered in the film. Parker's version has added a subplot, whereby the band has broken up just before the legendary American soul singer Wilson Pickett arrives at the club to jam with them. 'Success', even though it finally eludes them, is still very strongly defined in terms of being endorsed, not by a local audience, but by a living symbol of the multinational capitalist music industry, with its stars, its vast profits, its limousines and chauffeurs. As Jimmy, realising the lost opportunity, disconsolately walks through the Dublin night, he is given a platitudinous pep-talk by Joey the Lips: even though material success eluded them, Joey tells him, 'you raised their expectations of life [...] you lifted their horizons'. These comments are clearly central to Parker's own vision of the film; in a documentary on the making of *The Commitments* he remarked that the film was 'about kids who use music to get out of the world they're in [...] that's pretty relevant wherever you are in the world, I think'. Parker's comments in general are alarmingly stereotyped: if you want to get out of that working-class world, he says, 'you're going to have to be a professional boxer, a professional football player, or get into music'.

By their final concert the band has become a successful commodity, an identity which is emphasised by the way Parker films them through the conventions of 'real-life' concert documentaries and advertisements. Their musicianship is outstanding, they are smooth and professional, the three girls have donned short black dresses and become a visual commodity in the style of a pop video. Interestingly, for a short time after the success of the movie the actor playing Deco, Andrew Strong, starred in a glossy Coca-Cola ad, singing the company's jingle in the style of The Commitments, a transition which seemed astonishingly natural.

Where the ending of Doyle's book confirms the book as an affectionate and humorous depiction of adolescent naivety and immaturity, Parker's film turns the story into a kind of 1990s' teenage update of a familiar American narrative. Its conclusion, unlike Doyle's, is permeated with unproblematic assumptions about the ability to transcend one's environment through sheer perseverance, about international wealth and fame being the pinnacle of success, about real achievement consisting of successful commodity production in a multinational capitalist society. In the most clichéd way, Joey the Lips articulates the typical obfuscation of capitalism, whereby the spiritual and moral is held to be 'what really counts', while in fact it is material value and exchangeability which are directly rewarded in capitalist society. This fact is (probably unconsciously) pointed up by the series of vignettes which conclude the film. In these vignettes, it is suggested that for most of the band members, their experience as a Commitment has been a springboard to a musical career. Contrary to what Joey's 'soul talk' might imply, what really matters is not the moral or artistic quality of what they are now doing – what counts is that they are producing music in the acceptable, commodified form: Dean is a jazz musician, Natalie a pop star, Bernie a country singer, Mickah fronts a punk band. Those who do not go on to a musical career – James and Imelda – both take their places within the bourgeois economy as, on the one hand, a surgeon who sings, and on the other, a respectable middle-class wife. All have found productive rather than parasitical places in the economy, one might say. The only potentially jarring note is provided by Outspan and Derek, the kernel of the original band, who remain uncommercialised and unemployed, buskers on Grafton Street; but this is clearly their 'choice', one connected to their relative immaturity, something that has been emphasised during the film.

Of course, there is a similar dream of success presented in Doyle's book – Jimmy asks the band early on, 'Yis want to be different, isn't tha' it? Yis want to do somethin' with yourselves, isn't tha' it?'.[8] But, crucially, the book's ending provides a humorously ironic perspective on such sentiments; as readers we don't expect new band The Brassers to be any more successful than The Commitments were. Parker's film, on the other hand, doesn't want to explore such an unsettling possibility. Instead of modernity's myth of linear progress, which is what Parker, and Hollywood, and capital require, Doyle's book suggests a counter-narrative of circularity, where ideas of success may not merely be identified as a ruthless transcendence of the past.

Conclusion

I have been arguing that many of the aspects of these three literary works which are most challenging for a reader or an audience are transformed in their cinematic adaptations, where these adaptations have been aimed at, and largely financed by, a mainstream transnational film industry. Viewed together, these three films produce particular variants on 'romantic' myths of the premodern and the postmodern, myths that underwrite global capitalism in general and American mainstream cinema in particular. The challenges posed by the historical, the local, the culturally specific – all those elements which might prove difficult or opaque to the international viewer by disrupting such mythology – are foregone in the interests of reinforcing such myths. It is true that the literary works on which these films are based are not well-known or popular outside Ireland, but this ought not to mean that they have nothing to say to a non-Irish audience. On the contrary, such 'foreign' material might prove liberating in a postmodern world where the homogenisation of national cultures proceeds apace, and the production of a mass global audience (especially through cinema) threatens to accelerate the destruction of choices, the disappearance of shock, the domestication of the different, and the impossibility of learning anything new. Even the 'traditional' can sometimes be an instrument of radical challenge, where it exposes the limits and constructedness of that which is called modern.

Ironically, while Ireland is celebrated within the international cinematic frame (and not merely in *The Quiet Man*) as a place 'different' to modernity, a refreshing alternative to the worst of modern capitalist society, in a deeper sense the Ireland we see on screen is merely a reflection of the conservative myths that underpin that modern society

– the myths upon which Western capitalism has built itself, and through which it obscures its own contradictions. Thus, instead of being a place which might make an audience question the 'universality' of the values which capitalism cherishes – for example, the values of the nuclear family, individualism, self-improvement, and so on – Ireland on the screen turns out to be a place where those 'universal' values may be reassuringly observed, ultimately emerging intact or even strengthened against a background of the atavistic, the stultified, the backward-looking and immature, however charming such 'premodern' characteristics might sometimes be. What this means ultimately is that the international audiences of these films can experience the thrill of encountering an alien 'Other', while, in the end, feeling safely at home. Perhaps, to return to the Quiet Man's question at the start of this chapter, what we are watching in such films is absolutely real – not as an image of 'the real Ireland', but of the powerful and seductive operation of modernisation itself.

Endnotes

[1] Maurice Walsh, 'The Quiet Man' *The Quiet Man and Other Stories*. Original title *Green Rushes* (Belfast: Appletree Press, 1992 (1935)), p. 129.

[2] See Luke Gibbons, *The Quiet Man* (Cork: Cork University Press, 2002), pp. 24–39.

[3] Walsh (1992), p. 4.

[4] Quoted in Joseph M. Curran, *Hibernian Green on the Silver Screen* (New York: Greenwood, 1989), p. 84. See also Gibbons (2002), p. 16.

[5] See Gibbons, 'Romanticism, Realism and the Irish Cinema', in *Cinema and Ireland*, ed. by Kevin Rockett, Luke Gibbons and John Hill (London: Routledge, 1988), p. 200, and Gibbons (2002) for a detailed argument about the critical possibilities of Ford's film.

[6] See for instance David Lloyd, *Anomalous States: Irish Writing and the Post-Colonial Moment* (Dublin: Lilliput, 1993) and Gibbons, *Transformations in Irish Culture* (Cork: Cork University Press, 1996).

[7] John B. Keane, *The Field*. In *Three Plays: Sive, The Field, Big Maggie* (Cork: Mercier Press, 1990 (1965)), pp. 91-167.

[8] Roddy Doyle, *The Commitments*. In *The Barrytown Trilogy* (London: Secker & Warburg, 1992 (1988)), p. 11.

Echoes of *The Playboy*:
The Quiet Man and the Abbey

ADRIAN FRAZIER

The Quiet Man is often taken to be an idealisation of Ireland, even ridiculously so. That it is idealised is certainly true cinematographically. Although 1951 had been a good summer, the best the people of Cong had seen in years, it was not good enough for the cinematographer Winton Hoch. He photographed only when sunshine of Californian brightness broke out, so that the movie is made up of the best minutes of a fair season.

The Quiet Man also packs into its fictive little townland of Innisfree the sight-seeing splendours of three counties. The production company was based at Ashford Castle, but the film crew ranged around to all the beauty spots within a day's drive: Yeats's tower house, the Tully strand, the Maumturk mountains, Ballyglunin station, the streets of Tuam – they were all magically made part of the immediate vicinity of Innisfree (Cong village). *The Quiet Man* became the 'beautiful travelogue' that Ford intended: turn one way, and you are in Mayo, another and there is Galway; a short stroll, and you are standing on the sea-cliffs of Clare. But Ford did not just idealise Ireland, he critiqued it. The critique, like the idealisation, comes about through his practice of loading every rift with ore. Ford and Nugent drew into Walsh's basic tale references to many Irish literary classics. 'Innisfree,' the name of the townland, obviously alludes to Yeats's most popular poem, 'The Lake Isle of Innisfree.' *Innis* means 'island' in Gaelic, and the movie's village is on the mainland, so the name does not make sense. It is apposite as a literary allusion. Like the speaker of Yeats's poem, Sean Thornton was heartsick on the roadway and the pavements grey; he dreamed that he would arise and go to a small cabin. Indeed, Thornton not only dreamed of doing it, he did do it.

'To begin at the beginning,' as Father Lonergan says, the movie first introduces, though she has no particular plot reason for being there, May Craig at the 'Castletown' railway station. Craig was the Abbey's most veteran actor, someone present at the beginning of the Irish Dramatic Revival, and on stage in the first production of *The Playboy of the Western World* in 1907. That is why she is there.

Stepping off the newly arrived train, Sean Thornton (John Wayne) sparks off a complex little comedy just by asking the guard (Joseph O'Dea), 'Can you tell me the way to Innisfree?' Thornton gets a hilarious amount of useless help. O'Dea says, 'Do you see that road over there?' Yes. 'Well, don't take that one. It will do you no good at all.' As the train guard quickly falls into a fight with the railway porter about Irish history, May Craig butts in with her offer of assistance. Her sister's 'third young one' lives in Innisfree and will be only too glad to show Thornton the way. That's great. 'O, no, *if she was here*,' which she is not. The train driver is played by Eric Gorman (1882–1971), with the Abbey since 1909. He next steps to centre stage in the conversation, but then cannot get it out of his head that the Yank is not in the West of Ireland for the fishing. In his own tales of trout and salmon he has himself caught, 'as long as my arm' (he points with his right hand to the full length of his left arm, elbow to ring finger), he forgets all about Innisfree. The train porter joins in the melee, everyone talking at once, while the fireman watches closely. Finally, without a word, Michaeleen Oge Flynn (Barry Fitzgerald), arrives and walks off with Thornton's cases to his horse and buggy.

This comedy of country confusion is a skilful pastiche of a play by Lady Gregory, with her signature combination of condescension to, and appreciation of, Irish country people. *Spreading the News* (1904) works in ways similar to the opening episode of *The Quiet Man*. Eric Gorman, May Craig and Joseph O'Dea were old hands at playing Lady Gregory's one-acts; their performances in such plays were beloved by Abbey audiences and audiences across America during the Abbey's tours.

'Justified complaints about "American cultural imperialism",' Fintan O'Toole observes, 'can sometimes miss the point that American mass culture may well contain buried elements of other cultures.'[1] This Lady Gregory moment in *The Quiet Man*, of course, is hardly buried. It is a conscious tribute by John Ford, blazoned at the movie's beginning, to her type of comedy and the players who brought it to life again and again over the previous forty years. It is a Hollywood cover version of a popular hit from one's country's recent past.

The casting of Barry Fitzgerald as Michaeleen Oge Flynn manages to bring one of O'Casey's characters into play. The part of Michaeleen was expanded and diversified into a combination of jarvey-driver, family friend, match-maker, chaperone, bookie, veteran of the old IRA, secular priest, and boxing referee. He even has different costumes for different roles. When going about his business as a *shaughraun*, he puts on a top hat and great-coat like a character out of Boucicault (Fig. 1).

Fig. 1. Barry Fitzgerald as 'Shaughraun'; Maureen O'Hara as Mary Kate Danaher. (Courtesy Lilly Library, Indiana University, Bloomington, IN.)

It is by means of his vocabulary that Fitzgerald evokes Captain Boyle from *Juno and the Paycock*. In one of the best lines in the movie (*ad libb*ed by Fitzgerald),[2] Michaeleen, having carried the crib into the Thorntons' bedroom following their wedding night, sees that the bed has been toppled and a corner of the mattress has dropped to the floor. Ford allows Fitzgerald plenty of time to silently take in the scene, and set the stage for his first judgement, which he addresses toward the viewer as if from the apron of a stage: 'Impetuous!'

On further consideration of what he thinks must have been epic love-making, Michaeleen adds, 'Homeric!' The chief identifying feature of Captain Boyle in *Juno and the Paycock* is the utterance of the unexpectedly bookish polysyllable, an incongruous exactitude that is irresistibly comic.[3]

After Sean Thornton outbids Squire Danaher in the Widow Tillane's parlour for the 'White O' Morn,' Thornton proposes to Mary Kate Danaher, but the Squire, having lost to Sean Thornton a property he thought some day would be added to his own, will hear none of such a match. And Mary Kate could not, and would not, marry without her brother's consent. The Yank finds her deference to her brother and rejection of himself outrageous. We see how angry and frustrated he is by the way he rides his hunter. As if he were an eighteenth century Irish buck, he jumps gates, gallops through farmers' fields, spurs the horse on, then dragging hard on the bridle, pulls it to a painful stop beside Mary Kate, before digging the spurs again into its wet flanks.

Faced with the spectacle of such public passion, the priest, the vicar, the vicar's wife, and Michaeleen agree that something must be done. They concoct a plot to change Danaher's mind. The first part of the plot is to perpetrate a lie. They make out that Thornton is now aiming to marry the Widow Tillane, on whom (or on whose acres) Squire Danaher had always set his sights. At the Innisfree races, the custom is for the unmarried women of the parish to tie their bonnets on high stakes, and the riders in the order of their finish can snatch what bonnet they wish, and thus both prove their mettle and claim their prizes. Sean comes first at the finish, and leaves Mary Kate's bonnet untouched; he takes the Widow's instead. Mary Kate is distressed and Squire Danaher alarmed. Michaeleen and Father Lonergan then spring the second part of their plot. They tell Danaher that were Mary Kate out of his house, the Widow would be happy to come into it as Mrs. Danaher.

2

One of the biggest changes to Maurice Walsh's plot was the introduction of pony-racing on the strand. Nothing of the kind occurs in the short story; in the film, it is important both as spectacle and as a key part of the plot within the plot. It is also an obvious allusion to J. M. Synge's *The Playboy of the Western World*, where such a race occurs off-stage in Act III. A thing of this kind a film can do so well, especially one by John Ford (pastmaster of filming men on horseback), and a play cannot do it at all. *The Quiet Man* splendidly supplies a missing scene from a great Irish play. But there may be more of *The Playboy* to *The Quiet Man* than a pony race on the strand.

There is a rhyme between the premises of Synge's play and Ford's film. In Synge's plot, Christy Mahon arrives at a Mayo village having (he thinks) killed a man, his own father. Christy falls in love with the publican's daughter, while a widow also takes a fancy to him. He begins to prove his mettle – that he's not all talk, and a snivelling coward – by winning the races, but he cannot avoid a fight with the old man at the end of the play, watched by the whole village. Then, surprisingly victorious, he walks off alone, and Pegeen Mike is left to despair: 'I've lost the only playboy of the western world.'

Now compare the story of Sean Thornton. He arrives at a Mayo village having killed a man, the father of children. He falls in love with the local spinster, while it is falsely rumoured he is courting the village widow. He begins to prove his mettle by winning the races, but still ultimately has to fight old Squire Danaher. Here, however, there is an important change from *The Playboy* pattern: the movie does not end with sexual frustration, but fulfilment.

Some of these similarities between play and movie are also to be found between *The Playboy* and Walsh's story, which is riddled with recycled elements from the Literary Revival. Ford evidently perceived the similarities, and both underlined and extended them by the addition of the race scene. This enforcement of the parallel compels a comparison of Pegeen Mike with Mary Kate Danaher.

3

One of the elements that offended Irish nationalist audiences in 1907 when they saw Synge's play was its representation of women. Famously, rioting broke out at the verbal evocation by the playboy of himself being served up with 'a drift of chosen females standing in their shifts' (that is, in their slips). The alexandrine preciousness of the rhyme between *drift* and *shifts* did not mitigate the crime of conceiving of Irish women as willingly coming in a herd, like heifers, to service, or to be serviced by, the playboy. And how could Synge even use such a word as *shifts* or in any other way make mention of the undergarments of Catholic Irishwomen?

Synge's fantasies about country women did not stop there. Not a single passionate kiss (according to the stage directions) is exchanged between the actors, but Christy promises Pegeen that in days to come 'You'll feel my two hands stretched around you, and I squeezing kisses on your puckered lips, till I'd feel a kind of pity for the Lord God is all ages sitting lonesome in his golden chair.' Pegeen skips over the question of whether God might or might not regret His sexual solitude, and simply says, 'That'll be right fun, Christy Mahon.'[4] Pleased with her receptiveness, he next pictures the two 'making mighty kisses with our wetted mouths…, with yourself stretched back unto your necklace, in the flowers of the earth.' Pegeen, 'moved by his tone', murmurs: 'I'd be nice so, is it?' The readiness for love of Pegeen was Synge's wish and part of the point of his play. The audience got that point, and did not like it, especially coming from a Protestant author about characters who were Catholics. Catholic Irish country women were not like that. Not at all. Not a one of them. Never had been.

The riotous reaction to *The Playboy* pretty much put an end to stage representations of Irish women as sexual beings. Synge's play is unarguably a masterpiece, and it quietly took its place in the Abbey repertoire, after some bowdlerisations and the introduction of a demure tradition in the way Pegeen Mike was acted.

4

When Ford finally got around to making *The Quiet Man*, he decided it was going to be a sexy movie, not a movie about IRA heroics. This was not because Hollywood required it to be so, or because Ford needed to find a way to turn a profit on the movie, or because it was Ford's custom to dwell on the sexual side of things (it was not), or even because the IRA activities were small beer after Ford's experiences in the Office of Strategic Services (OSS). *The Quiet Man* is far and away the sexiest movie that Ford ever made. Indeed, he claimed it is 'the sexiest picture ever […] all about a man trying to get a woman into bed'.[5] He had a reason for making it such.

Sean Thornton's first physical encounter with Mary Kate occurs just after he buys 'White O' Morn'. He is left home by Michaeleen Oge Flynn for his first night in his new property, a quite Gothic, Sheridan Le Fanu, ghostly ruin. Yet as he approaches the abandoned house, he sees turf-smoke coming from its chimney. Thornton opens the cottage door, and the gale outside rushes in, disturbing a little heap of dust beside an abandoned broom. He tiptoes in and fastens the door. He does not (as we do) see Mary Kate Danaher crouching in the shadows, but he does sense the presence of someone else in the building. He gives an Indian war-cry and pitches a stone through a window-pane. Mary Kate (who has been preparing the place for his arrival) gasps, turns, sees her own image in a dusty mirror, screams, and runs for the door, where she is intercepted by the Yank. He pulls the beautiful woman into his arms for a kiss. She, having taken the kiss, stands back, considers her position, then wallops him with a round-house punch.

> *Mary Kate Danaher*: It's a bold one you are! Who gave you leave to be kissin' me?
>
> *Thornton*: So you can talk!
>
> *Mary Kate Danaher*: Yes I can, I will and I do! And it's more than talk you'll be getting if you step a step closer to me!
>
> *Thornton*: Don't worry – you've got a wallop!

Mary Kate Danaher: You'll get over it, I'm thinkin'.

Thornton: Well, some things a man doesn't get over so easy.

Mary Kate Danaher: Like what, supposin'?

Thornton: Like the sight of a girl coming through the fields with the sun on her hair ... kneeling in church with a face like a saint...

Mary Kate Danaher: Saint indeed!

Thornton: ... and now coming to a man's house to clean it for him.

Mary Kate Danaher: But ... that was just my way of bein' a good Christian act.

Thornton: I know it was, Mary Kate Danaher. And it was nice of you.

Mary Kate Danaher: Not at all.

'Saint, indeed!' She both rebukes him for the impiety and phoniness of his courtship metaphor, and indignantly denies being any such thing as a saint. This Irish woman is no puritan. After she is done talking, Mary Kate turns to leave, then darts her head back inside the door for one last quick kiss on the lips of the Yank before taking her leave.

When the official courting commences (Fig. 2), Mary Kate is as eager as Sean Thornton is to escape the eye of their chaperone Michaeleen.

Together they steal a tandem bicycle – the riding of which even more than paddling a canoe together traditionally symbolises successful marital relations. Having gotten clear of onlookers, they pause, and Sean wishes to point out aspects of the scenery. Not Mary Kate.

Fig. 2. John Wayne, Barry Fitzgerald as chaperone, and Maureen O'Hara, at the beginning of the courting (Courtesy Lilly Library, Indiana University, Bloomington, IN).

She runs off across a field. At a river's edge, she kneels to peel off her silk stockings. Sean catches a glance of her thighs, she catches him looking, and returns to her undressing, then bare-footed prances across the stream. He gives his usual John Wayne double-take, throws one shoulder back, then rears forward to stomp still wearing his shoes splashingly after her. Up ahead, she does a Daphne-like pastoral strip-tease – with her stockings in one hand, she takes off her bonnet with the other, casting flirtatious looks backward at him. He shows he is as game as she is by hurling his derby into the next field over. Then she leads him by the hand up the incline. They arrive at a hilltop churchyard with a ruined chapel.

> *Thornton*: If anybody had told me six months ago that today I'd be in a graveyard in Innisfree with a girl like you that I'm just about to kiss, I'd have told 'em...

> *Mary Kate Danaher*: Oh, but the kisses are a long way off yet!
>
> *Thornton*: Huh?
>
> *Mary Kate Danaher*: Well, we just started a-courtin', and next month, we, we start the walkin' out, and the month after that there'll be the threshin' parties, and the month after that ...
>
> *Thornton*: Nope.
>
> *Mary Kate Danaher*: Well, maybe we won't have to wait that month ...
>
> *Thornton*: Yup.
>
> *Mary Kate Danaher*: … or for the threshin' parties …
>
> *Thornton*: Nope.
>
> *Mary Kate Danaher*: … or for the walkin' out together...
>
> *Thornton*: No.
>
> *Mary Kate Danaher* :.. and so much the worse for you, Sean Thornton, for I feel the same way about it myself!

She opens her arms to be embraced, and he gathers her in to himself. Thunder rolls. Frightened by the lightning-bolts, Mary Kate hugs closely to the broad chest of Sean Thornton. He puts his suit coat round her shoulders as the winds rise. Then big raindrops splat one by one on his white nylon shirt, and each makes a little nude pool of transparency, over which Mary Kate spreads and tenses her fingers. Finally, they do kiss. The experience leaves Mary Kate limp. During its shooting, Ford did take after take trying to get the pair to be more passionate.[6] Though only involving a kiss and a rain-shower, the action is metaphorically pre-coital, coital, and then post-coital. It is as sexual as a Hollywood movie in 1951 could be.

For the rest of the movie, Ford makes the audience interested in one chief question: when will Sean Thornton and Mary Kate Danaher get on with the consummation of their love? They get married in due course, but at the wedding reception Squire Danaher finally realises that he has been tricked by a community plot against himself; he punches Sean and scatters the coins across the floor.

Fig. 3: The Rev. Playfair (Arthur Shields), Mary Kate Danaher Thornton (Maureen O'Hara), and Michaeleen Oge Flynn (Barry Fitzgerald) attend to Sean Thornton (John Wayne) after he has been knocked cold at his own wedding reception (Courtesy Lilly Library, Indiana University, Bloomington, IN).

Mary Kate makes it known to Sean that she will not sleep with her husband until she gets her dowry, and locks herself in the bedroom.

In a new scene suggested by John Wayne (unless he got to do it, he feared he would appear to have 'no balls'),[7] Sean Thornton kicks the bedroom door down, picks his bride up into his arms, and says, 'There'll be no locks or bolts between us, Mary Kate Danaher, except those in your own mercenary little heart,' then tosses her, panting with anger and sexual frustration, onto her own marriage bed, breaking it. So when Michaeleen Oge Flynn says their love-making has been impetuous and Homeric, we know it has as yet been nothing of the kind. They both want it, but because of the missing dowry, they cannot have it.

Each goes to talk to a man of the cloth – Thornton to Church of Ireland Reverend Playfair (Arthur Shields); Mary Kate to Father Lonergan (Ward Bond). Reverend Playfair knows all about Thornton's history in the ring, and has a scrapbook to illustrate it, but he also knows a lot about local customs of marriage and, though Protestant, respects them. He gently takes it for granted that now Sean will have to fight for the dowry. By showing a picture of himself on the Trinity College Dublin boxing team, he subtly shifts the context from boxing as a fight to the finish to boxing as an athletic competition. That is all the persuasion required. The tact and economy in the script are admirable, as is Shields's performance. His message is, You must fight for that dowry, and it will be good sport on the day.

Mary Kate happens to catch Father Lonergan just as he is stalking a trophy salmon. She whispers to him in Irish of her plight (as if dirty things become clean when spoken *as gaelige*): no dowry, no consummation, husband in sleeping bag. 'Sleeping bag' in Irish is unfamiliar to Lonergan (a joke on the language revival?), but when he does get the meaning, he is outraged: 'Ireland may be a poor country, God help us, but here a married man sleeps in a bed and not a bag.' His implied message is, Go home and bring your husband to your bed. Which she duly does.

We do not witness the long-delayed nuptials, but the next morning Sean Thornton appears to be mighty pleased with how the night was passed. He is cock of the walk and calls for his wife, but she is not to be found in the kitchen. Michaeleen Oge Flynn, waiting at the cottage door, is all so ready to explain that she is so ashamed of loving a man of whom she could not be proud, she has run away to Dublin. It all has to do with the dowry, and a woman's rights. Thus, the final fist-fight is precipitated, more or less as in the story by Maurice Walsh, apart from Ford's innovation of having Sean Thornton drag his wife brutally from the train station across half the parish to Squire Thornton's fields, where he throws her violently back into the hands of the squire.

It is hard to see what this picturesque and vaudevillian violence is meant to be except either a comic critique of the widespread wife-battering in the Irish Free State, an endorsement of it, or the public, spectacular, erotic entertainment of a Trojan's rape of the local Sabine.[8]

Fig 4. Publicity still of Mary Kate Danaher (Maureen O'Hara) being violently dragged along by Sean Thornton (John Wayne); the use of the image for publicity suggests an expectation that this 'taming of the shrew' will become a favourite part of the movie (Courtesy Lilly Library, Indiana University, Bloomington, IN).

The fight with Red Will Danaher sportily (if not sportingly) won, peace settles back on Innisfree, according to the narrator, Father Lonergan. The whole story has unfolded as if it were his home movie ('See, that's me there...'), and now he is folded back into it in a playful device. In a theatrical 'curtain call' – as Luke Gibbons calls it – the characters each get a final close-up (all pretending to be Protestants, for the benefit of Reverend Playfair and the visiting Bishop).[9]

The last to take a bow are Sean Thornton and his wife in their cottage garden. Then Mary Kate whispers in Sean's ear. He is amazed by what he has heard. She sprints off toward the cottage and, once again rearing back one shoulder, then plunging forward, John Wayne follows after her.

A cult-movie secret is what Ford told O'Hara to whisper in John Wayne's ear before she dashes off – something she at first said she would not dare to say, and then did say. If her words did not have to do with some very pleasurable thing that Wayne has always wanted and will get if he just comes inside, it would be a big surprise. Ford has made the audience wait and wait. Just as the curtain falls, they know impetuous, Homeric consummations are very soon to resume and will long continue.

5

What is even more noteworthy than Ford's thoroughgoing characterisation of the Irish woman as a fully adult, pleasure-loving person is how few objections were raised by Richard Hayes, the Irish censor. He cut to ribbons most Hollywood movies submitted for Irish circulation. In the case of *The Quiet Man* Hayes scissored out Michaeleen's two best lines – 'Homeric!' 'Impetuous' – about the presumed feats of love that broke Sean Thornton's big bed, and the appraisal by Feeney (Jack McGowran) of the bed itself: 'Ah, a man'd have to be a sprinter to catch his wife in a bed like that.'[10] While these excisions are ridiculous, they are mild exactions by the standards of the time in Ireland, which were the strictest in the world.

Ford was, unlike Synge, a Catholic. Also, the sex that occurs in *The Quiet Man* occurs within marriage, off-screen, and for the most part after the end of the story. Nudity is never an issue. But still it is surprising that no whisper was raised about the 'unhealthiness' of the way Mary Kate is depicted. She is often filmed from low down and in half-profile, so as to make Maureen O'Hara, already well-endowed, appear heroically voluptuous. It would have been silly to make a stink about what is overall such a light and affectionate portrait of Ireland, simply because Mary Kate Danaher's breasts appear to be cinematically large, but the fear of being silly did not always stand in the way of Irish censorship.

The failure to register the film's two major innovations, its sexualisation of Irish womanhood and its thematic concentration on the importance of regular and mutually joyful sexual intercourse to a happy marriage, meant that Ford's chief criticism of Ireland went unnoticed. Like Synge, he saw the Irish rural population as starved of joy by Catholic sexual repression and nationalist chauvinism. He wanted to replace those false images with more natural truths and healthy teachings. A man would not have to be a sprinter to catch his wife in a big bed, because she would most likely not be running away from his embraces, but warmly returning them. This view of women was Ford's gift from America to his homeland, but Ireland was not quite ready to accept the offering, or even to acknowledge it.

The Irish response to *The Quiet Man* was often embarrassment. It was commonly said to be all stereotypes. Squire Danaher, as if on cue, even produces an Irish bull: 'He'll regret it til his dying day, if he lives that long.' The characters, situations, and gags of *The Quiet Man*, however, are not so much stereotypes of a socially regressive kind, as 'old chestnuts' – oft-told tales and pieces of theatrical lumber. Ford's Irish movie is like a Christmas pudding made from an ancient recipe, stuffed with nuts and fruits and coins and candies of every description, then soaked in liquor.

The cast was conscious of the twice-told character of the tale, and they gave to their playing the quality of an encore. They gloried in the recherché quaintness of the game. The quality of acting is quite in the spirit of that Friday night in March 1935 when the Hollywood actors joined the Abbey regulars in a performance of *The Playboy of the Western World*. In *The Quiet Man*, however, the stars are not lost in the crowd; they come forward into central roles. Admittedly, those film-stars playing Irish people ham it up in sometimes corny fashion, but Abbey actors had always done that too. Fifteen years after the Abbey actors had come to Hollywood for *The Plough and the Stars*, the dramatic furniture and playing style of the Irish Revival had been taken up into the working vocabulary of international performance. It is remarkable how well Victor McLaglen does as Squire Danaher, and how brilliantly the old football player and cowboy actor Ward Bond pulls off Father Lonergan. Irish priests aren't like that? More's the pity.

In a surprising coincidence, just as Ford was making *The Quiet Man* into one of 'the greatest hits of the Irish revival,' and Hollywood stars were demonstrating that the Abbey playing styles had been affectionately taken up into the vocabulary of global entertainment, the Abbey Theatre itself burned down. As its home burned, the style took wing.

The *Irish Independent* caught up with the *The Quiet Man* cast on the runway of Shannon Airport, just before their return to Hollywood, and asked them their reactions to the fire. John Wayne said he had known the Abbey actors since they began touring America in the 1930s, and they had become some of his best friends, often visiting his home, so he felt terrible for them; it was as if their own home place had been burnt. Yes, it was a terrible shock, Shields admitted, but the place was always a tinderbox. Anyway, 'fire won't stop the Abbey.'[11] Barry Fitzgerald agreed. The old, beloved costumes were gone, and perhaps some valuable unpublished scripts, but the actors are still here to act and the playwrights were not going to vanish. It was past time for the government to build and new and bigger theatre in Dublin.

John Ford had the last word. The Irish people could expect the film he was making in Galway to appear in Irish picture houses the following March or April. The greatness of the Abbey Theatre, it was implied, had been captured and, in some degree, immortalised in *The Quiet Man*.

Endnotes

[1] Fintan O'Toole, *The Ex-Isle of Erin: Images of a Global Ireland* (Dublin: New Island Books 1997), p. 21.

[2] Gerry McNee, *In the Footsteps of the Quiet Man* (Edinburgh: Mainstream Publishing, 1990), p. 132.

[3] Fitzgerald himself made this point about Captain Boyle: 'he was a Dublin original, a strutting Paycock, fond of his drink and vociferous with malapropisms,' 'Star System Opposed by Celebrated Irish Comedian,' *Los Angeles Times* (3 March 1935): A10. Fitzgerald gets the same sort of O'Casey quality into his pronunciation of the syllables of Sean Thornton's supposed American home city: 'Pittsburgh, Massachusetts' and his disgusted one-word comment on America: 'Pro-hi-bi-tion!'

[4] J.M. Synge, *The Playboy of the Western World. A Comedy in Three Acts* (Dublin: Maunsel, 1907), p. 67.

5 Qtd., Des MacHale (ed.), *Picture The Quiet Man: An Illustrated Celebration* (Belfast: Appletree Press, 2004), p. 131.

6 McNee, *In the Footsteps*, 133.

7 Randy Roberts and James S. Olson, *John Wayne: American* (New York: Free Press, 1995), p. 365.

8 At the end of *The Quiet Man*, Mary Kate significantly throws the stick away – the same stick that the old woman gave Sean 'to beat the lovely lady with', and that, after her rebuke from the parish priest, Mary Kate herself handed to Sean for that purpose.

9 It is tempting to suggest that this scene of the Innisfree villagers pretending to be Protestants is John Ford's inside joke on the Abbey custom of Protestants pretending to be Catholics, with a kind of triumphalist smirk at the fact that there were a scant few Protestants left in Ireland after thirty years of predominantly Catholic self-rule, but the tone of the scene is in fact simple and cheerful. There is, however, a Hollywood inside joke on the name of the Innisfree pub, Cohan's. 'We pronounce it,' Michaeleen says, 'Co-Hans,' a slightly anti-semitic, because unnecessary, correction. Would Michaeleen be likely to know much of Cohens or Cohns? Or that a prominent Hollywood producer was Harry Cohn? Shortly after completing *The Quiet Man*, John Wayne formed a production company with Robert Fellows, saying 'it had to be better than working with men like Yates and Cohn' (Ronald Davis, *Duke: The Life and Times of John Wayne* (Norman, Oklahoma: University of Oklahoma Press, 1998), p. 164).

10 See Kevin and Emer Rockett, *Irish Film Censorship: A Cultural Journey from Silent Cinema to Internet Pornography* (Dublin: Four Courts Press, 2004), p. 13.

11 'Former Players High Hopes for the Future,' *Irish Independent* (20 July 1951): 7.

6

The Quiet Man, Brigadoon and Scottish and Irish Film Criticism

FIDELMA FARLEY

This chapter will compare *The Quiet Man* to its Scottish counterpart, *Brigadoon* (Minnelli, 1954). There are many similarities between the two films, in terms of style and content, in the place each occupies within the history of cinematic representations of Ireland and Scotland, and within the history of film criticism in each country. Both films are key reference texts for Irish and Scottish filmmakers, whether through resounding rejection of their romanticism and 'inauthenticity' (e.g. Bob Quinn's *Poitín* (1978) was conceived in part as a riposte to *The Quiet Man*)[1], or affectionate engagement with their elements of spectacle and comedy (e.g. Bill Forsyth's *Local Hero* (1982)), or in replaying the theme of the Irish west and the Scottish Highlands as places of refuge and redemption.

Both films are also key texts in the inauguration and growth of Irish and Scottish film criticism: *The Quiet Man* is central to Luke Gibbons's analysis of romanticism and the Irish landscape in *Cinema and Ireland* (1988), the founding text of Irish Film Studies; Colin McArthur used *Brigadoon* to identify the enduring phenomenon of 'Tartanry' in his chapter in *Scotch Reels* (1982), the founding critical text of Scottish Film Studies. Indeed, both Gibbons and McArthur have revisited the films in recent publications, expanding upon and developing their original arguments.[2]

I will argue here that a comparative analysis of the two films serves to highlight the similarities and differences between representations of Scotland and Ireland in film, and between conceptions of the relationship between tradition and modernity in Irish and Scottish cinema.

Scottish and Irish Film Criticism

A shared feature of Irish and Scottish films is the narrative of the American visitor who invariably makes his way to the west and encounters there stunning natural scenery and odd but lovable natives. Scottish examples include *The Maggie* (Mackendrick, 1954), *Trouble in the Glen* (Wilcox, 1954) and *Loch Ness* (Henderson, 1996), and some examples set in Ireland include *The Luck of the Irish* (Koster, 1948), *Widow's Peak* (Irvin, 1993) and *The Nephew* (Eugene Brady, 1998). *The Quiet Man* and *Brigadoon* are particularly well-known and influential examples of the genre, not least because of the authorial talents of John Ford and Vincente Minnelli and the star images of John Wayne and Gene Kelly.

Despite the enduring popular success of both films, they have consistently provoked considerable ambivalence about their representations of Ireland and the Irish and Scotland and the Scottish. Since their respective releases, *Brigadoon* and *The Quiet Man* have figured high on the cultural cringe factor, provoking embarrassed and angry rebuttals of their false and 'stereotypical' portrayals of the Irish and the Scottish.[3] Indigenous filmmakers and some critics have regarded the films as serious impediments to the development of native film industries, and to the development of national cinemas that address the concerns of the nation.

The films have occupied a more complex position in academic film criticism in Ireland and Scotland. *The Quiet Man* was one of the key films in Luke Gibbons's essay, 'Romanticism and Realism in Irish Cinema', in *Cinema and Ireland* (1988), and *Brigadoon* featured in Colin McArthur's essay, 'Scotland and Cinema: The Iniquity of the Fathers' in *Scotch Reels* (1982). In their respective essays, Gibbons and McArthur argue that films about Ireland and Scotland construct each country, and in particular the landscapes of the west coasts, as refuges from modernity, from the fast-paced, distracted, mechanised nature of modern urban life. *The Quiet Man* and *Brigadoon* are exemplary films in constructing Ireland and Scotland as places that are locked forever in a past characterised by the traditional and the rural: travelling to Ireland or Scotland is not simply a movement across space to a different location, it is also a movement backwards through time.

Gibbons' essay argued that cinematic Ireland was constructed as a pre-modern realm, depicted positively as 'soft primitivism', that is 'civilised life purged of its vices'[4] or negatively, as 'hard primitivism', that is, 'civilised life purged of its virtues'.[5] *The Quiet Man* is discussed at length by Gibbons as an example of soft primitivism, a prelapsarian Eden untouched by the stress, rigidity and greed of modernity.

In *Scotch Reels*, Cairns Craig and Colin McArthur identify two recurring cinematic discourses about Scotland, Tartanry and Kailyard, which draw on wider cultural discourses about Scotland generally. Tartanry constructs a Scotland of mists and heather, mountains and lochs, populated by fey maidens and noble warriors, an image given enormous resonance and popularity by the novels of Sir Walter Scott. Kailyard, on the other hand, is small-town Scotland, depicting a tight-knit, insular community inhabited by such figures as the minister, the schoolteacher and the 'lad o' pairts' whose move to the big city and subsequent return underlines the values of his community. Both discourses are, argues McArthur, anti-modernity; both construct a lost world that is infused by nostalgia, and both lock Scotland into a static past, with no engagement with the dynamics of history or prospect of progress. The majority of films about Scotland are 'tartan exteriors with kailyard mores',[6] i.e. articulating conservative, small-town values with the external trappings of tartan, highland landscapes and so on, with *Brigadoon* named as the 'cinematic apotheosis'[7] of this hybrid of Tartanry and Kailyard.

While both critics agree that Ireland and Scotland are constructed as 'primitive' spaces, their analyses diverge in their assessments of the consequences of this. For McArthur, the majority of popular films about rural Scotland contribute to damaging 'myths' that distort and therefore inhibit constructive creative and artistic engagement with the realities of contemporary Scotland.

A considerable part of Gibbons's analysis of *The Quiet Man*, however, is devoted to the film's self-ironising tendencies, which prevent it from being read at face value as a realist text. Irish romanticism, argues Gibbons, is consistently undercut by foregrounding its romanticism. By foregrounding the artificiality of film conventions such as mise-en-scène and the illusion of an autonomous fictional world, the naturalisation of the film's romanticism is undone. Thus the film's fantasy of escape from the hell of modernity and recovery of the lost motherland is exposed as a fantasy, even as the desire that fuels the fantasy is still present. Ireland's status as a fantasy space is simultaneously reinforced and exposed in the film's playful acknowledgment of its fictional status.

This recognition of the complexity of popular texts does not, generally, occur in *Scotch Reels*, heavily influenced as it was by the structuralist approach current in UK critical writing and thinking at the time. For McArthur and other critics writing on Scottish culture in the 1980s, representations of Scotland had been consistently 'colonised' and misappropriated by American and British films, and thus served the interests of those dominant cultures, rather than the interest of Scotland and the Scots. Although McArthur recognises *Brigadoon* as a deconstruction of the Romantic myth, the overall condemnation of popular cinema in *Scotch Reels* had a lasting effect on Scottish film criticism, which has, until quite recently, favoured cinematic realism and experimentation.[8] It is only in the last few years that Scottish film criticism has begun to adopt the kind of approach instigated by Gibbons in relation to Ireland and film, with the result that popular films that had previously been dismissed, such as *Local Hero* (Forsyth, 1982), *The Wicker Man* (Hardy, 1973) and *Whisky Galore!* (Mackendrick, 1949) have increasingly been reclaimed for critical interest. The evident self-reflexivity of *Brigadoon* (acknowledged but not discussed in any detail by McArthur in *Scotch Reels* and his latest book, *Braveheart, Brigadoon and the Scots*), its construction of Scotland as a pre-modern utopia brought into being by the protagonist's (and audience's?) intense yearning to transcend the material, the rational and the banal,[9] serves as a template for identifying the ways in which later Scottish films using the 'outsider' narrative template play around with conventional romantic themes and images of Scotland, managing to reiterate and undermine them at the same time.

The Wicker Man is a dark reworking of the outsider narrative, in which a dour Calvinist policeman from the mainland enters the pre-modern, pagan community, only to be burnt as a sacrificial offering to the gods.[10] *Local Hero* is another 'outsider' narrative that draws on the conventional romantic images of rural Scotland in a knowing fashion. Objects of modernity, such as the wrist watch and the motor car, are rendered inoperable by the forces of nature; frequent long shots and long takes demonstrate the beauty of the landscape; the two principal female characters are named Stella and Marina, evoking the sky and sea; and the film is populated by quirky locals. But its whimsical charm is interspersed with shrewd observations on the difficulties faced by contemporary rural communities and the simultaneous rapaciousness and sentimentality that result from the relentless spread of global capitalism. The outsider, Mac, a representative of an American oil company, while deeply affected by his sojourn in the village of Furness, does not, after all, become part of the community, returning instead to his life in modern America. The final shot shows him in his American apartment, looking at a photo of Furness. Acknowledging and analysing the occurrence of elements of irony and textual play enable films like *Local Hero* to be critically recuperated as examples of present-day Scottish films that successfully engage with, rather than simply rejecting, the familiar, and formerly much-despised, narrative and visual templates for representing rural Scotland.

Nostalgia

In his recent short book on *The Quiet Man*, Luke Gibbons discusses how nostalgia functions in relation to modernity in *The Quiet Man*, arguing that the hazy perfection with which nostalgia covers its object operates as compensation for its loss. Nostalgia, Gibbons argues, undergoes a significant change in the late eighteenth century, being defined initially as a pathology, an over-attachment to birthplace and homeland that hinders integration into other places, a vital skill in the rise of mobility that accompanied the spread of modernity. Gradually, however, the past recedes and is idealised to the extent that nostalgia becomes a 'consoling fiction', pleasurable reminiscence rather than painful memory:

> Crucially, there is an experience of trauma in both cases except that, the second time round, dimmed by romantic nostalgia, the past is recreated in the image of a dream world and wrapped in a golden haze which all but removes the source of pain at the outset.[11]

The Quiet Man, argues Gibbons, has both forms of nostalgia. Sean's journey to the homeland was preceded by his killing of a man in the boxing ring and is thus motivated by the desire for a cure from the resulting trauma. The second form of nostalgia is also present in *The Quiet Man*, in the romantic haze that surrounds Innisfree and that signals the impossibility of return. Escape from Pittsburgh and industrialised, urban US is both possible and impossible, an illusion that might just be real.

If we look at these arguments in relation to *Brigadoon*, it is striking how apt they are – indeed, they are probably even more applicable to *Brigadoon* than to *The Quiet Man*. They also allow us to explore how the image of Scotland functions, rather than simply dismissing it as a false and inauthentic distortion of the truth. *Brigadoon* has both forms of nostalgia identified by Gibbons, the first form evident in Tommy's yearning to escape the superficiality of his life in New York. But the emphasis is more strongly on the second form of nostalgia, whereby the 'homeland' is idealised and romanticised to the extent that it is, ultimately, inaccessible. The nostalgia in *Brigadoon* is for a world that is long gone, never to be seen again. Comparing *Brigadoon* to *The Quiet Man*, it is notable that the disconnection between the modern hell of America and the pre-modern Utopia of Scotland is much starker in *Brigadoon*, exemplified by a dramatic cut from the misty heaths of Scotland as the village of Brigadoon disappears for another hundred years, to the vertiginous skyscrapers of New York and then its noisy, crowded bars, making a striking contrast between the open

spaces and stillness of Brigadoon and the noisiness and overcrowd-
ing of the city.

Most significantly, however, is the literal severance from modernity required to enter Brigadoon. While Sean Thornton's journey to
Ireland is a journey across space but (metaphorically) backwards in
time, Tommy Allbright's journey to Brigadoon is literally backwards
in time, as Brigadoon exists in a permanent past that can be accessed
only by an irrevocable rejection of modernity. Given that Brigadoon
is clearly an imaginary construct, the past, *Brigadoon* tells us, can be
accessed only through the imagination. From the perspective of critics of Scottish cinema, the film also tells us that cinematic Scotland is
also a beautiful illusion, a 'consoling fiction' of unspoiled nature,
community and belonging.

Tradition and Modernity in Irish and Scottish Cinema

The dramatic gulf between the traditional and modern, the rural and
urban, and the past and present that is evident in *Brigadoon* is also to
be ascertained in more recent Scottish films. Irish films, by contrast,
tend to complicate the opposition between tradition and modernity.

The differential treatment of the relationship between tradition
and modernity in Irish and Scottish cinema is rooted in the historical
development of the ideas of nation and national identity in relation
to landscape. In Irish national discourses, the true heart of the nation
lies in its rural west and a traditional way of life, an association that
began to shift only in the mid-twentieth century with the belated beginnings of the modernisation process. By contrast, the Scottish Lowlands underwent intensive industrialisation from the late eighteenth
century, creating a split between the modern, industrialised lowlands
and the rural, traditional Highlands that was exacerbated by the defeat of the Jacobite cause and its aftermath and the Highland Clear-
ances of the mid-nineteenth century. In Scottish popular, and indeed
some critical, discourses, the rural Highlands are associated with the
past and the urban Lowlands with the present and future. In cinema,
the Highland landscapes are either imbued with a sense of loss (of
the true heart of Scotland, of a traditional way of life), or are rejected
as projecting a 'false' and 'distorted' version of Scotland that detracts

from the problems of the real Scotland of the industrialised (now post-industrial) Lowlands. Scottish cinema's expression of that sense of loss has crystallised around the story of the evacuation of the island of St Kilda in 1930, the subject of several documentaries, Michael Powell's *Edge of the World* (1937) and more recently, Bill Bryden's *Ill Fares the Land* (1983). In the final shots of *Ill Fares the Land*, we see the evacuated islanders arrive at the mainland by boat, the hymn 'The Lord is my Shepherd' on the soundtrack. The silence is broken when they land by the noise of the crowds, who stare, jeer and shout, and by the flash of newspaper cameras. As they prepare to leave, a voice-over recites the names of the rest of the islanders, most of whom became ill or died shortly after leaving the island. The young boy looks back to the island from a car window, picturing the rural, traditional past that is now gone forever, as the car moves forward to the modern, urban future.[12] The transition from the traditional to the modern is abrupt and destructive, with the traditional world eradicated by the forces of modernity.

A film such as *Trainspotting* (Boyle, 1996) represents the other side of the coin, the rejection of the Highlands, or more generally, rural Scotland, as the 'real' Scotland. In a now (in)famous scene, the protagonist, Renton, rants 'It's shite being Scottish', in response to his friend Tommy's pride in the beauty of the natural landscape. In an inversion of the usual way of framing the Highland landscape, where nature predominates over the human, Renton's face dominates the frame during his monologue. Here, the experience of Lowland, urban, working-class Scotland is contrasted to the inauthenticity of the romantic Highland landscapes.[13]

While contemporary Irish films also mount a challenge to the identification of the west of Ireland as the authentic heart of the nation, they do so in a more nuanced way that is less rejection than subversion. Examples include using different landscapes that do not have the same connotations as the west, such as the midlands in *Eat the Peach* (Ormrod, 1986) and *I Went Down* (Breathnach, 1997); characters who do not conventionally 'fit' the landscape, such as the Chinese immigrant in *Yu Ming is Ainm Dom* (O'Hara, 2003), the Ulster Presbyterians of *December Bride* (O'Sullivan, 1990); introducing surrealism, as in the scene in *The Butcher Boy* (Jordan, 1997) where an atomic mushroom cloud explodes in a lake; or deliberately de-romanticising the landscape of the west, as do the films of Bob Quinn, especially *Poitín*. In other words, the split between rural and urban, traditional and modern, past and present is dramatic in Scottish films, whereas the Irish films do not necessarily even perceive them as oppositional.

Conclusion

On the evidence of recent Irish films, it seems as though Irish cinema, having effectively ignored Irish cities for decades, is now focusing overwhelmingly on the urban experience, and reinstating the countryside as a place of refuge and escape from the city (*The Honeymooners* (Golden, 2004), *The Trouble with Sex* (Connolly, 2005)). By contrast, Scottish cinema, while still retaining a strong focus on the urban Lowlands, has produced films that increasingly complicate the conventional opposition between rural/urban, traditional/modern, particularly in *Breaking the Waves* (von Trier, 1996), but also in films such as *The Last Great Wilderness* (Mackenzie, 2002) and *Morvern Callar* (Ramsay, 2002). Looking at *The Quiet Man* and *Brigadoon*, and the critical writings spawned by them, enables these kinds of comparisons to be made. It also enables fresh perspectives to be brought to bear on Irish and Scottish film, and Irish and Scottish film criticism and history.

Endnotes

[1] See Robert Quinn's documentary, *Cinegael Paradiso* (2004).

[2] Luke Gibbons, *The Quiet Man* (Cork: Cork University Press, 2002). Colin McArthur, *Brigadoon, Braveheart and the Scots: Distortions of Scotland in Hollywood Cinema* (London: I.B. Tauris, 2003).

[3] See James MacKillop's essay on responses to *The Quiet Man* among the Irish and Irish-American diaspora, 'The *Quiet Man* Speaks', in James MacKillop (ed.), *Contemporary Irish Cinema: From The Quiet Man to Dancing at Lughnasa* (Syracuse, New York: Syracuse University Press, 1999).

[4] Luke Gibbons, 'Romanticism, Realism and Irish Cinema', in Kevin Rockett, Luke Gibbons, John Hill, *Cinema and Ireland* (Syracuse, New York: Syracuse University Press, 1988), p. 198.

[5] Ibid., p. 200.

[6] Colin McArthur, 'Scotland and Cinema: The Iniquity of the Fathers', in Colin McArthur, ed., *Scotch Reels: Scotland in Cinema and Television* (London: BFI, 1982), p. 41.

[7] Ibid., p. 47.

[8] See Jonathan Murray, 'Straw or Wicker? Traditions of Scottish Film Criticism and *The Wicker Man*', in Jonathan Murray, Lesley Stevenson, Stephen Harper and Benjamin Franks (eds.), *Constructing The Wicker Man: Film and Cultural Perspectives* (Dumfries: University of Glasgow Crichton Publication, 2005), for a detailed discussion of the development of Scottish film criticism. See also John Caughie's 'Representing Scotland: New Questions for Scottish Cinema', in Eddie Dick (ed.), *From Limelight to Satellite: A Scottish Film Book* (London, Glasgow: BFI/SFC, 1990), one of the earlier critiques of the *Scotch Reels* position (Caughie, 1990).

[9] *Brigadoon* falls into the third category of musical identified by Richard Dyer in his article 'Entertainment and Utopia', in which 'utopia is implicit in the world of the narrative as well as the world of the numbers. The commonest procedure for doing this is removal of the whole film in time and space [...] to places, that is, where it can be believed (by white, urban Americans) that song and dance are "in the air"' [Richard Dyer, 'Entertainment and Utopia', in Bill Nichols (ed.), *Movies and Methods Vol. II* (Berkeley: University of California Press, 1985), p. 231].

[10] Philip Kemp, in his biography of Alexander MacKendrick, the Scottish director of *Whisky Galore!* (1949) and other Ealing films, notes that *The Wicker Man* is, effectively, *Whisky Galore!* made as a horror film (Kemp, Philip, *Lethal Innocence: The Cinema of Alexander Mackendrick*. London: Methuen, 1991).

[11] Gibbons, *The Quiet Man*, p. 49.

[12] Colin McArthur sees the shot of the young boy looking out of the car window at the island he has just left as emblematic of Scottish cinema's enchantment with the past and corresponding inability/unwillingness to engage with the present or future (Colin McArthur, 'Tendencies in the New Scottish Cinema', *Cencrastus*, 13 (Summer 1983) 33-5).

[13] A scene in *My Name is Joe* (Loach, 1998), in which Joe takes a break at a scenic spot during a drug run, foregrounds the packaging of Scottish landscape for the tourist and thus rejects its 'inauthenticity' in favour of real life in working-class Glasgow.

7

The Quiet Man Resurrects
Waking Ned Devine

MICHAEL PATRICK GILLESPIE

Despite its widespread application, 'Irish' remains a term defined subjectively rather than by broadly accepted criteria. Consequently, a film in which individuals, seemingly behaving like caricatures, stand in as representations of a national character can take on a threatening quality, and provoke reactions devoid of a sense of humour and with a high level of indignation. That disposition may explain responses to the seemingly innocuous film *Waking Ned* (1998) (released in the United States as *Waking Ned Devine*). Though the film was marketed as a slapstick comedy, a number of viewers have seen it as much more, taking offense at what they perceived as stereotypical portrayals and manipulative screenwriting.

For example, in the opening paragraph of a relentlessly acerbic review posted on his website, Harvey O'Brien, who teaches film at University College Dublin, ably illustrates the animus that many critics of Irish film feel towards *Waking Ned*:

> Worthless comedy shot in the Isle of Man but set in Ireland which attempts to capture the feel of Ealing films from forty years ago, but fails miserably to achieve their tone, pace and humour. This film is transparently desperate in its appeal to sentimentality and it is offensive in assuming that the sight of Ian Bannen and David Kelly romping naked on a motorbike

along the roads of an ersatz Ireland is actually funny. Its makers seem to presume that audiences will allow any amount of
bad dialogue, poor plotting and mawkish drivel to pass for
entertainment in the name of 'old fashioned' comedy, and that
playing the Irish card will excuse the absence of any kind of
intelligence.[1]

O'Brien's reaction highlights the volatility of opinions about depictions of Irishness and its sputtering tone underscores his emotional
investment in his own sense of the concept. Neil Jackson, writing the
Waking Ned entry for *Contemporary British and Irish Film Directors*, perhaps feels less threatened by the implications of the film's treatment
of Irish identity, but cannot get beyond criticism through under-
statement. He calls the film 'not as saccharine as it might have been'
with 'a strain of black humour that provides a welcome relief'.[2]

Martin McLoone, in *Irish Film: The Emergence of a Contemporary
Cinema*, presents a less outraged response than O'Brien, but at the
same time proves far more inclined to articulate specific, splenetic
criticism than does Jackson:

> The problem with a film like *Waking Ned* is that it lacks any
> degree of self-consciousness or internal subversion that might
> rescue it from the charge of 'paddywhackery'. The mythical
> rural community that is created, with its wily and resourceful
> inhabitants, stands unproblematically for an authentic organic
> community that outfoxes the po-faced representative of urban
> modernity. The film's celebrated leads, two old men on an
> outrageous scam to defraud the national lottery, certainly add
> an original element to the story (no doubt achieving in the
> process a significant blow against the ageism of much con-
> temporary cinema). However, the series of oppositions that
> the film sets up – between tradition and modernity, between
> Tullymore and Dublin – are almost exactly the same as those
> we located in *The Quiet Man*, but without the latter's ironic
> self-subversion as compensation.[3]

McLoone's sweeping dismissal evokes the sort of generalisations
about Irishness that need more concrete evidence to be sustained.[4] At

the same time, like O'Brien, his critique points to the very features that determine whether or not the film succumbs to stereotypical silliness – slapstick humour, sentimentality and the manipulation of stereotypes. While I do not agree with McLoone's unfavourable comparison with *The Quiet Man*, I do feel that it highlights an effective gauge for *Waking Ned* and other films of this sort. In the half-century that has elapsed since its release, the subversive qualities of John Ford's motion picture have established an interpretive paradigm that allows viewers, who might otherwise be inclined to dismiss Kirk Jones's film, to see a narrative complexity that manipulates rather than panders to national stereotypes.

A number of striking production parallels facilitate the comparison between *Waking Ned* and *The Quiet Man* even as they raise fundamental questions of identity.[5] Both films take a seemingly predictable narrative structure, and use it to evoke a more complex interpretive response than one might initially suppose is supportable. They play on assumptions that viewers will make when presented with seemingly stereotypical situations and characters, and they facilitate an alternative interpretive response by allowing audiences to engage the conflicted natures and conditions that lurk beneath the façades.

As other chapters in this collection make abundantly clear, from its appearance in 1952 John Ford's film has become a paradigm of a non-indigenous approach to Irish film-making. It engages most of the conventional stereotypes – the naïve Yank, charming rascals, the gombeen man, and the hot-tempered redhead. And its narrative shows that critiques of dominant views function as effectively when they take a subversive approach as they do when they unfold with sledge-hammer determination. Since many of the same types of criticism levelled at *Waking Ned* have been applied to *The Quiet Man*, I think a reminder of the subversive techniques of Ford's film can provide a helpful interpretive introduction to Kirk Jones' efforts.[6]

Although *The Quiet Man* has been a popular success from its release, the evolution of positive attitudes toward the film among critics has developed more slowly.[7] The breakthrough came with Luke Gibbons's seminal essay, and from there a tolerance of romanticism grew through acceptance and ultimately to an admiration of its subversiveness.[8] No matter what one's view along this spectrum, a growing number of critics have dismissed as reductive the idea of *The Quiet Man* as simply a collection of stereotypes.

Certainly, *The Quiet Man* is a film very much aware of the burden of stereotypes, and indeed the title character, Sean Thornton, works mightily to project the traits of a stage Irishman and to impose his stereotypical views on others. However, it is a grave mistake to equate Thornton's perception of Ireland and the Irish with the point of view that dominates the film, for the film's narrative undermines his clichéd views from the opening scenes. In the trip from the railway station to Innisfree, for example, Thornton asks Michaeleen Oge Flynn to pause at a bridge overlooking White O'Morn, the cottage in which Thornton was born. The shot of Thornton on the bridge gazing at the home he had idealised, obviously filmed on a soundstage, announces the artificiality of his world, underscored by the outdoor shots that pepper the rest of the scene. Indeed, that seems to be the point. While other outdoor scenes, particularly those that do not include Thornton, are shot on location, representations of Thornton are consistently set in the clichéd ethos of his simplistic view of Ireland.

Actions as well as attitudes reflect Thornton's limited sense of the Irish ethos. Not only does Thornton come to Ireland with naïve views that seek to legitimise stereotypes, he continually misconstrues his understanding of the culture which confronts him every day. He knows a few odd customs – dipping his hand in holy water for Mary Kate or attempting to treat the patrons of Cohan's pub – but he misses the full implications of these gestures and, more significantly, of rituals like courting or traditions like dowries. As the narrative makes clear to viewers, at least to those sensitive to the nuances of the plot, practices that Thornton takes as quaint local colour stand as life and death issues for the people of Innisfree.

Most significantly, Thornton grievously misjudges the effect that Ireland will have on him. He arrives at Innisfree seeking the solace offered by a gentler world than the mills of Pittsburgh or the boxing rings of American prize-fighting. Instead, in his first interaction with the locals, he precipitates a violent argument by simply asking directions. By the end of the film, Thornton has become all that he sought to escape. He has abused his wife, beaten his brother in law, and become roaring drunk. In the process, this has gained him the measure of acceptance that he sought from the start. In fact, while Thornton, and unsophisticated viewers, may remain ignorant of the changes that have occurred in his nature, the narrative of *The Quiet Man* uses this transformation to present a much more sinister, much more corrosive sense of rural Ireland that lurks beneath a veneer of charm.

I see *Waking Ned* operating according to these same narrative principles, and for that reason I find O'Brien's objections insufficiently specific and reflecting prejudices more than considered opinions. They echo a number of the disparaging responses that critics have voiced of *The Quiet Man*, reflecting an ongoing hostility to anything reminiscent of the broad slapstick of the Christmas pantomimes or the sardonic parodies of the stage Irishman who dominated plays and novels from the eighteenth century to well into the twentieth. In fact, the narrative complexity of *Waking Ned* comes closer to the corrosive self-examinations of *The Quiet Man* than to the simpleminded stereotypes that punctuated the pages of *Punch* throughout the nineteenth century, and this structure demands more series attention than O'Brien seems prepared to exert.[9]

Like *The Quiet Man*, objective measures establish *Waking Ned* as a typical Irish film. In fact, it addresses several of the key issues that McLoone, in his well-received book, *Irish Film*, lays out as essential to any motion picture claiming an indigenous Irish connection:

- an interrogation of the rural mythology which underpinned cultural nationalism and is encapsulated in the use of landscape [...]

- a consequent desire to reveal the social and political failures of independent Ireland and latterly to probe the failures and contradictions of the Irish 'economic miracle'

- an interrogation of religion in Ireland [...]

- the question of women in Ireland [...] [10]

Viewers may debate the effectiveness of *Waking Ned* in taking up each of these topics, but the narrative's concern for the same subjects that McLoone privileges gives the film, according to his own standards, a formal legitimacy. In the plot, the rural mythology of the de Valera era – young women dancing at the crossroads – is shouldered aside by images of middle-aged and elderly peasants grasping at the chance to commit fraud for the sake of the lottery money. Ireland's economic miracle has clearly bypassed the village of Tullymore with few young people, no children aside from Maurice, and little sign of any economic activity – outside the pub and the grocery. The facile attitudes of the local parish priest, who specialises in trips to Lourdes, and the easy moral relativism of the curate, who stands in for him, highlight a cynical and ineffectual religious institution. Finally, Maggie O'Toole, a single mother at peace with herself and the community, articulates a characterisation that works against stereotypes without becoming polemical.

A trickier issue turns on the question of whether or not the film itself is worth watching, whether one calls it Irish or not. In the passage quoted above, Harvey O'Brien dismisses the movie with a series of scathing generalisations: 'Its makers seem to presume that audiences will allow any amount of bad dialogue, poor plotting and mawkish drivel to pass for entertainment in the name of "old-fashioned" comedy'. Setting aside the sweeping subjectivity of such judgments, certain analogies make it easier to assess the validity of O'Brien's charges.

Generic features play an important role in shaping *Waking Ned*. I assume by the term old-fashioned comedy, O'Brien means that the film follows the slapstick conventions that the Marx Brothers made famous in their films of the 1930s and that the Ealing comedies celebrated in the 1950s. They remain evident in contemporary films such as *Animal House* (1978), *Raising Arizona* (1987), *The Full Monty* (1997), *Analyze This* (1999) and *Snatch* (2000). Irish motion pictures like *Eat the Peach* (1986), *The Snapper* (1993), *Puckoon* (2002), and *Intermission* (2003) follow this tradition without evoking the same level of scorn. Nonetheless, in every film of this type the plots are predictable and the action often plays upon sentiments.

A more telling critique made by O'Brien, and one echoed by McLoone, though not with the same ferocity, is that the dialogue is weak and the characterisation facile. Again, that statement disregards the genre, for in slapstick films it is the exchanges between characters and the promise of complexity beneath the surface that carries the action. In the remainder of this chapter, I will outline that complexity in *Waking Ned*.

As in so many slapstick comedies, much of the film's humour turns upon the interaction of a sweet-natured straight-man Michael O'Sullivan (played by David Kelly) and his conniving partner Jackie O'Shea (Ian Bannen's character). In consequence, it would be easy to see these roles degenerate into stereotypes. However, key features in Jackie's nature prevent this.

From the start of the motion picture a cynical predatory impulse informs Jackie's behaviour. He has a marvellous eye for human weakness, and he exploits it ruthlessly in any situation, great or small. In addition, he exudes a boundless hypocrisy that allows him to undertake the most devious plans with a straight face and no indication of anything but the best of intentions. Most significantly, Jackie has an endearing charm that invites people to forgive or ignore his most egregious acts, even as he perpetrates even greater depravities.

The opening scene amply illustrates all these attributes. In tricking his wife, Annie, into bringing him an apple tart, Jackie indulges in a seemingly harmless bit of marital subterfuge, the sort of game that one might expect to go on between any couple long married. That may well be the case, but that is not the narrative point. The triviality of the stakes, the ardour of Jackie's performance when he pretends to win the lottery, and the obvious delight he takes in fooling his wife, underscore for viewers his nature as rogue and trickster. Further, Annie's sharp rebuke, punctuated by a slap, suggests numerous, exasperating experiences with this sort of manipulation. (The fact that it was the tart that Annie had been eating adds to Jackie's pleasure and her frustration.)

However, the narrative quickly announces that Jackie is more than simply a carnivalesque figure. As soon as he learns that a local has won the national lottery, the narrative begins to sketch a picture of a man whose nature is informed by greed and a predatory nature. It begins in a tentative, indirect fashion with his sounding out Michael about winning and continues with the extravagance of provid-

ing a feast for all potential winners. In short order, Jackie emerges as
the consummate con man, able to pull in accomplices (Michael and
Annie) and willing to risk a relatively small outlay, the cost of the
chicken dinners, in the hopes of gaining much larger rewards by
swindling the lottery winner.

Like any good narrative, the plotline offers other views, and one
might point to Jackie's early enlistment of Michael O'Sullivan as
proof against an avaricious nature. In fact, I believe, his gesture simply underscores a cold-hearted calculation that the job is too much to
be taken on alone and he has no compunction about drawing in his
naïve friend. In the bedroom scene that takes place before Jackie's
final commitment to the plot, Annie lays out the possible consequences with great clarity when she tells Jackie that Michael could
not survive prison, a statement that Jackie simply brushes aside.

To my mind, however, the most overt demonstration of Jackie's
manipulative, predatory nature comes during the funeral oration that
he delivers in the local church. Ostensibly meant to be a eulogy for
Ned Devine, Jackie finds himself momentarily at a loss for words
when the Dublin lottery man appears at the back of the church. After
some initial hesitation, however, Jackie not only recovers but uses the
occasion to cement the loyalty of his accomplices. He offers an ex-
temporaneous tribute to Michael O'Sullivan that seems on the surface to affirm the ideals of friendship, but, given Jackie's record of
manipulation, can more accurately be read as a marvel of hypocrisy.
The speech is an inside joke for the congregation, since they realise
that Jackie is duping the man from Dublin by praising a friend who is
actually alive. By the same token, viewers are invited to take an
equally cynical view of the sincerity of a man who thinks nothing of
putting his best friend at risk, blithely engaging in sacrilege, and
making the entire village complicit in his actions.

Even the scene in the pub, near the end of the film, showing
Jackie's reaction when he learns that Ned Devine is the father of
Maurice (itself, admittedly, given the age disparity and Ned's general
scruffiness, a highly improbable occurrence), is open to a sceptical
interpretation. Given his behaviour throughout the film, Jackie's urging of Maggie O'Toole to take all the lottery money is highly out of

character and more likely simply a calculated gamble. The news that Ned had a child confronts Jackie with the possibility of losing the portion of the money he had worked so diligently to acquire. (He has already been forced by circumstances to include the village in the division of the spoils.) In fact, advocating that she share the money would run the risk of antagonising Maggie and confirming her determination to secure it all for Maurice. Whereas, seeming to be magnanimous (I say seeming since there was nothing he could do to stop her, no matter what her decision) by urging Maggie to keep the money, plays upon her own generous nature. The way that he responds shows the same calculation that he used in his oration for Michael O'Sullivan. As always, Jackie is in control of the action.

In the end, whatever judgment one wishes to make of *Waking Ned* must take into consideration the approach of *The Quiet Man*. Ford's film has shown what can be done with a manipulation of familiar stereotypes. Truncated reactions by reviewers to a film, no matter how banal the movie may be, always run the risk of oversimplification. People of goodwill may well disagree about the aesthetic value of *Waking Ned*. However, I think that detractors simply take the easy way out by resorting to critical name-calling. For all the flaws in *Waking Ned*, I think viewers take a reductive perspective by lumping all of the characters under the term stereotype.

Endnotes

---

[1] Harvey O'Brien, 'Waking Ned', *Harvey's Movie Reviews*, 1999 <http://homepage.eircom.net/~obrienh/wn.htm> 27 October 2005.

[2] Neil Jackson, 'Kirk Jones', *Contemporary British and Irish Film Directors* (London and New York: Wallflower, 2001), p. 170.

[3] Martin McLoone, *Irish Film: The Emergence of a Contemporary Cinema* (London: British Film Institute, 2000), p. 59.

[4] Space does not permit a discussion of the nature of Irishness. For a survey of diverse attitudes and recent opinions, see the following. *The End of Irish History: Critical Reflections on the Celtic Tiger*, ed. by Colin Coulter and Steve Coleman (Manchester; New York: Manchester University Press, 2003); *Being Irish: Personal Reflections on Irish Identity Today*, ed. by Paddy Logue (Dublin: Oak Tree Press, 2000); Murray G.H. Pittock, *Celtic Identity and the British Image* (Manchester; New

York: Manchester University Press, 1999); Richard Kearney, *Postnationalist Ireland: Politics, Culture, Philosophy* (London: Routledge, 1997). See also Declan Kiberd, *Inventing Ireland* (Cambridge, Mass.: Harvard University Press, 1995); Desmond Fennell, *The Revision of Irish Nationalism* (Dublin: Open Air, 1989); Dennis Donoghue, *We Irish* (Berkeley: University of California Press, 1988).

[5] Both owe their existence to non-indigenous investment. The former derived its financing from French and English sources, while the American company Republic Pictures bankrolled Ford's film. One of the stars of *Waking Ned*, Ian Bannen, is a Scotsman, and its director, Kirk Jones, is English. In *The Quiet Man* non-Irish actors – John Wayne, Ward Bond, and Victor McLaughlen – have prominent roles (one could argue that, by the time she appeared in this film, the Dublin born Maureen O'Hara no longer qualified as Irish). While the topic of what constitutes an Irish film remains both important and conflicted, it is simply too large to engage in a paper of this length. Rather than concern oneself with the question of whether or not these are Irish films, I would prefer here simply to deal with them as Irish-themed films, and develop their similarities from that perspective. For details, see *Film Ireland*, 69 (February/ March 1999).

[6] Lance Pettitt offers a good survey of these views in his *Screening Ireland* (Manchester and New York: Manchester University Press, 2000), pp. 64–67. Lee Lourdeaux offers a harsher view in *Italian and Irish Filmmakers in America* (Philadelphia: Temple University Press, 1990), p. 109.

[7] See Des MacHale, *The Complete Guide to The Quiet Man* (Belfast: Appletree Press, 2000).

[8] Luke Gibbons, 'Romanticism, Realism and Irish Cinema', *Cinema and Ireland* (Syracuse: Syracuse University Press, 1988), pp. 194-257. James McKillop '*The Quiet Man* Speaks', *Contemporary Irish Cinema*, ed. by James MacKillop (Syracuse: Syracuse University Press, 1999), pp. 169–81. Michael Patrick Gillespie, 'The Myth of Hidden Ireland: The Corrosive Effect of *The Quiet Man*', *New Hibernia Review*, 6 (Summer 2002): 18–32.

[9] For a detailed examination of this phenomenon, see L. Perry Curtis' *Apes and Angels: The Irishman in Victorian Caricature* (Washington, D.C.: Smithsonian Institute Press, 1997).

[10] McLoone, *Irish Film: The Emergence of a Contemporary Cinema*, p. 128.

II

Language, Style and the Visualised Nation

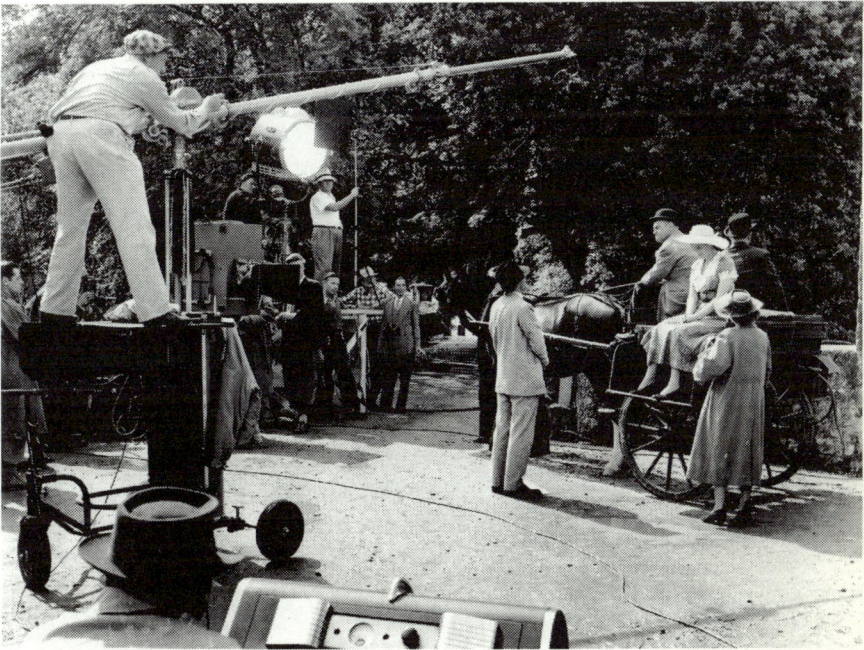

8

John Ford, the Irish Language and the Linguistic Politics of Multiculturalism

Caitríona Ó Torna and Brian Ó Conchubhair

'I was born in Cape Elizabeth, Maine, but I went to school in Ireland for a while and was brought up to speak both English and Gaelic.'[1]

This chapter examines the roles and functions of the Irish language in the blurred life and vivid cinematic work of movie director John Ford, aka John Feeney. While precise details are as elusive and as contested as the wild frontier depicted in his classic westerns, his life offers a revealing case study in identity formation. The difficulty, in part, stems from conflicting anecdotal evidence and from what Tag Gallagher, one of several biographers, describes as Ford's 'tendency to shroud himself in mystery', while 'his life and personality remain inscrutable'.[2] Ford created a public persona to promote a particular self-image by manipulating biographers, journalists and public events. In many regards, he is a case study of what Barbara Meyerhoff refers to as those who became 'authors of themselves'.[3] Such individuals and groups actively and consciously reconstruct their identity:

> One of the most persistent but elusive ways that people make sense of themselves is to show themselves to themselves, through multiple forms: by telling themselves stories; by dramatizing claims in rituals and other collective enactments;

by rendering visible actual and desired truths and the significance of their existence in imaginative and performative productions. Self-recognition is accomplished by these showings
and is, as George Steiner says, a 'formidable, difficult and perpetual task.' More than merely self-recognition, self-definition is
made possible by means of such showings, for their content
may state not only what people think they are but what should
have been or may yet be. Evidently, interpretive statements are
mirrors for collectives to hold up to themselves; like mirrors
they carry, and they need not be isomorphic with 'nature'.[4]

By defining himself as the man he might have been, or wanted to be,
Ford persistently and repeatedly rendered visible Ford the Irish-
speaker. In this regard Ford deployed the Irish language to effect, not
only in his cinematic work but in his life, to bequeath himself a distinct cultural identity and heritage that underlined his Irish ethnicity
but also allowed him to claim kinship in the brotherhoods of ethnic
minorities marginalised in the dominant WASP narrative. To appre-
ciate the functions of the Irish language in the life and cinematic
work of John Ford requires a brief summary of his life, his exposure
to Irish and its importance not only to him, but to his projected self-
image. Intimately connected to this function and no less important is
the role Irish played in shaping and facilitating Ford's attitude to
submerged and marginalised cultural and ethnic groups in American
society with whom he identified.

Born John Martin[5] Feeney on 1 February 1895 in Portland, Maine,
Ford was the eleventh child of native Irish-speakers, Barbara 'Abbey'
Curran and Seán Ó Feinneadha/John Feeney. His mother, a relative
of the bilingual author Liam Ó Flaithearta/Liam O'Flaherty, was born
in Cill Rónáin, Inis Mór, the largest of the three Aran islands in Galway Bay.[6] She grew up, however, on the mainland in Coill Rua, close
to An Tuar Beag, An Spidéal/Spiddal, where her future husband was
born and raised.[7] Despite this proximity, their paths would cross only
in the state of Maine in the US. In 1878, eight years after John Feeney
had emigrated, Barbara Curran alighted in the United States. Having
met and married, they raised eleven children on Cape Elizabeth,
Maine. McBride and Wilmington describe him thus: 'a first genera-

tion American Sean Aloysius O'Fienne [sic] in 1894, he grew up speaking both English and Gaelic, and spent much of his childhood making visits to the family hearth.'[8] Irish, it appears, was common in their home. Gallagher claims that 'Gaelic was often spoken in the house, midst frequent spats over pronunciation'[9] and Andrew Sinclair, another biographer, recounts: 'The teacher there [on the Cape] seemed to pick on the elder Feeneys, and their playmates baited them for being Catholics and speaking the few words of Gaelic they had picked up from their parents.'[10] In later years, Ford waxed lyrically of the time, around 1906, when reportedly he accompanied his father to his boyhood home in the Irish-speaking region near An Spidéal/Spiddal in west County Galway. Remaining there for several months, Ford claims he attended a local national school where, as a result of the recently introduced bilingual programme, instruction was now in Irish, the vernacular of the pupils.[11] This exposure to Ireland, the Irish language and to the culture which formed his parents, Ford subsequently implied, marked him in an indelible and enduring fashion. Indeed, if he is to be believed, it may well have bolstered whatever knowledge of the language he accrued from his parents and their conversations in New England. He again returned to Ireland during the War of Independence and, if folklore is correct, may have been arrested by Black-and-Tan troops in Galway city.[12]

The Irish language appears to be a core element of the adult Ford's view of Ireland and of himself. While his awareness and exposure to Irish is undeniable, his linguistic competence is ambiguous and the subject of dispute. Faced with the uncertainty of this narrative, we find rumour, folklore and anecdotal evidence compensating for the void in factual information, offering 'plausible yet unauthenticated explanations'.[13] Such intimations may be interpreted as evidence of Ford's status as a heritage-speaker or attest to his desire to render 'visible actual and desired truths and the significance of their existence in imaginative and performative productions'.[14] A reporter for the local Galway newspaper *The Connacht Tribune*, reporting from *The Quiet Man* set, wrote of his astonishment in 1951 'to hear the Hollywood director drop into Irish in an interview, unaware that Ford's parents were from the Gaeltacht, or that Irish had been spoken in his home in Portland, Maine'.[15] During filming the same newspaper reported:

Director Ford's association with the people of Spiddal is already well-known, still a *Connacht Tribune* representative was surprised to hear a Hollywood Oscar winner, in his American accent, tell him he was still 'cineál bodhar' (deafened) from the drone of the plane engines on his journey to Ireland and that he was a 'col cúigear' (cousin) of Micheal Droighnea [sic], a teacher from Furbough. Those who would like to have a long chat with Mr Ford would be well advised to forget all about Hollywood and film stars and be prepared to discuss the people of Connemara, the Cong struggle towards Irish Independence, the Irish language and his Irish relations.[16]

Ford's use of Irish on the film set is collaborated by an interview Mike P. Ó Conaola conducted with Máirtín Ó Droighneáin[17] (aka Martin Thornton), who remembered Ford speaking Irish on *The Quiet Man* set. He writes:

Is fiú a lua go raibh beagán Gaeilge ag John Ford agus go ndearna sé iarracht í a labhairt go háirithe agus é ag scannánaíocht. In agallamh a rinne an dornálaí Máirtín Ó Droighneáin liom do Raidió na Gaeltachta in 1973 dúirt sé go mbíodh Ford ag fógairt air féin as Gaeilge nuair a bhíodh sé ag dornálaíocht sa scannán – 'an dorna a Mháirtín, dorna, tabhair an dorna dhó.' Thaitnigh an ceol Gaelach le Ford freisin go háirithe agus é casta ar an mbosca ceoil agus déarfadh sé as Gaeilge ar an seit 'cáil an ceoltóir, cáil an ceoltóir.'[18]

[It is worth mentioning that John Ford had a little Irish and he made an effort to speak it especially when filming. In an interview I conducted with the boxer Máirtín Ó Droighneáin for *Raidió na Gaeltachta* in 1973 he said that Ford used to exhort him in Irish when filming the boxing (scenes) in the film – 'the fist, Máirtín, (the) fist, give him the fist.' Irish music also pleased Ford especially when played on the accordion and he used say in Irish on the set 'where's the musician, where's the musician?']

In addition, Robert Parrish, who acted as an assistant editor to Ford on *Drums Along the Mohawk* (1939) and *The Grapes of Wrath* (1940), wrote of his aunt conversing with Ford in Irish: 'after chatting in Gaelic with Ford, she remarked he was among the most delightful people she had ever met – but it was a pity he had not continued his studies for the priesthood.'[19]

Conversely, Maureen O'Hara, an iconic Irish actress, star of several Ford films and a core member of his 'company', is adamant, however, that, unlike her, Ford could not speak the language.[20] Her autobiography, *'Tis Herself*, recounts an 1950 incident during the production of *Rio Grande* (1950), starring O'Hara and John Wayne in the post-Civil War era, with Wayne training young recruits, including his son, to fight Apache native Americans. Suggesting that Ford's posturing as an Irish-speaker was a sham, performed for the benefit of others, she writes:

> He'd pretend that he could speak Gaelic – which he could not; he knew only some words and phrases – and made me have mock conversations in Gaelic with him. He would say something to me in fake Gaelic and I would answer affirmatively, '*Seadh Seadh*,' while nodding my head. Everyone on the set thought we were speaking Gaelic with each other the entire time we shot *Rio Grande*, but we weren't – it was mostly gibberish. He seemed to revel in his trickery and was pleased that I did not expose him. Then thirty minutes later, after making him look good and Irish in front of the crew, he'd ridicule me under his breath while I was performing.[21]

Years later, on 31 March 1973, with Ford terminally ill, the American Film Institute presented 'A Salute to John Ford' in Los Angeles, five months prior to his death. Nationally televised, the award ceremony honoured an individual's lifetime contribution to enriching American culture through motion pictures and television. Hollywood stars and celebrities attended and listened to President Richard M. Nixon laud Ford's cinematic achievement and present him with the Medal of Freedom. O'Hara, as her tribute to Ford, sang from *The Quiet Man* score:[22]

When I returned to the dais, my songs seemed to have breathed
new life into the old man. It gave him the yearning to pull one
last John Fordism with me. Making sure President Nixon could
see and overhear him, Ford leaned over and began speaking in
my ear in bogus Gaelic. I knew my cue and wasn't about to let
him down. As I always had, I nodded softly and replied, '*Seadh.
Seadh.*' He went on and on until getting precisely the reaction
from the President that he wanted. Nixon leaned over and
asked, 'What are you two doing over there?' I could almost hear
the giddiness in Pappy's voice as he answered gruffly, 'We're
speaking in our native language.'[23]

O'Hara's memoir, which reveals several aspects of Ford's character
previously unknown, also sheds light on the complicated nature of
her relationship with the director.

Part of the problem in unravelling the extent of Ford's linguistic
ability with regard to Irish or any other language may be glimpsed in
his confession to Hopper, a future biographer, of being able to speak
German, but adding 'You know, I don't want this to get out – I pose
as an illiterate'.[24] McBride and Wilmington reiterate this notion, arguing that 'this self-perpetuated image as an illiterate cowboy is belied
by the testimony of his scriptwriters and actors...'[25] and Gallagher
buttresses this opinion:

Because John Ford shrouded himself in mystery, his life and
personality remain inscrutable. His was a complex, perhaps
multiple, individuality. Direct and devious, charismatic and
sardonic, amusing and caustic, he generally dominated those
around him, or at least retained his independence [...] But he
posed as illiterate, hiding his erudition, as he hid his wealth
under baggy clothes and his sensitivity under a tough crust.
He was a man of many masks, a joiner who stayed an outsider, a man of action, self-consciously reflective, a big man,
Irish and Catholic.[26]

Despite O'Hara's denunciation, other accounts bolster Ford's linguistic claims as a heritage speaker of Irish and other languages. Andrew
Sinclair believes that Ford cultivated an image of some fluency in

Navajo: 'He was chosen as an honorary chief with the name of *Natani Nez* or Tall Soldier ... He even spoke a few sentences of Navajo, enough to give the impression that he knew the language if the words could be gotten out of him.'[27] Ford's biographer, Tag Gallagher, asserts that: 'He read voraciously, history especially, surrounding himself with books; his memory was virtually photographic, and he could get by in French, German, Gaelic, Italian, Spanish, Yiddish, Japanese, Hawaiian, and Navajo.'[28]

Ford, whatever his command of Irish, was certainly aware of and sensitive to the language. The Irish language features in several of his movies, the best known of course being the confessional scene in *The Quiet Man* where Mary Kate Danaher (Maureen O'Hara) admits to the Catholic priest, Father Peter Lonergan (Ward Bond), a failure to consummate her recent marriage. In an earlier version of the movie, however, the Irish language also featured when the sheep-herding Mary Kate first greets Sean Thornton (John Wayne). This scene, subsequently deleted, was among those scenes cut in a well-known incident featuring Herb Yates.[29] According to film critic Rob Nixon:

> Several scenes were shot that never appeared in the movie: O'Hara speaking Gaelic to greet Wayne for the first time [to which he famously replies – "is it real?"] [...] a scene where Father Lonergan and Michaeleen discuss betting on horses (deemed offensive because he is a priest); Wayne's first scene on the train, where he speaks to a mother, and her child gives him an apple (in the existing opening scene, Wayne deboards the train holding the apple and thanks the unseen child).[30]

Des MacHale corroborates this claim in his study of *The Quiet Man* script: 'Surprisingly, however, these scenes bear very little resemblance to the ones envisaged in Nugent's original screenplay. In this version, Mary Kate speaks mostly in Gaelic, hence Sean's line "So you can talk" when she speaks in English.'[31] The sole surviving Irish-language scene is a conversation between the recent bride and priest and is interpreted in various manners: Ford's homage to his parents and relatives, a sop to Irish cultural nationalist aspirations, an alternative to the prevailing conservative Catholicism of 1950s' Ireland,

and/or a deliberate snub to those who might consciously or unconsciously denigrate the west of Ireland, whence Ford's parents had emerged. Filmed in 1951, *The Quiet Man* marked a time of crisis for the Irish national project.[32] By inserting the confessional scene into *The Quiet Man* and by transacting it through the medium of Irish, not to mention the initial Irish-language scene with O'Hara, Ford signals the existence not alone of Irish, but of a distinct cultural pedigree. The scene's very linguistic nature, however, undercuts such readings. The cleric's failure to comprehend 'mála codlata' requires Mary Kate to translate it as 'a sleeping bag'.[33] This act signals the linguistic history of Irish, a language, lacking much if not most of modernity's lexicon. Such hybridity as the scene achieves rests on the priest's failure to comprehend the lexical term and forces Mary Kate to resort to English, the dominant linguistic register. This simple interaction draws attention to a post-colonial inability to simply replant or transplant one set of cultural values on another. The failure of Irish to keep pace with modernity requires recourse to English translation. Even in this briefest of brief vignettes, Ford dispels any hope of purity – linguistic, cultural or racial. His gospel, as ever, is hybridity.

Luke Gibbons views this scene, in which the Irish language emerges temporally from its subaltern role, in tandem with Sean Thornton's confession to Reverend Playfair and deems them both '… parodic to the point of being counter-confessional: Mary Kate's muffled confession in Irish to Father Peter simply distracts him from his fishing …'[34] William C. Dowling, however, sees this scene as fundamental and as marking *'The Quiet Man'*'s great countermovement toward a vision of innocent or ludic violence' and 'signals a break or rupture in cultural time'.[35] 'Yet from the moment that Mary Kate switches from English to Irish', he argues, 'the rules governing life in Innisfree will be those of an earlier Irish society where property has no meaning outside communal values and where, within a closely related context of festive or Bacchic release, certain ritualized forms of violence or abuse have a power to regenerate community'.[36] Des MacHale, while acknowledging 'Ford spoke a little Irish, but liked to give the impression that he was fluent in the language'[37] argues that it was not included in the original scripts, but was later included to 'introduce an element of mystery into the proceedings but it also gets around any censorship difficulties that might have arisen because of the delicacy of the subject matter'.[38] The mystery factor, as MacHale points out, is important not for an Irish audience but for the North American audience. We can only speculate on Herb Yates's reaction to the deleted scene in which O'Hara spoke in Irish and Ford's rationale for the scene, but the decision to foreground Irish in such an undertaking not only reiterates the symbolic importance of Irish for Ford, but underscores his desire to give the language a significant role in a film he had planned and striven to make over many years.

The Quiet Man, however, is not the sole Ford film where the issue of language looms large. *Cheyenne Autumn* (1964) – the final Ford western – is considered his apology to Native Americans, reversing the viewpoint and ethos of his previous westerns. '*Cheyenne Autumn* was not just a departure in terms of theme', writes Lindsay Anderson, 'it also represented severe problems of dramatization and performance. Ford's Indians had never lacked dignity, but he had never attempted familiarity either: he had always respected the privateness of their world, and its integrity [...] But the heroes of *Cheyenne Autumn* are the Cheyenne.'[39] The oft-cited notes which Ford's son, Patrick Ford, produced for the film, reveal Ford's attitude and challenge:

> The Cheyennes are not to be heavies, nor are they to be ignorant, misguided savages without plan or purpose to their warmaking. Their motives must be clearly expressed in the beginning of the picture [...] My father and I agreed that the Cheyenne should not speak English in the picture. They should serve, in his words, as a 'Greek Chorus.' Since lack of communication was one of their chief causes of trouble, it would be ridiculous to show them speaking the national language [...] The Indians as a people, are to be portrayed as Indians [...] unable to speak English or to communicate their thoughts to the Whites, but magnificent in their stoical dignity.[40]

This idealistic and laudable aspiration inevitably led to difficulties. As Anderson notes, if the Cheyenne's motives are to be expressed, how can English be avoided in a Hollywood movie? To treat them as a Greek Chorus would reduce them to 'dignified abstraction' and render them 'passive monuments to injustice'.[41]

Ford's attitude towards Native Americans and their language provides a possible context by which to read not alone the use of Irish in *The Quiet Man*, but also in *The Long Gray Line* – Ford's 1955 depiction of a non-commissioned officer's fifty years at West Point military academy, based on Marty Maher's 1951 memoir *Bring Up the Brass*. Marty Maher (Tyrone Power), a son of Tipperary, arrives at West Point straight off the emigrant ship, identification card still attached. Securing a menial position, serving cadets as a waiter/cleaner in the kitchen, he fails spectacularly. Possessing an impressive array of stereotypical 'Irish' traits, he displays his abilities to all and sundry: clumsiness, awkwardness, boastfulness, verbosity, pugnacity and an inability to follow orders or take direction. He is, in short, utterly lacking in practical skills. Despite these inherent short-comings, his embrace of military ethos earns him a home at West Point. And as the army makes the man regardless of nationality or flaws, he becomes an integral part of the military academy as a non-commissioned officer. Despite personal tragedy and hardship, he serves for fifty years as athletic trainer and football coach. He meets and falls in love with Mary O'Donnell (Maureen O'Hara), and their on-base quarters becomes an oasis of familial warmth and humanity. It offers succour to various military waifs and diverse nationalities struggling with the academic rigors demanded by West Point. In-deed, such is the depiction that Sinclair complains that 'he [Maher] made it an Irish enclosure, as if the Academy was situated on the west point of the Ould Sod'.[42]

Faced with mandatory retirement, Maher realises that West Point and the army have become his life and without them he has nothing. As the movie opens, we see Marty Maher in the White House. Still the emigrant, his lack of etiquette betrays him as he lights his pipe and commences his autobiographical tale. Startled on realising his *faux pas*, he is reassured by the voice of an unseen former West Point pupil, now president of the United States and Commander-in-Chief. Marty, as a permanent fixture at West Point, has seen many officers pass through his hands: some falling on foreign battlefields, some rising to high office. Introducing the Irish language in this movie, Ford complicates the immigrant experience, destabilises myths of racial purity and humanises the military. The military presented here is an army emerging from various and disparate cultural histories and origins; the Irish and the Irish language constitute but one among many ethnicities and languages that bob and weave beneath the surface of American identity. In Ford's extended world, the Irish language circulates in West Point, Hollywood, Los Angeles and at dinner tables with US presidents. Gibbons reads Ford's life and cinematic corpus as a life-long engagement with redefining the American dream. It is, he opines, an attempt to translate the WASP narrative to a wider, more fluid and inclusive version that includes those marginalised, rejected and erased in the standard WASP text. Ford's Irishness in this endeavour was paramount.[43] Inherent in his work, Gibbons argues, is an understanding of 'the dispossessed im- migrants, migrant workers, Native Americans, African-Americans, the unemployed, whiskey doctors, fallen women, rebels – to renew the search for home this side of paradise'.[44] Charles Ramirez Berg re- iterates this idea, arguing that Irishness for Ford is less an 'intro- verted ethnicity' centred on shamrocks and shillelaghs, but rather a space 'for a host of socially (and geographically) marginalized Oth- ers, among them various tribes of Native American, Mexicans and Mexican-Americans, women and African-Americans, Slavs and Poles, Frenchmen and Italians, Swedes and Germans, poor whites and Southerners'.[45] Rejecting the assimilationist ideology that frowned on the hyphenated American, Ford contested such defining limits: 'Instead of narrowing cultural vistas, as the assimilationist ideology of the melting-pot would have it, the appropriation of mod- ernity in the name of one's own culture led to new forms of diversity and tolerance that extended beyond the expansionist designs of the frontier ethic.'[46] Consequently, if 'the procession of rambunctious and feckless Celts through Ford's films, Irish and otherwise, was meant to cock a snoot at WASP or "lace-curtain Irish" ideas of respectability, thrift and propriety',[47] how much an affront to monoglot Anglo- phones was the insertion of the stigmatized, maligned and largely discarded Irish language in a panegyric to the US military? Into West

Point, the inner sanctum of the US military, where future presidents learn to fight and die for the Stars and Stripes, Ford infuses not only German, Swedish and Hispanic immigrants, but Irish-speakers.

In a poignant scene, Maher's father and younger brother arrive unexpectedly from Ireland. When O'Hara opens the door to reveal his father and son, Maher identifies his father by the Irish-language affectionate name for 'grandfather', 'Daideo, daideo, ... sure it is a thing out of my dreams to look upon the face of my beloved father again ...' Maher may have left Tipperary a long, long way behind, but when family links are heightened and at moments of crisis, identity is performed and social order reinforced through communal practice, ritual and language. Maher's reference to a dream recalls Sean Thorton's question on encountering the Irish-speaking Mary Kate, '– is it real?' in *The Quiet Man*. 'Ford's favourite device for heightening the meaning of the commonplace', write McBride and Wilmington 'was the ritual'[48]: 'A person involved in ritual is celebrating the solemnity of his own actions, and at the same time is bowing to something greater than himself. The ritual becomes most vital when we sense that the characters are improvising it in reaction to a crisis.'[49] The crisis here stems from the brief emotional reunion of the family unit before its imminent dispersal. The patriarch, Old Martin (Donald Crisp), enquires of his daughter-in-law: 'Do you have the Irish, woman of the house?' And on receiving an affirmative answer, announces, 'Then it's for you to say the words'. The quartet enter an adjoining room, and O'Hara, with head covered, 'prays' as follows: 'Céad míle fáilte romhaibh is beannacht Dé oraibh ar do [sic] chéad chuairt go tigh m'fhir céile, a athair is a dheartháir fosta'. ['One hundred thousand welcomes and God's blessing on you on your first visit to my husband's house, (his) father and (his) brother also'].

Similarly, Irish appears in *The Informer* (1935), based on a 1925 novel of the same title by Irish-speaker Liam O'Flaherty/Liam Ó Flaithearta, a relation of Ford's mother. In this film, where identity is in flux and allegiance is temporary, Ford roots Irish in the heart of the hero's home and family. After Frankie McPhillip (Wallace Ford) is betrayed by Gypo Nolan (Victor McLaglen) and subsequently shot by Black-and-Tans, his grieving mother (Una O'Connor) and sister

(Heather Angel) wake their dead brother in the family home. As Gypo Nolan enters the wake-house to convey his condolences at this time of familial and organisation crisis, communal strains of 'Ár nAthair atá ar neamh go naofar d'ainm...' ['Our Father who art in heaven, hallowed by thy name ...'] hover in the air. A group of men, with their backs to the viewer recite the 'Our Father' over the corpse. Again in a Ford film, the Irish language appears at a time of crisis and is intricately connected with ritual and rites of passage. The language forms the background to this scene and when Gypo loudly disrupts the ritual performance of grief and ceremony, the group of men turn their attention from the corpse to Gypo, and a *fáinne* – a circular pin symbolising an Irish-language advocate – is clearly visible.[50] As if the aural element was insufficient, Ford also provides a visual representation of Irish.

Focusing solely on whether or not Ford spoke Irish, debating whether he possessed fluent or halting Irish or spoke just a few words or garbled nonsense, is ultimately to miss the point. Ford created myths. He directed, produced and lived them. As Gallagher admits: 'There will probably never be an adequate biography of John Ford, nor even an adequate character sketch, for there were as many of him as there were people who knew him.'[51] Ford, having run away from Portland and abandoned his Irish-American family, fell back on his Irish heritage when faced with the distinctively modern popular art form in Hollywood. The WASP narrative excluded minorities who held allegiances and practical connections to European homelands. In the Irish language, Ford found not only a distinction that distinguished him from the WASP narrative, but provided a bond with ethnic minorities and a sense of empathy; a rock onto which he could graft his identity and anchor his alternative vision of the United States.

As James Clifford observes perceptively: 'Peoples whose sense of identity is centrally defined by collective histories of displacement and violent loss cannot be "cured" by merging into a new national community. This is especially true when they are victims of ongoing, structural prejudice.'[52] 'When Ford was young,' argue McBride and Wilmington, 'the American Irish were still climbing up the ladder to social acceptance ... Ford never stopped considering himself a rebel.'[53] In his life-long engagement with American politics, culture and society, time and time again Ford deployed the Irish language – meaningfully and symbolically – to signal difference and ethnicity, to flag his distinctiveness from the WASP homogeneity and simultaneously from the 'lace-curtain' Irish. In associating himself with the Irish language and by cultivating an image of linguistic fluency, he affirmed his allegiance to, and allied himself with, the marginalised, forgotten and occluded. For Ford, Irish was an immediate and intimate link not only to his Irish-born parents, but to his extended family in Connemara and that link allowed him to claim in a letter to Lord Killanin, 'But thank God I am THE Irish peasant of the peasants...'.[54] Such a declaration mirrors the attitude and message found in so much of his cinematic work. Faced with a demand for homogeneity and a narrow exclusionary nationalism, he responded with hybridity and inclusiveness. Reacting against those who saw monolingualism as a precondition for national unity and strength, Ford articulated a broader, more humanistic and more global agenda.[55] To paraphrase Mary Evans's critique of Simone de Beauvoir, Ford, in order to achieve his own heroism, had to continue to invent, and to invest in promoting the perception of him as an Irish-language speaker.[56] The self, in the modern era, is more fractured and fissured than at any historical period. The Irish language functioned as a bridge between Ford, the hyphenated Irish-American, and a host of ethnic American groups. In the Irish language Ford found a link to his family and heritage. He found not only a means to provide himself with a linear continuity, but also a sense of ethnicity that permitted him to form an ideological kinship with minority groups traditionally marginalised in the American dream.

Endnotes

---

[1] Tag Gallagher, *John Ford: The Man and His Films* (Berkeley: University of California Press, 1986), p. 279.

[2] Ibid., p. 3.

[3] Barbara Myerhoff, 'Life not Death in Venice: Its Second Life', *The Anthropology of Experience*, ed. by Victor W. Turner and Edward M. Bruner (Chicago: University of Illinois, 1986), p. 263.

[4] Ibid., pp. 261–2.

[5] Sinclair (p. 9) states that he was named 'John Augustine Feeney'. McBride and Wilmington (p. 17) claim that he was christened 'Sean Aloysius O'Fienne,' [sic] while Gallagher (p. 2) notes that 'although Ford went through his youth as John Augustine Feeney, and later claimed even on passports that his name was Sean Aloysius O'Feeney, and although most references, including Ford himself, cite the year as 1895, the town clerk registered him as John Martin Feeney, born February 1, 1894 and this information appears also on his tombstone and baptismal records. John was baptized March 13, 1894, at St. Dominic's, 163 Danforth Street; Edward and Julia Feeney were the sponsors, Aloysius was the name John chose at Confirmation.'

[6] Several biographers make the strange claim, given the educational practices of her youth and the state of the Irish language in the educational system in Ireland, that while unable to read or write English, she could read Irish. See Gallagher, p. 2 for one example.

[7] See Mike P. Ó Conaola, 'An Quiet Man', *Picture The Quiet Man: An Illustrated Celebration*, ed. Des MacHale (Belfast: Appletree Press Ltd., 2004), pp. 120–2.

[8] Joseph McBride and Michael Wilmington, *John Ford* (New York: Da Capo Press, 1975), p. 17.

[9] Gallagher, *John Ford: The Man and His Films*, p. 2.

[10] Andrew Sinclair, *John Ford: A Biography* (New York: The Dial Press/James Wade, 1979), p. 11. 'So, because of social conflict and bad times, the Feeney family gave up the farm and moved back to Gorham's Corner, where they bought a house at 48 Danforth Street. But the neighbour was being flooded by the new immigrants from Europe, so John A. Feeney bought another large house on Monument Street. Unfortunately, he could never make his wife and family move there from the large family apartment at 21/23 Sheridan Street on respectable Munjoy Hill, which they rented in 1903.' For Ford's subsequent academic progress, see Sinclair, p. 14.

[11] Ibid., p. 4. In 1904 Patrick Pearse reported in *An Claidheamh Soluis* that many teachers employed a bilingual method of instruction in 'Aran, the whole of Iar-Chonnacht, practically all of Conemara, the Joyce Country, and large tracts east and south of Lough Corrib'. *An Claidheamh Soluis*, 8 October 1904. [cited in Thomas A. O'Donoghue, *Bilingual Education in Ireland, 1904-1922* (Murdoch University: Centre for Irish Studies Monograph Series, 2000), p. 36]. Domhnall Ua Duibhne, a teacher in Spiddal Male National School, attests to the implementation of the bilingual programme in his school in 1904 and those in the

surrounding areas. (Domhnall Ua Duibhne, 'The Bilingual Programme in Operation', *An Claidheamh Soluis*, 15 November 1904. [Cited in *A Significant Irish Educationalist: The Educational Writings of P.H. Pearse*, edited by Séamus Ó Buachalla (Cork: Mercier Press, 1980), pp. 58-9)].

[12] See Mike P. Ó Conaola, 'An Quiet Man,' pp. 120–22. For Ford as a fundraiser for the IRA, see Andrew Sinclair, *John Ford*, pp. 31–3.

[13] Ron Robin, *The Making of the Cold War Enemy* (Princeton, New Jersey: Princeton University Press, 2001), p. 3.

[14] Barbara Myerhoff, 'Life not Death in Venice: Its Second Life', *The Anthropology of Experience*, ed. by Victor W. Turner and Edward M. Bruner, p. 263.

[15] William C. Dowling, 'John Ford's Festive Comedy: Ireland Imagined in *The Quiet Man*', *Éire-Ireland*, 36.3 & 4 (2001) p. 197.

[16] *The Connacht Tribune*, 'Hollywood Take Over Village of Cong,' cited by Gerry McNee, *In the Footsteps of The Quiet Man* (Edinburgh: Mainstream Publishing, 1990), p. 78.

[17] See Des MacHale, *The Complete Guide to The Quiet Man* (Belfast: Appletree Press, 2000), p. 215. 'Wayne, it seems, played himself in most of the fight scenes, but McLaglen's double was Martin Thornton from Spiddal, a professional boxer himself and allegedly a cousin of Ford's. He was a 'character' and a hard drinker who was involved in some outlandish sessions with Wayne and other members of *The Quiet Man* cast […] Thornton, on whose family name Sean's was probably based, appears prominently as an extra in the later fight scenes.'

[18] Mike P. Ó Conaola, 'An Quiet Man,' p. 122.

[19] Robert Parrish, *Growing Up in Hollywood* (New York: Harcourt Brace Jovanovich, 1976), cited in Tag Gallagher, p. 344.

[20] Nora Ní Chonghaile (Uí Chualáin) tutored O'Hara in Irish during the filming of *The Quiet Man*. See Mike P. Ó Conaola, 'An Quiet Man', p. 121. The fact that O'Hara required Irish tutoring for such a brief scene calls into question her ability to assess Ford's command of Irish. Would her exposure to Irish in primary and secondary school enable her to comprehend snatches of colloquial speech possibly retained by Ford from his childhood?

[21] Maureen O'Hara, *'Tis Herself: A Memoir* (New York: Simon & Schuster, 2004), p. 139.

[22] For Nixon and the Irish language, see http://www.presidency.ucsb.edu/ws/index.php?pid =2695

[23] O'Hara, *'Tis Herself: A Memoir*, p. 260. In Des MacHale's account, Ford delivers his acceptance speech by reciting the Lord's Prayer in Irish. See Des MacHale, *The Complete Guide to the Quiet Man*, p. 187.

[24] Unpublished conversation with John Ford, 13 April 1962. Cited in Tag Gallagher, *John Ford: The Man and His Films*, p. 381.

[25] McBride and Wilmington, *John Ford*, p. 19.

[26] Gallagher, *John Ford: The Man and His Films*, p. 1.

[27] Andrew Sinclair, *John Ford: A Biography* (New York: The Dial Press/James Wade, 1979), p. 83. When Peter Bogdanovich was introduced to Ford, he impressed the future biographer by demonstrating knowledge of Serbian, albeit only a single word.

[28] Gallagher, *John Ford: The Man and His Films*, p. 1.

[29] Herb Yates decreed that the movie not exceed 120 minutes. During the screening for Republic distributors, however, the film unexpectedly ended just as the climactic fight between Wayne and McLaglen commenced. The point made, Yates relented and *The Quiet Man* ran at 129 minutes. Despite the inclusion of the fight scene, several other scenes, including those featuring the Irish language, were sacrificed.

[30] For additional information, see Rob Nixon 'The Quiet Man' *Turner Classic Movies*, 15 November 2004. <http://www.turnerclassicmovies.com/ThisMonth/Article/0,,71710,00.html> Our thanks to Rob Nixon for providing additional information in private correspondence.

[31] MacHale, *The Complete Guide to the Quiet Man*, p. 97.

[32] See Gearóid Ó Tuathaigh, 'Language, Ideology and National Identity,' *The Cambridge Companion to Modern Irish Culture*, ed. by Joe Cleary and Claire Connolly (Cambridge: Cambridge University Press, 2005), p. 53.

[33] For a full transcript, see MacHale, *The Complete Guide to the Quiet Man*, p. 187. It should be noted here that the cleric's initial response of '*sea*, '*sea* echoes Ford's own pet phrase when 'speaking' Irish. It is unclear if this is a case of self-parody or unfortunate repetition.

[34] Luke Gibbons, *The Quiet Man* (Cork: Cork University Press, 2001), p. 61.

[35] See William C. Dowling, 'John Ford's Festive Comedy: Ireland Imagined in *The Quiet Man*', *Éire-Ireland*, 36.3 & 4 (2001), p. 206.

[36] Ibid., pp. 206-7.

[37] MacHale, *The Complete Guide to the Quiet Man*, p. 187.

[38] Ibid., p. 187.

[39] Lindsay Anderson, *About John Ford* (London: Pexus, 1981), p. 172. Tag Gallagher argues that 'critical essays rarely deal with the film itself. They deal with obstacles Ford encountered,' p. 429.

[40] Sinclair, *John Ford: A Biography*, p. 198.

[41] Anderson, *About John Ford*, p. 172.

[42] Sinclair, *John Ford*, pp. 173-4.

[43] See Gibbons, *The Quiet Man*, p. 104.

[44] Ibid., p. 105.

[45] Charles Ramirez Berg, 'The Margin as Centre: The Multicultural Dynamics of John Ford's Westerns', *John Ford Made Westerns: Filming the Legend in the Sound Era*, ed. by Gaylyn Studlar and Matthew Bernstein (Bloomington: University of Indiana Press, 2001), pp. 75-101, cited in Gibbons, *The Quiet Man*, pp. 15-6.

[46] Gibbons, *The Quiet Man*, p. 16.

[47] Ibid., p. 13.

[48] McBride and Wilmington, p. 28.

[49] Ibid., p. 29.

[50] Later in the movie, Commandant Dan Gallagher also wears a *fáinne*, thus firmly linking the language with republicanism and the Irish Republican Army.

[51] Gallagher, *John Ford: The Man and His Films*, p. 1.

[52] James Clifford, 'Diasporas', *The Ethnicity Reader: Nationalism, Multiculturalism and Migration* ed. by Montserrat Guibernau and John Rex (Malden, MA: Polity-Blackwell, 1997), p. 286.

[53] McBride and Wilmington, p. 18.

[54] Cited in Sinclair, *John Ford*, p. 199.

[55] Donna C. Stanton, 'On Linguistic Human Rights and the United States "Foreign" Language Crisis', *Profession 2005* (New York: Modern Languages Association, 2005), p. 73.

[56] Mary Evans, *Missing Persons: The Impossibility of Auto/biography* (London: Routledge, 1999), pp. 50–1.

9

The Quiet Man in Technicolor: Aspects of Film Style

TOM PAULUS

The majority of the contributions to this volume look at *The Quiet Man* from a cultural perspective and seek to interpret it in either broad or specific cultural terms. This seems unobjectionable: films are meant for audiences and there is no doubt that social and cultural factors or traditions shape the creation of artworks, in this case a film, in many ways. Still, in the concluding chapter to his most recent book on film style, *Figures Traced in Light*, David Bordwell takes issue with what he calls a 'culturalist perspective'. Bordwell lists the various ways in which cultural factors shape artworks – subjects and themes come directly or indirectly from a cultural milieu; social and cultural factors can be considered pre-conditions for artworks (no Hollywood movies without capitalism); sometimes social and cultural institutions explicitly mandate the forms or materials or functions of artworks – only to conclude that it is still the filmmaker, not culture, who turns on the camera.[1] What Bordwell means is that the explanation of a cinematic phenomenon, of a film, should not necessarily look first or in many cases even exclusively to cultural factors. There are a number of smaller questions to be examined, mainly related to internal patterns of film style and the filmmaker's craft. This chapter aims to raise such a small question and will present it as crucial to our understanding of the film's style, the way it appears to us and expresses the aesthetic choices of its director, John Ford.

The Quiet Man is a Technicolor film, shot in the three-strip (combining negatives sensitive to red, green and blue), dye-transfer process invented by Dr. Herbert T. Kalmus. Winton Hoch, the head cameraman on the film and a key staff member of the Technicolor corporation with whom Ford had made two pictures previously, *Three Godfathers* (1948) and *She Wore a Yellow Ribbon* (1949), received an Oscar for his cinematography in the same year the Academy bestowed a special Honorary Award on the film's producer, Merian C. Cooper, for 'his many innovations and contributions to the art of motion pictures'. One of Cooper's contributions to cinema was that in 1936, when Technicolor was still young, he had formed a production company with wealthy financier John Hay 'Jock' Whitney, named Pioneer Pictures, to make films in the new three-strip process. Cooper later became vice-president of Selznick International Pictures and persuaded David Selznick to try the three colour process for *Gone With the Wind*. The phenomenal success of *Gone With the Wind* then convinced the hesitant majors to take up Technicolor. So, in a sense, Cooper can be said to have 'pioneered' Technicolor. While Ford was still at RKO, he had signed a contract with Cooper to make two Technicolor films for Pioneer Pictures. Nought came of it: the first Ford/Cooper collaboration, *Stagecoach* (1939), was made for independent producer Walter Wanger and shot in black and white by Josef Von Sternberg's regular cameraman, Bert Glennon. After World War II, when Ford got out from under his contract with Darryl Zanuck at Fox and Cooper separated from Selznick, the two became producing partners in a new company, Argosy Pictures. Still, only the third Argosy production, *Three Godfathers*, was shot in Technicolor.

Ford never liked colour, not even 'Glorious Technicolor'. He had tried the three-strip process in *Drums Along the Mohawk* (1939), but the effect, as biographer Joseph McBride describes it, was colour 'so lush, so pop-artish in its boldness and intensity, that the costumes and décor count as much as the people'.[2] Ford told Peter Bogdanovich that he found colour facile and

… much easier than black and white for the cameraman; it's a cinch to work in, if you've any eye at all for color or composition. But black and white is pretty tough – you've got to know your job and be very careful to lay your shadows properly and get the perspective right. In color – there it is; but it can go awfully wrong and throw a picture off […] You'll probably say I'm old-fashioned, but black and white is real photography.[3]

Ford is referring to the fact that in colour photography the colour areas could distinguish planes, eliminating the need for edge lighting. Technicolor was shot with soft, flat light, using less backlighting, because now colour could separate foreground and background in the frame. The choice for softness was as much a matter of letting colour do all the work in guiding the viewer's attention in the frame, as of responding to the intrinsic qualities of the Technicolor negative film stock, which remained fairly slow even with the more sensitive emulsions of the early fifties. When we say that the Technicolor camera negative was 'slow', we mean this relative to the fast black-and-white emulsions developed during the late thirties, like Eastman Plus X and Super XX, culminating in Eastman's Tri-X stock introduced in 1954. 'Slow' film needs a lot of evenly spread light (almost twice as much as black-and-white); in the case of Technicolor, the three-colour system was arranged to give correct colour balance under sunlight, which was best matched in the studio by powerful arc lamp illumination and by shooting at a large lens aperture.

Now Ford had all but abandoned the low-contrast, high-key lighting style (with very little strong shadow present in the image, which was always fairly bright all over) which was typical of the early sound era and made a comeback with colour photography. In his films of the mid- to late thirties with progressive cameramen like Bert Glennon, Joseph August, Arthur Miller and especially Gregg Toland, Ford had experimented with the rendering of depth in a low-key style. Even in his 'soft style' films with George Schneiderman as cameraman, Ford had always tried to compose the image in depth, but it was only through working with the innovators mentioned above that he became aware of the possibilities for producing depth through choice of lens, aperture and film stock. Bert Glennon used lenses much wider than the 50mm norm in *Young Mr. Lincoln* (1939) and *Stagecoach* (1939), while Arthur Miller coated lenses to increase light transmission and enable the cameraman to stop down the aperture and thus increase depth of field in *Tobacco Road* (1940) and *How Green Was My Valley* (1941). But it was Gregg Toland who was boldest in exploring the dramatic possibilities of staging in depth. His two films with Ford (not counting the US Navy films *The Battle of Midway* and *December 7th*), *The Grapes of Wrath* (1939) and *The Long Voyage Home* (1940), feature several examples of the characteristic Toland shot: a low-angle shot, lit low-key with little fill or backlighting (Toland let the fast film stock do the work of picking out the various planes), with several planes in depth, all in focus, and an enlarged foreground plane.

With Technicolor, most of these contributions to Ford's deep staging style were invalidated: Technicolor film was slow – the supersensitive stock released in 1950 (speed equivalent to around 50 ASA) was barely as fast as the Eastman Plus X Toland used to shoot *The Grapes of Wrath* (speed around 80 ASA), and positively geriatric compared to the Super XX (160 ASA) of *The Long Voyage Home*. Moreover, wide-angle lenses were scarce among the special set designed for the Technicolor camera, necessitating greatly increased light levels if the cameraman wanted to stop down the aperture and achieve a modicum of deep focus. In any case, Ford saw little use for colour in his films: just as he had passed on Merian Cooper's proposal to make *Stagecoach* in the three-strip process, Ford had disregarded Darryl Zanuck's vision of *How Green Was My Valley* and *My Darling Clementine* as Technicolor epics. Ford's only colour film for Zanuck, *Drums Along the Mohawk*, was one of his weakest, 'artful naiveté' according to Tag Gallagher.[4]

Still, as Ford told Bogdanovich, '[t]here are certain pictures, like *The Quiet Man*, that call for color – not a blatant kind – but a soft, misty color'.[5] The distinction is an important one, since, as David Bordwell points out, like certain kinds of music or lighting, the use of Technicolor was governed by genre conventions: from the start, the Technicolor boom was associated with musicals, comedies, romances, westerns, historical spectacles and fantasies.[6] When Ford made *The Quiet Man* at Republic Pictures, it was no longer *The Informer* (1935)-like dark political drama of the Irish 'Troubles'; it was in Richard Llewellyn's adaptation of Maurice Walsh's novella. This was to be a money-maker, a way to salvage what was left of Argosy after the box office disaster of that other *Informer*-like drama of redemption, *The Fugitive* (1947). But neither did Ford want to *over*-emphasise the fantasy part, the 'pop-artishness': compared to the other Technicolor spectacles of 1952 – *Singin' in the Rain, Ivanhoe, The Greatest Show on Earth, Hans Christian Anderson* and *The Million Dollar Mermaid* – this colour production was to be more, well, quiet.

In her wonderful autobiography, *'Tis Herself*, Maureen O'Hara (no stranger to Technicolor, Herbert Kalmus called her the 'Queen of Technicolor' because her red hair, hazel-green eyes and fair complexion photographed so well in the three-strip process) lays to rest the myth, perpetuated mainly by Ford himself, that it rained so hard while filming *The Quiet Man* that they almost stopped shooting the picture: 'We had so much sun,' as Maureen tells the story, 'that we used to ask the cameramen Winton Hoch and [assistant cameraman] Archie Stout if they were putting sunshine pills in the camera. The single time that it did rain was just when Mr. Ford needed it', in the scene where she and Duke kiss in the windy cottage.[7] The exteriors for that scene were shot day-for-night in the kind of weather that recalls the famous lightning storm sequence in *She Wore a Yellow Ribbon*. Ford always told the story that Winton Hoch had to shoot that scene under protest because he thought it would not come out. This yarn about the rain seems meant to excuse the softness of the picture, an aesthetic choice from the start to distinguish this melancholy piece from the 'Glorious Technicolor' of a pure fantasy like *Ivanhoe*.[8]

Since two-thirds of *The Quiet Man* was shot on location in the kind of bright sunlight occasionally found in County Galway, and we know that the three colour system was arranged to give perfect colour balance under sunlight, you would expect an overall sharp definition of the colour tones (especially after the relative sharpness of the image in *Three Godfathers* and *She Wore a Yellow Ribbon*, both shot for the most part on sun-drenched locations in the Mojave Desert and Monument Valley respectively). The fact that the film looks more 'misty' therefore reveals an aesthetic choice on the director's part: Ford did not want this film to resemble the average Technicolor fantasy. By either diffusing the lens or generally shooting at a larger aperture to lower definition, however, Ford and Hoch lost even more depth in the frame. This loss of depth did not bring about any *radical* change in shooting style: this film has an average shot length (ASL) of 9.4 seconds, close to the usual figure of around 9 seconds Barry Salt has found for most Ford films of the late thirties,[9] and mixes classical editing with long-take scenes in a recognisably Fordian way. The windy cottage scene mentioned earlier by Maureen O'Hara has an ASL of almost 12 seconds, with the actual clinch going on for almost thirty seconds. But there is a higher proportion of reverse-angle cuts (both over the shoulder shots and eye-line matches, i.e. cuts between a watcher and her point of view) than in Ford's work up to this point, and therefore fewer scenes to highlight Ford's skill in blocking and moving the actors and staging in multiple depth planes. This becomes especially evident if we compare this film to a later Technicolor production, *The Searchers*, in which the large format negative and short lenses of the VistaVision process allow for a much greater depth of field. We should also mention that in both *The Quiet Man* and *The Searchers* there is very little camera movement in these long takes other than some reframing. This is mainly owing to the monstrous size of the three-strip camera ('blimped' for sound recording), which discouraged elaborate dolly shots.

The number of depth compositions decreases as the film goes on, and the more striking instances of Ford's painterly set-ups in depth clearly suffer from lack of sharpness. Here are some examples from the first half of the film, in which Ford and Hoch use deep space to compose the image: both contrasting and intersecting movement is created in the low-angle opening shot, in which the train moves slightly diagonally downwards into the frame, while the attendant moves upwards into depth, and the woman with the basket intersects his movement by walking into the frame and towards the train from left to right; in a succession of 'aperture framings' (an open door or open window shot that frames the characters) we first get a medium-long shot of Michaeleen Oge framed in the open door of the

Castletown station hall, then an eye-line match from a medium shot of Sean looking for Michaeleen, to a long shot, framed in the open window, of Michaeleen loading the sleeping bag onto the buggy, then a more ambitious depth shot involving a number of 'frames within the frame': looking through the doorway that first framed Michaeleen, we see Sean exit the station through a doorway opening on the left, while Michaeleen and buggy are still visible in the window on the right; in a later low-angle long shot, our view of Sean hurrying back to Michaeleen's buggy in the background of the frame, after having witnessed the 'pastoral' entrance of Mary Kate, is framed in the foreground and middle ground by overhanging trees, creating the kind of natural theatrical space widely adopted in American landscape painting. On the other hand, we need only look at a medium close-up of Mary Kate spying on Sean from behind the church gate to ascertain how hard it was for the cinematographer working in Technicolor to keep more than one plane in focus.

Keeping focus was even harder in the interior scenes shot at the Republic studios (16 days of shooting out of 51), especially since Ford generally insisted on shooting in his usual low-key style, lowering the number of arc floodlight units and opening the lens to maximum aperture. In fact, interiors in the film are almost evenly split between scenes lit with arc floodlights in the rather flat Technicolor mode (like the scene at the Widow Tillane's), and scenes with a bit more chiaroscuro reminiscent of Ford's earlier work, lit with incandescent spotlights (most scenes in which 'source lighting' – light apparently coming from a nominal source within the scene – is emphasised). Scenes at the Hotel Sarsfield bar are extremely dark for a Technicolor film, an autumnal palette further accentuated by the muted colours of the costumes, mostly greys, browns and tweeds, belying Republic Chief Herbert Yates's famous reaction to the rushes of *The Quiet Man*: 'It's all green. Don't they have any browns or blacks in Ireland?'[10] The most famous instance of low-key lighting in the film is an interior shot on location inside Cong's Catholic church. Rather than boost the light levels, Ford instructed Winton Hoch to lower the camera speed to about twelve frames a second, allowing more light into each frame. Of course, this kind of 'under-cranking' would produce a fast-motion effect when projected at the regular speed of twenty-four frames per second. Ford therefore had John Wayne rise from his pew and walk down the aisle past the camera in slow motion. The ploy almost succeeds, but there remains a kind of unnatural jitteriness to Wayne's movement in the scene.

Although superficially the composition of interior scenes from *The Quiet Man* resembles Ford's work with Bert Glennon from the late thirties, especially in their resumption of the deep stage schema with an object in the foreground to accentuate recessional depth, what is immediately striking is that the angles used in *The Quiet Man* are in general more straight-on than the low angles that characterise a film like *Stagecoach*. In the latter film, low angles made with the wide-angle lens show the low ceilings, whereas in this film ceilings are generally left out of the frame. In *Stagecoach*, of course, low angles combined with low ceilings and slightly raked floors were used to emphasise the claustrophobic tightness of living quarters on the frontier; there is no need for this in an 'airy' film like *The Quiet Man*. But if we look at Ford's later films – like *The Searchers* (although again a more 'claustrophobic' film than *The Quiet Man*) – we find a general predilection for slightly lower angles, especially in those films in which depth is an important compositional schema. But in *The Quiet Man* angles are more straight-on than usual, further proof that Technicolor demanded a revision of compositional principles.

Ford disliked colour photography because it made the kind of low-key chiaroscuro effect that he preferred more difficult, and given that his only Technicolor films up to *The Quiet Man* were made reluctantly either as an assigned picture (*Drums Along the Mohawk*) or as a commercial strategy given the popularity of colour films in the late forties and early fifties, it seems reasonable to assume that the original *Quiet Man* conceived by Ford, Maurice Walsh and Richard Llewellyn was a topical picture in the vein of *The Informer*, and would not have been made in colour. Argosy's threatened demise after the failure of *The Fugitive* necessitated a sound commercial decision, even on this long-cherished personal project. Nevertheless, by diffusing colour definition in the exterior scenes, shooting low-key in some interior scenes and refusing coloured lights, Ford and his cameraman

Winton Hoch succeeded in making a different kind of Technicolor film. Shooting exteriors at a larger lens aperture and interiors at reduced light levels, however, aggravated one of the intrinsic problems of the very slow Technicolor film: a loss of depth in the frame that affects the staging of the action on different planes. A critical question worth asking about *The Quiet Man* is to what degree the kind of choices inspired by commercial necessity and technological circumstance determine a director's style and the way the finished film appears to us.

Endnotes

[1] David Bordwell, Janet Staiger and Kristin Thompson, *The Classical Hollywood Cinema* (London: Routledge, 1996), pp. 242–43.

[2] Joseph McBride, *Searching for John Ford: A Life* (London: Faber and Faber, 2003), p. 306.

[3] Ibid.

[4] Tag Gallagher, *John Ford: The Man and His Films* (Berkeley, Los Angeles, London: University of California Press, 1986), p. 174.

[5] McBride, *Searching for John Ford: A Life*, p. 306.

[6] Bordwell, Staiger and Thompson, *The Classical Hollywood Cinema*, p. 355.

[7] Maureen O'Hara (with John Nicoletti), *'Tis Herself': An Autobiography* (London, Sydney, New York, Toronto: Pocket Books, 2005), pp. 199–200.

[8] The 'softness' of the film is often wrongly attributed to the recent restoration having been based not on the original three-strip negative but on a composite Eastman colour print.

[9] Barry Salt, *Film Style and Technology: History and Analysis* (London: Starword, 1992), p. 200.

[10] Scott Eyman, *Print the Legend: The Life and Times of John Ford* (New York: Simon & Schuster, 1999), p. 402.

Narrative Pleasures of the Visualised Nation: *The Quiet Man* and Disruptive Systems of Viewing

BARRY MONAHAN

A significant scene in Neil Jordan's *Breakfast on Pluto* (2006) shows the protagonist, Patrick 'Kitten' Braden, writing an amusing school essay about the circumstances of his conception. As Kitten recreates imaginatively the autobiographical moment when his father, the local priest, Father Liam, is seduced by his house lady, the sequence of events is depicted with a narrative voice-over and humorous over-acting by Liam Neeson and Eva Birthistle. Significantly, the fantastical reconstruction of a past moment – simultaneously nostalgic and unfamiliar for Kitten – is underscored by music from John Ford's 1952 film *The Quiet Man*. By evoking the earlier film as Kitten reconstructs his personal history, Jordan acknowledges both Ford's imaginary rendering of Ireland and the status of *The Quiet Man* in the broader historical context of cinematic representations of the country. In Pat Murphy's film *Maeve* (1981), a scene occurs which, although constructed without Jordan's calculated intertextuality, is relevant here for its juxtaposition of image and word to create narrative instability. As the young eponymous heroine travels through the countryside in her father's van, the lush verdant landscape is framed momentarily by the van window, with colours and composition reminiscent of the scene in which Sean

Thornton first catches sight of Mary Kate. In a reverse shot containing young Maeve and her father, she asks him about his claim to the witnessing of supernatural phenomena on the mound across the field. In an instant that acknowledges the unreliability of narration (the way many other moments of the film have undermined, specifically, patriarchal narrative), he answers:

> You know the way these things are exaggerated. A man sees a light in a field ... and the next thing is he's swearing he's seen the Virgin Mary. And then the next fella tellin' the story ... he'll not only have seen the Virgin Mary, but the baby Jesus as well. And then Saint Joseph will be dragged into it, and before you know where you are you'll have half of the heavenly host out there in the field.

Structurally both of these moments call to mind not only tonal qualities of *The Quiet Man*, but also the dialogical interplay of sound and picture, and the disruption of narrative seamlessness that Ford's film continually performs. If, as one commentator has noted, 'The real significance of the film is [...] the dialogue it makes with its audience',[1] then this quality has its origin in a series of formally discursive features that work across different levels of the text. I want to propose here that these dialogues create a disruption that provides narrative pleasure for spectators, and goes some way toward explaining the enduring popularity of the film for an eclectic range of audiences over the last half-century of screenings.

As the boundaries of the film's plot are established – precisely delineating character, event, location and time – two narrative modes of address are left open-ended. Corresponding to what Edward Branigan has called 'levels of narration' and 'focalization' and 'interdependence',[2] the film enacts dialogues between the diegetic image and extra-diegetic sound, and between characters' and audiences' point of view. These binaries are maintained within the overarching structure of inside/outside, and they are dramatised by aspects of seeing, watching and the gaze. From the beginning, *The Quiet Man* disturbs 'the look' by pitting aural and visual cues against one another. It allows the subsequent disruption to blur the division between the outside (visitor/narrator/spectator) and the inside (local/story/performer). The merging of these positions is rendered by the character of Sean Thornton, placed within, yet at one remove from, the narrated world of Innisfree. It is only when he has been accepted into that community – a position occupied when authorised by Mary Kate – that the character is sutured into the story world. The diegetic split representative of Thornton's position is dramatised visually – through his, other characters' and the film spectator's look – in ways that are significant for how Ireland as an 'imagined community' was being perceived at the time the film was made.

The Quiet Man was produced in Ireland at the mid-point of two significant historical moments. Saint Patrick's Day 1943 and the accession of Seán Lemass as Taoiseach on 23 June 1959 are often cited as representative of two ideological moments in the history of Ireland in terms of international relations and political outlook. The former has been noted for then Taoiseach Eamon de Valera's radio broadcast that was ideologically imbued with a conservative inward-looking national, cultural and economic protectionism, based on a favouring of anti-materialist values and a general mistrust of the processes of modernisation. Lemass, on the other hand, was noted for his outward-looking internationalism and his association with the progressive economic plans of T.K. Whitaker.[3] This shift in political perspectives on nationalism and internationalism was accompanied by two parallel sociological developments. Between 1945 and the late 1950s, while emigration figures rose from an annual 30,000 to above 43,000,[4] the tourist industry grew at an enormous rate.[5] The historical moment was thus marked by alternative and simultaneous ways of looking at Ireland and 'Irishness': perceived both from the outside by recently emigrated natives, but also increasingly through the expectations of visiting tourists. This was to have a number of significant political and social effects. In the case of Dr Noel Browne's proposed state subsidised Mother and Child medical scheme, for example, J.J. Lee noted 'the disparity between the treatment of the sick in Ireland and in Britain was brought increasingly home to the Irish by their emigrant relatives'.[6] There were also cultural incidents that contributed to new ways of displaying the nation. Not only did the 1950s see the establishment of Bord Fáilte – the Irish Tourist Board – the body responsible for coordinating Ireland's international image, but the decade also witnessed the beginnings of a new framing of cultural performance with the setting up in 1951 of the cultural festival An Tóstal, the Wexford Opera Festival and Comhaltas Ceoltóirí Éireann (established to promote Irish music), the Cork Film Festival and the Arts Council (1956) and the Dublin Theatre Festival (1957). The new developments in the cultural performances of 'Irishness' often capitalised on the nostalgia of Irish descendants returning to the country so that a certain kind of imagery was selected and amalgamated into the idealistic framework.[7] This was embodied most evidently in the founding of the Rose of Tralee Festival in 1958, where the nostalgia of returning Irish descendants was contained within a structured ceremonial celebration of national, cultural and historical identification. A similar structural arrangement had been dramatised and rendered cinematically along lines of perception at the beginning of the decade in Ford's film.

In *The Quiet Man*, the Irish-American returning to his birthplace helps establish our frequently altering viewpoint: sometimes aligned with, sometimes divergent from that of Sean Thornton. We accept the performative excesses of the film and the non-fictional qualities that provide contexts for them because we occupy variously altering positions of spectatorship in relation to the presentation. This is most evident in the scene on the bridge when authentic landscapes that represent Sean's point of view are intercut with a false studio backdrop that problematically disrupts our position as sutured spectators. A heavily orchestrated soundtrack, a richly coloured landscape, and moments of melodramatic dialogue are framed alongside diegetically performed songs, authentic locations, and moments of intimate and understated performance. The fantastical combination of elements that are otherwise stylistically incongruous provides some degree of comic effect or dramatic lightening and, therefore, pleasure for the spectator. *The Quiet Man* manifestly subverts the typical procedures of seamless integration that produce narrative homogeneity within contemporary mainstream cinema. Accepting that operations of the

classical Hollywood film are guided by an imperative of verisimilitude, Colin MacCabe addresses the position of the spectator, suggesting that 'representation masquerades as presentation, the fictional
diegesis as the real world. The spectator is invited to attend to the
unfolding of the story, not to the way in which it is told'.[8] Inasmuch
as it disrupts this position of unacknowledged spectatorship, Ford's
film can be understood to be working syntactically – if not always
semantically – like a musical: foregrounding performance, establishing a fourth wall point of view, and presenting multiple levels of narration. Spectator satisfaction occurs at the point of audiences' awareness of their watching the performance, their engagement with star
personalities as performing entities, and the knowledge of the
framed theatricality of the event. Audience investment and pleasure
are not fed by seamless verisimilitude, as in the typical classical film,
and, like the musical, *The Quiet Man* draws attention to the audience's 'fourth wall' perspective – a position of pure watching – towards which action is always addressed. As in musicals like *An
American in Paris* (1951, Minnelli) and *Singin' in the Rain* (1952, Donen
& Kelly), throughout *The Quiet Man* there occurs a recurrent combination of narration and narrative. The amalgamation of 'teller' – a
position simultaneously established and undermined by involvement
in the diegesis – with 'told' – the linear development of the plot – facilitates the operation of a number of playful cinematic features. The
earliest example that demonstrates the film's status as fiction is the
voice-over introduction by Father Lonergan, whose chatty informal-
ity invokes the action of story-telling from the outset:

> Well then, now, I'll begin at the beginnin'. A fine soft day in
> the spring it was when the train pulled in to Castletown, three
> hours late as usual, and himself got off it.

His next vocal interruption has the peculiarity of covering a shot that
contains him – a device most frequently used in the *film noir* genre by
the narrating detective, or the protagonist of the musical[9] – but marks
an even greater disruption of the diegetic and extra-diegetic separation by virtue of the fact that he introduces himself in it. As the trap
carrying Michaeleen Óg and Sean Thornton moves along a quiet

country lane, and the priest walks into the shot towards them, his voice-over declares: 'Now, then, here comes myself. That's me there walking: that tall saintly-looking man. Peter Lonergan, Parish Priest'.

The most unusual and cinematically subtle example of this device is the voice-over that occurs at the end of the film. The text is delivered in the usual tone of resolution, but the monologue is abruptly interrupted by the rapid entrance into the frame of Mrs Playfair, as she cycles into the village and towards a gathered crowd. Not only does the action break the narrative commentary momentarily (another rupture of diegetic and non-diegetic, *and* a narrative impossibility) but, when Lonergan resumes his speech, he appears from the crowd, his voice now diegetically motivated:

> Well, then, so peace and quiet came once again to Innisfree, and we were up … [*Playfair cycles into the village, centre shot and the camera pans to follow her*] … Good Heavens! What's that woman up to now? Make way! Make way! She'll be running you down with that juggernaut … [*Shot of crowd gathered, bicycle moves in among them, Lonergan emerges from the group and stands on the wall to address them*] … Ah sure! Now, when the Reverend Mr Playfair, good man that he is, comes down, I want you all to cheer like Protestants.

The transfer from off-screen voice-over to on-screen address is subtly made by disguising the character in the crowd, and his presence is marked when he rises above it to speak to those gathered. This transition visually objectifies the syntactic acoustic register of the musical that Bordwell and Thompson have called 'progressive diegeticization'.[10] In this instance, an alteration in narrative levels allows an acceptance of a combination of soundtracks from sources that are both diegetically and extra-diegetically motivated.

The film displays a series of performances within its story as it frames musical numbers (sometimes by pub revellers, at others by Mary Kate or Michaeleen Óg Flynn), minor narrations and other tangential narratives. A connection is emphasised between diegetic levels since these performances provide entertainment for both the diegetic on-lookers and extra-diegetic spectators. Inasmuch as they

play like the theatrical asides or performances of the musical, many
of these moments suspend narrative action and take the form of spectacle. Such spectacular instances emphasise a particular relationship
between story world and audience along lines of visualisation. Steven Neale has noted that:

> Spectacle is content neither with simple rendering visible the
> observable, nor with inscribing the spectating subject simply
> in position as observer. It is much more concerned with the
> processes of rendering visible and looking themselves. What
> counts in spectacle is not the visible as guarantee of veracity
> (of truth, or reality) but rather the visible as mask, as lure.
> What counts is not the instance of looking as observation, but
> rather as fascinated gaze.[11]

The onlookers of the village – themselves notably performers within
the fiction – are central elements in the 'processes of rendering visible' of our film viewing. As outsider, Sean Thornton's position is
problematised and underscored for us when we are told that, unlike
other visitors 'He didn't have the look of a tourist about him', and
that he didn't have a camera: marking his being one step closer to
entering the represented (symbolic) world of Innisfree. His first
point-of-view shot further emphasises this division as he looks
through the window frame of the train station, watching Michaeleen
loading his belongings onto the trap. An important moment of interior focalization occurs during the flashback sequence to Sean's last
fist fight. In the wedding photograph scene immediately before the
flashback, Mary Kate and Sean stand still in a typical bride and
groom pose, while we occupy what appears to be the position of the
wedding photographer's camera. Ford does not use a still-to-action
transitional cut after the wedding shot, as Welles does in *Citizen Kane*
(1941). Instead, after a brief pause, the camera tracks back rapidly to
reveal left-of-shot the real still camera and photographer whose position we had occupied. This movement motivates a change in audience perspective which is normally accomplished by a cut: the fact
that it is accomplished here with the added framing of a diegetic
(still) camera further emphasises the dramatic transition. Elsewhere,

commenting on Michelangelo Antonioni's use of a similar device in *Blowup* (1966), Sam Rohdie notes the potential tension inherent in alternating cinematic 'looks':

> When the camera looks on its own, it is outside the fiction; in that place it comes to regard and contemplate not simply the photographs and the photographer, but its own gaze, until it seems that the film you are watching is a documentary of itself. It is a film encountering itself and, thereby, encountering the cinema.[12]

During the subsequent flashback sequence, Ford draws attention to the split point of view that has been established at the beginning of the wedding scene. Just as the film encounters itself, the spectators also become aware of their unsutured position; effectively, another 'encountering'. Here, again, perspectives are confused as we presume that we are being informed by Sean's memory (and therefore point of view) despite the fact that we actually see him in the remembered scene.

Otherwise invisibly sutured in classical cinema, conventional shot/reverse shots and clearly motivated point-of-view set-ups are extremely infrequently used by Ford in the film. Andrew Higson remarks upon the ubiquity of undisturbed visual matches in films of the time when he notes that:

> The classical film generally attempts to give the impression of there being a match, a perfect fit, between the look of individual characters within the world of the fiction and the look of the camera at this performance.[13]

Ford constantly creates tensions across any such expectations of 'a match' or 'perfect fit' and this is done in varying modes of empowerment shifting from sets of protagonists, to ensemble characters, to spectators. Working from the notion that he is neither absolute outsider nor strictly native, Sean's position is formally echoed in point-of-view shots that represent his perspective. A disruption occurs as his position and viewpoint are frequently undermined cinematically for the audience. His first three direct point-of-view shots, for example, are unconventionally ruptured from the typical diegetically closed shot/reverse shot set-up. The first of these occurs when he watches through the station house window as Michaeleen Óg climbs into the trap, literalising a framing of the story world that he has yet to enter. The second and third, in which he looks from the bridge to White O'Morn and across the fields at Mary Kate, are cynically undercut by Michaeleen Óg's comments that immediately undermine any romantic or nostalgic illusions entertained by Thornton. Pointing out that the first is 'nothing but a wee humble cottage', he adds that Sean's perspective of Mary Kate framed against the idyllic Irish landscape is 'only a mirage brought on by [his] terrible thirst'. In this example there is ostensible camera restraint when, as Mary Kate comes down the hill and looks back at Sean, a spatial tension is produced as her head descends mid-frame until it occupies the cinematically imbalanced position of lowest central point on the screen. The presence of the camera is conspicuous since it refuses to tilt in order to keep her in the more traditional position within the frame, and thus avoids imitation of the naturalistic movement of Sean's eye-line. Ubiquitous on-lookers in the story world of the film perform spectatorship as it occurs in the musical. Villagers gather (like French bystanders on the streets of *An American in Paris*) to watch many of Thornton's activities, most notably his arrival, the horse race, the announcement by Red Will of his giving Sean permission to court Mary Kate, and the climactic fight scene.

In contrast, Mary Kate is empowered by direct alignment with audience point of view. Her gaze (as Irish-American) also significantly bridges the outsider/insider dichotomy, thus resolving many of the mentioned tensions of perspective. Unlike Sean, as both local and visitor, she holds a more coherent 'gaze', watching the action and dramatically 'looking'. Her position is securely fixed within the diegetic space, and her actions and performances are matched by a repeated returning of the gaze. So potent is her position that at one moment she even terrifies herself as she catches sight of her reflection during a flash of lightning in the darkly lit cottage she later occupies with Sean. Mary Kate's position is not one of the fetishised females of Laura Mulvey's classical cinema 'as erotic object for the characters within the screen story, and as erotic object for the spectator within the auditorium, with a shifting tension between the looks on either side of the screen'.[14] It is apposite, therefore, that Ford's film equally disobeys the separation of cinematic 'looks' that Mulvey has defined elsewhere. Delineating the three looks as 'that of the camera as it records the pro-filmic event, that of the audience as it watches the final product, and that of the characters at each other within the screen illusion', Mulvey continues:

> The conventions of narrative film deny the first two and sub-ordinate them to the third, the conscious aim being always to eliminate intrusive camera presence and prevent a distancing awareness in the audience.[15]

By drawing attention to what is normally denied in the functioning of cinematic looks, *The Quiet Man* dramatises a particular mode of viewing the nation which is appropriate to the historical moment of its production. In doing this, it requires a consciousness of seeing: point of view, aspect, looking, observing, empowerment of the gaze, and framing are all parts of how this document captures the way Ireland was being encapsulated in the early 1950s and how cultural commodification has occurred through mediation since then. As Linda Hutcheon defines the moment when cultural texts enact a merging of fictional and historical narration, she points to benefits of such 'historiographic metafictions' which 'enact the problematic nature of the relation of writing history to narrativization and, thus, to fictionalization, thereby raising [...] questions about the cognitive status of historical knowledge'.[16] By undermining its visual codes and framing its inauthenticity, *The Quiet Man* dramatises and exhibits 'a deliberate contamination of the historical with the didactic and situational discursive elements, thereby challenging the implied assumptions of historical statements: objectivity, neutrality, impersonality, and the transparency of representation'.[17] *The Quiet Man* is not merely a piece of cinematic history: it is an example of Irish cinematic historiography, showing us Ireland in the process of being represented, representing itself, and being watched on screen. It is constructed formally around the gaze of the outsider and insider, and dramatises the reception of the foreigner into its community along lines of visual empowerment. The final shot of the film shows Mary Kate and Sean, arm in arm, walking through their garden: the action in the upper section of the frame is reflected in the river that surrounds their cottage. This shot echoes the ones behind the opening credits, composed of a castle landscape on the top half of the screen which is reflected in a lake in the bottom half. The division implied, between reality and its reflection, in the closing and opening images, marks the thematic operation of visualisation which is important for the whole film. Ultimately, Sean is accepted into the community and his secured status as 'local' is registered formally when he, with the other characters, lines up to wave towards the camera (and us), in what Luke Gibbons has referred to as the 'curtain call'.[18] Like the hero of the Coen brothers' *Barton Fink* (1991) who arrives in Los Angeles from New York, uncomfortably alien in his new surroundings, Sean Thornton is framed in the closing sequence within the representation outside of which he had remained as observer for the earlier part of the film.

Endnotes

[1] James MacKillop, 'The Quiet Man Speaks', *Contemporary Irish Cinema*, ed. by James MacKillop (New York: G. Crowdis, 1999), p. 179.

[2] Edward Branigan, *Narrative Comprehension and Film* (London, New York: Routledge, 2004), pp. 87, 100.

[3] J.J. Lee, *Ireland, 1912–1985: Politics and Society* (Cambridge: Cambridge University Press, 1989), pp. 341–59.

[4] Ibid., p. 288.

[5] A point made by the managing director of the Shelbourne Hotel on a special St. Patrick's Day edition of *The Ed Sullivan Show*, 1959.

[6] Lee, *Ireland, 1912–1985*, p. 314.

[7] Luke Gibbons, *Transformations in Irish Culture* (Cork: Cork University Press, 1996), pp. 82–93.

[8] Colin MacCabe, 'Realism and the Cinema: Notes on some Brechtian theses', *Screen*, 15.2 (Summer 1974) 12 (7–27).

[9] *An American in Paris* (Minnelli, 1951) plays with this convention throughout, though most extensively during the opening sequence when Gene Kelly's voice-over is heard during the Paris montage that ends with his self-introduction.

[10] Robert Stam, Robert Burgoyne and Sandy Flitterman-Lewis, *New Vocabularies in Film Semiotics: Structuralism, Post-Structuralism and Beyond* (London, New York: Routledge, 1992), p. 92.

[11] Steven Neale, 'Triumph of the Will – Notes on Documentary and Spectacle', *Screen*, 20:1 (Spring) 85 (63–86).

[12] Sam Rohdie, *The Passion of Pier Paolo Pasolini* (Bloomington, Indianapolis: Indiana University Press, BFI Publishing, 1995), p. 17.

[13] Andrew Higson, *Dissolving Views: Key Writings on British Cinema*, ed. by Andrew Higson (London: Cassell, 1996), p. 150.

[14] Laura Mulvey, 'Visual Pleasure and Narrative Cinema', *Movies and Methods Volume II*, ed. by Bill Nichols (Los Angeles, London: University of California Press, 1985), p. 309.

[15] Ibid., p. 314.

[16] Linda Hutcheon, *A Poetics of Postmodernism: History, Theory, Fiction* (London, New York: Routledge, 1988), p. 92.

[17] Ibid.

[18] Kevin Rockett, Luke Gibbons and John Hill, *Cinema and Ireland* (London: Routledge, 1988), p. 240.

III

Landscape, Politics and Identity

11

The Hidden Landscape Aesthetic of *The Quiet Man*

EAMONN SLATER

When Edmund Burke, the Irish philosopher and aesthete, wished to illustrate by example his theory of beauty, he did not choose a piece of classical statuary, an inspiring ode, nor even a beautiful woman, but one of the experiences of a Brownian park.[1]

Luke Gibbons dramatically proposed that landscape as it has been represented in Irish cinema tended to play a leading role, to such an extent that it 'upstaged' the main characters and narrative themes in the construction of Ireland on the screen.[2] John Ford's movie *The Quiet Man* was no exception in this regard. Gibbons backs up his assertion by referring to a contemporary reviewer's commentary on the movie:

> … there can be no quarrel with Ford's fine treatment of the scenery he found in the West [West of Ireland]. It is a lovely background caught in soft shades of technicolour and as real as one could wish. The camera lingers on it lovingly, almost reluctant one would imagine at times, to be getting on with the story.[3]

To begin, I want to 'quarrel' with Ford's representation of Irish land-scape by suggesting that what gets depicted as authentic Irish land-scape in the movie is atypical, rather than the more prevalent land-scape of bog and mountain in the West of Ireland. Ford's 'lovely background' to his action is generally a parkland garden, an Anglo-Irish landlord landscape. The reason for this has to do with the com-plex relationship between landscape appreciation, Romanticism and landscape gardening.

However, before we explore this crucial relationship, let us con-tinue our examination of the structure of cinematic representation of Irish landscape through the work of Gibbons. He goes on to suggest that this preoccupation with Irish landscape dates back to the emer-gence of Romanticism in the eighteenth century. Des Bell has argued for a direct historical link between Romanticism and film.[4] In a more recent article, Gibbons cites the work of Raymond Immerwahr in suggesting that the opening up of picturesque locations of Ireland to the modern traveller in the 1740s was one of the founding moments of European Romanticism.[5] European Romantics constituted a daz-zling assortment of artistic talents and classes which came together in their opposition to the apparent rationalism of the Enlightenment and their rejection of urban industrial life.[6] Therefore, the inherent anti-urbanism of the early Romantics determined that as an intellec-tual movement Romanticism was going to have its emotional 'home' in the rural countryside. The countryside through the Romantic per-spective was to embody the lost virtues of simplicity and natural harmony. However, according to Gibbons, the Romantic relationship to nature was not a simple one, but a mediated relationship, which can take on many forms. He himself identified two, the American and the Irish form.

In American Romanticism, nature was to be experienced in a raw elemental condition, more or less in the state in which God had left it.[7] Nature and wilderness in this perspective were to be devoid of any symbolic associations with history or legend. Language and society were not permitted to enter this 'natural' terrain of the Ro-mantic. In these circumstances, the Romantic quest was to be ex-perienced in silence and in solitude.[8] Recently, John Urry has described this condition as the Romantic gaze.[9] In contrast to American Romanticism, Gibbons suggests that:

> Irish romanticism, though no less concerned with the celebra-
> tion of wilderness and natural disorder, is from the outset
> characterised by an aversion to individualism and the clarity
> of vision required by the puritan ideal. Perception is accorded
> no primacy over language, so that there is little evidence of
> any wish to apprehend nature in a pristine unadulterated
> state, free from any symbolic or linguistic contamination.[10]

Therefore, in Irish Romanticism nature and landscape can never be reduced to mere scenery but always bear some traces of cultural meaning. This symbolic meaning to landscape can be given by the presence of ruins in that landscape or by narrative accounts (both oral or written). Gibbons draws the following important implication from his analysis:

> The point of drawing attention to this interpretation of nature
> as a symbolic field is to underline the case for treating land-
> scape in Romantic images of Ireland not merely as a pictur-
> esque backdrop, but as a layer of meaning in its own right, a
> thematic element which may cut across the other levels of
> meaning in a text.[11]

But the picturesque backdrop can have its own symbolic field when we are able to read the text inscribed in the landscape.

Gibbons concludes this section by suggesting that landscape can operate on two levels, one that conforms to a realist, pictorial aesthetic and which represents the vantage-point of the outsider, and the other which refuses instant or immediate access and the kind of transparency which is integral to the tourist or colonial vision.[12] The latter can be interpreted as the insider's or native gaze.[13] But the crucial point to be grasped from Gibbons's analysis is that there are not only two differing forms of Romantic interpretations of landscape, but they can also be competing with each other for dominance. And the structure of the contest between these competing interpretations and the subsequent emergence of one as dominant may depend on the actual context (and crucially the text) in which this struggle is fought out.[14] We also should be careful in not accepting the idea that the American version of Romantic appreciation of landscape is without its own symbolic associations, that is, is not mediated through a language or a framework. Even the landscape connoisseur of the American puritan mould did not stand in front of a scene without thoughts and concepts passing through his or her head. On the contrary, according to John Barrell, the contemplation of the landscape was not a passive activity but involved reconstructing the landscape in the imagination according to the principles of composition of the picturesque. And these principles had to be learned and were indeed learned so thoroughly that in the later eighteenth century it became impossible for anyone with an aesthetic interest in landscape to look at the countryside without applying them, whether s/he knew s/he was doing so or not.[15] Therefore, the appearance of silence from a landscape connoisseur does not imply the absence of language or cultural symbols but can imply the diametrical opposite. As a consequence, the dualism of language/silence has to be superseded as a way of making sense of how we relate to nature and wilderness. I want to argue that it is better to investigate how the landscape is constructed as a cultural object, either ideologically or physically, or both. With this approach in mind, let us return to the 'lovely background ... of soft shades' in *The Quiet Man*.

Here, I want to examine some backdrop scenes from the movie. One of the first scenic locations of the movie is when Michaeleen Oge (Barry Fitzgerald) and Sean Thornton (John Wayne) meet Father Lonergan (Victor McLaglen) on the way to Innisfree. Michaeleen is seen driving Sean along through the countryside in a jaunting cart as is depicted in the following still (Fig. 1):

Fig. 1. The Quiet Man (Republic Pictures, 1952)

There are a number of things I find rather curious about this particular setting. The first is the way we are able to see the jaunting car moving through the landscape from a side angle, as if it is sailing through a vast sea of grass. What is unusual about this depiction of the West and especially Connemara is the actual vastness of the field which allows us such an uninterrupted long shot. The typical Connemara landscape is made up either of a patchwork of small fields divided by small stone walls,[16] within which grass is produced as a crop, or of a vast expanse of poor unproductive bog without any walls.[17] The latter is held in commonage by the local farmers, from which they produce turf. Secondly, we as spectators are placed under a clump of trees, as indicated by the dark shadow falling over the grass in the foreground. The background is similarly made up of tree clusters or clumps. All these tree clusters seem to consist of differing species, as indicated by the contrasting shapes of the tree trunks in the foreground and varying colour tones in the background. But trees, and especially clusters, are not typical of the West of Ireland. Where trees do exist, they do so in industrial-type plantations set out in linear rows and are of one particular species, but never in clusters of broadleaf and evergreen. This setting therefore indicates that the land is being underutilised for productive purposes, either for forestry or agricultural production. In fact the mixing of the two suggests an extravaganza.

The following scene has another example of visual extravaganza. As Michaeleen and Sean pass along the now visible road, an old Celtic cross comes into view (Fig. 2):

Fig. 2. The Quiet Man (Republic Pictures, 1952)

There are two odd things about this scene. Firstly, with regard to the cross, there are no religious icons depicted on it. Also, it has extremely elaborate art work for a mere boundary cross, and therefore it should be in a graveyard, not on the side of the road. This oddity begs the following question: Is this an authentic ruin or is it a folly, constructed to look like a ruin? I suggest that we see it as a folly and therefore its value to the scene cannot be judged from the viewpoint of historical accuracy or authenticity. It merely stands as a token of historical development, but also, because it is seen to be leaning over, this historical legacy is itself seeming to be deteriorating. And, as a folly, the cross's function in the shot is to exude an air of decay. Secondly, with regard to the roadway, it appears to be sunken into the ground on both sides. The consequence of this is that there is a good likelihood that this road would flood in heavy rain, unless there is extensive underground draining provided. The sunken aspect of this roadway implies that someone has constructed it this way in order to hide it. This is no ordinary landscape!

Sean and Michaeleen continue their sojourn through this exotic landscape until they meet the local priest. The next still depicts the jaunting car approaching the priest.[18] Here, we are provided with the most panoramic view of the landscape in this sequence (Fig. 3):

Fig. 3. The Quiet Man (Republic Pictures, 1952)

What is unusual about this view in the Irish context is the sense of freedom which it conveys, freedom with regard to a person's ability to move from the public highway into the surrounding countryside without being impeded by fence or a stone wall. Fences and walls are the physical manifestation of private property and society's attempt to control access to rural space. But here these normal rural bounda-

ries do not exit, suggesting that private property may also not be operating in this mysterious place. These depictions are getting close to
a pre-modern world, a world without constraint, an arcadia. This ar-
cadian theme is continued in the next still and final scene in this sequence. Here, Sean Thornton has dismounted from the car and sees
Mary Kate Danaher (Maureen O'Hara) for the first time (Fig. 4 depicts this moment during the making of the film).

*Fig. 4. The filming of the moment Sean Thornton first sees Mary Kate Danaher
in* The Quiet Man

Gibbons has subtitled this particular shot as 'paradise regained'[19] and
states the following:

> Here, in John Ford's most memorable evocation of the pastoral
> ideal, we see a radiant Mary Kate (Maureen O'Hara) driving
> sheep through a primeval forest in luminous sunlight, a per-
> fectly realised image of woman at home with nature.[20]

It could be stated against my approach that this is just one ideological
reading of *The Quiet Man* among many. But there is a material basis
for my interpretation of the landscape depicted in this movie. The

reason for this is that the backdrop to this sequence of events (and many subsequent ones) from the movie were filmed in the parklands of Ashford Castle, Co. Mayo. As a parkland, it is a garden, designed by landscape gardeners according to certain principles and therefore was conceived to have a predetermined effect on the viewing subject. In short, it is an ideology 'made flesh' by the 'natural' forms of recon-structed terrain and selected species of vegetation. Therefore, the visible oddities that we have highlighted are a result of an estab-lished set of meanings that are fixed before the construction of these pleasure parklands.[21] Within such vast stretches of pasture, pano-ramic vistas of uninterrupted landscape can be got from sunken ser-pentine-like roadways. Such spectacular views were only interrupted by obvious artificial follies and by clumps of trees scattered through the landscape without any apparent order to them. Therefore, these landscape 'oddities', as depicted in the movie, are a result of garden-ing. But, crucially, this type of gardening was not an attempt to high-light the exotic features of the Irish landscape, but to make those 'natural' Irish features look like an English landscape, a little England in Ireland. To make sense of this contradiction, we need to go back beyond Ford's time in the West of Ireland to the eighteenth century and to the world of art.

According to John Barrell, the word landscape is originally a painter's word,[22] first introduced from the Dutch language in the six-teenth century to describe a pictorial representation of the country-side. Later the word came to include within its meaning both the sense of countryside represented in a picture, and another, of a piece of countryside considered as a visual phenomenon. In the latter sense, the concept has jumped from its pictorial frame, to mean all that could be seen at one glance from a fixed position, usually from an eminence. But not only did it go into commonsense understand-ing of landscape, it also emerged within philosophy, with the ap-pearance of Edmund Burke's work in 1757, *A Philosophical Enquiry into the Origin of our Ideas of the Sublime and Beautiful*. Burke was the first to develop philosophical ideas in the appreciation of scenery. Beauty was smooth, rounded, and induced feelings of peace and well-being. Sublime, on the other hand, was rugged, 'awe-full', and produced feelings of horror and fright.[23] Therefore, these categories created a dualism, the dualism of the beautiful and the sublime, and this became identified in the public mind as a pair of binary opposites from the 1760s onwards.[24] Parallel to this movement of aesthetic categories between painting, philosophy, and scenery appreciation was a more mundane development in landscape gardening. All these developments were intrinsically connected with each other. But the emergence of the new English-style garden of the mid-eighteenth century was a further development because the abstract categories of the beautiful and the sublime were now going to be made manifest in a concrete form, the form of a garden. This new revolutionary-style garden, which emanated from England, was also known as the Informal style garden. As a design, it demanded that flowers, fruit and vegetables be banished to walled gardens away from the house and that formal features, such as parterres, avenues and canals, be swept away and replaced with an idealised conception of 'natural' landscapes.[25] According to Gallagher, the emergence of the Informal English garden indicated a crucial change in man's relationship to nature. Now the perspective was to see man's position as being within nature itself, rather than as an agent to tame and regulate its forces, as in the old Dutch and French formal gardens.[26] But not only did the change in the ideological outlook influence the new style, but it also had an impact on the adoption of new media techniques of representation, notably the compositional techniques of landscape painting. In particular, the English Informal garden owed much to the portrayal of idyllic Italian scenery in the paintings of Nicholas Poussin and Claude Lorrain.[27] The greatest exponent of the English garden was Capability Brown. Brown applied the compositional principles of Poussin and Lorrain and worked them through three basic mediums of wood, water and grass. However, it was the tree which became the essential tool of Brown and his followers.

Although, in spatial terms the Brownian landscape was dominated by grass and water (lakes), it was the tree that created the dramatic effect in this 'natural' garden. Grass and water tended to be monotonous in tone and lacking in visual variety. In contrast, the tree, because of its physical variety and differing colour tones, became the actual 'brush strokes' of the landscape gardener, as the following advice of Uvdale Price suggests:

> Consult the works of painters, and learn the principles which guided them in their combinations of natural and artificial objects. Group your trees on the principles they do. Connect your masses as they do. In short, apply their principles of painting whenever you intend any imitation of nature; for the principles of nature and painting are the same.[28]

Trees, therefore, became the most useful and the most manageable material on the palette of the Brownian landscape gardener. And by mixing deciduous with evergreen trees and by placing them along differing planes in the landscape, the landscape gardener was able to achieve the same effect as the paintings did in perspective. In attempting to replicate the same optical illusion of the landscape paintings of Lorrain and Poussin, the gardeners had to follow the very rigid compositional structure of their work:

> A landscape by Claude [Lorrain] employs, in the first place, a fairly high viewpoint – high enough, that is, for a distant horizon to appear above any rising ground between it and the viewpoint: and the first impression which everyone must receive, I imagine, on seeing a Claude landscape, is one of tremendous depth [...] The eye, attracted by an area of light usually set just below the horizon, travels immediately towards it over a long and often steeply contoured stretch of intervening land [...] The initial movement in all Claude's landscapes is this one, from the foreground straight to the far distance; [...] The foreground itself is usually in the shade of the coulisse – a group of trees, or a building, to the right or left of the picture, and framing the landscape behind. There is, therefore, a band of fairly dark colour at the bottom of the picture; and, dropping below the level of the land in the foreground, and deeper into the picture, is the second plane, of ground more exposed to the sunlight. A third plane beyond this will be darker again, overshadowed by trees or a cloud which is understood to have come between this patch of land and the sun. The next plane will be the one that first attracts the eye, and usually suf-

fused with a clear yellow evening light; and the last will often
be blue, and connects the landscape with the colour of the
sky.[29]

By mixing the colour tones of the differing tree species and placing
them along differing planes, the gardener was able to reproduce the
compositional techniques similar to a Claudian landscape painting.
But crucially, this reproduction was not a mere representation of a
landscape, it was the real thing, a real landscape designed to look
picturesque.

However, not only were the compositional techniques of Lorrain
and Poussin adopted to a new medium, but also some of the painterly categories used to describe their work and the work of Salvator
Rosa. These were the old aesthetic dualism of the beautiful and the
sublime. The beautiful in this type of garden tended to be associated
with the cultivated parts of the demesne, those of the parkland itself.
On the other hand, the sublime applies to wilderness, in spatial
terms, the area beyond the parkland of the beautiful. As a consequence, the sublime aspect of the picturesque could be visually appropriated into the overall framework only as a background to the
beautiful. The landscape gardener could only physically reshape the
beautiful aspects of the picturesque. This he did by planting alternating bands of grass and trees in the foreground and middle-ground of
the picturesque.[30] The sublime features could not be successively
planted in the parkland without losing those characteristics which
defined them as sublime, i.e. being truly 'natural' and creating 'awe-
inspiring and fearful feeling', which could be achieved only by looking into vast uncultivated wastes beyond the comforting confines of
the beautiful. In terms of terrain, the sublime appeared as high jag-
ged mountains, and with regard to flora, the sublime was generally
indicated by the presence of bogland, especially mountain blanket
bog.[31] However, there was a way in which the sublime could enter
the garden of the beautiful, but not as a living plant or as prospect
but as a decaying man-made object, – a 'historical' ruin. The existence
of a ruin, whether real or artificial (therefore a folly) was an important feature of the picturesque experience. Ruins became nodes for

the contemplation of the transient nature of life by the way they exude an air of decay. According to Andrews, ruins create a feeling of
'awe and agreeable horror', similar to looking at the wild desolation
of the sublime.[32] Therefore, the ruin and its artificial variant, the folly,
become the physical icon of the forces of sublimity within the beautiful parkland.

Accordingly, the picturesque landscape within the estate parkland was designed to impress the mind of the viewer. These disguised gardens are about the consumption of views. And, in this respect, the most important subject in the picturesque does not actually
appear in the landscape, because that person is doing the viewing.
The social vision to be viewed, although actually hidden from view
because the culturally designed framework is enveloped in the natural forms of grass, water and the tree, can be explicated from these
physical forms by the application of the appropriate interpretative
device, the ideological categories of the picturesque. Therefore, the
landscape in the parkland was not just a physical backdrop but also a
medium that was full of aesthetic icons that needed to be interpreted,
to be read. And this reading depended on acquiring the skill to make
sense of the 'natural' hieroglyphics thrown about the landscape. Interpreting the view is not only a mediated relationship, but that
process of mediation involves an acquired connoisseurship of the
arts, i.e. painting, poetry, garden design and travelogue reading.
Therefore, this form of landscape appreciation was an essential aspect of an elite culture. The essential philosophical endeavour of the
picturesque centred on an attempt to restore the harmony between
society and nature. But the experience of this restorative harmony
was to be exclusively visual. And since the process of viewing is inherently an individual activity, any attempt to grasp nature through
the visual had to be conceived of as an individual experience. It is not
a collective experience. As a consequence, viewing the picturesque
can be seen as constituting a form of bourgeois individualism, an
ethic where the emphasis is on consumption and the activity of the
individual subject.[33] But in the consumption of the picturesque view,
a state of harmony is sought between the individual and the 'natural'
surrounds, an Arcadia without anomie. Therefore, for this experience

of harmony to be achieved, any form of disharmony must be excluded from the garden. Disharmony cannot be natural – of nature –
since in the picturesque, nature, as in the sublime, is given. The idea
of disharmony could be ascertained only as being determined by social factors, those which involve people interacting with nature or
with other people, in the sense that people or objects constructed by
people can ruin the view. Therefore, people must be kept out of the
frame, detached from the picturesque.

The detaching of the local people from their native habitat is itself
a complex process and in many instances replicates the movement of
ideological concepts between differing mediums within the overall
framework of the picturesque. J.B. Harley, in his essay 'Maps, Knowledge and Power', has suggested that the nineteenth century rural
maps impinged on the daily lives of the ordinary rural people.[34] Since
the clock had brought a form of time discipline on the new industrial
workers, maps introduced a dimension of space discipline on the rural
peasantry. Following this line of argument, it could be suggested that
the picturesque framework introduced a dimension of aesthetic discipline on the Irish peasantry. Defining an area as picturesque within the
domain of an improving landlord meant that the peasantry could
never hope to gain access to that land for productive purposes. Even
more harmful was to have a sitting tenant's land defined as picturesque by a landscape connoisseur. This surely meant eviction for the
sitting tenants as the landlord cleared these unsightly objects from the
picturesque landscape.[35] It could be argued that this process of de-
tachment is an essential feature of colonialism and imperialism.
Edward Said would certainly suggest so. He has argued that imperialism is an act of geographical violence through which every
space in a country is explored, charted, and finally brought under
control.[36] The picturesque as we have described it fits into the
Saidian idea of imperialism, in that the picturesque, as part of Romanticism in general, explored the globe in search of picturesque
spots. It charted those spots through various forms of representations.
As a cultural and social movement with a strong ideological framework, it had the power to control access to those areas identified as
picturesque.

The ideology of the picturesque was an essential aspect of the Anglo-Irish elite in Ireland. It, as an ideological support, had the ability to justify the prevention of the native population from occupying the land. In a sense, the picturesque as an ideological apparatus defined the terrain as a landscape to be viewed, rather than as a place to be lived in. Finally, as part of this wrenching of control over the land from the native population, the picturesque landscape movement changed the ecology of the local habitat by introducing foreign plant species into the gardens. Trees, such as beech, lime, horse chestnut, sycamore and walnut were all foreign exotics introduced by the landscape gardener of the eighteenth century.[37] Edward Said argues that the colonialists in general had a conscious plan to transform the colonised territories into images of what they have left behind. Therefore, the appearance of the English informal garden in Ireland can now be seen in a different light, in the political light of British colonialism of Ireland. If Said is right, the picturesque framework is a crucial element in the colonialist mind-set, and an important part of the ideology of the planter colony, an ideology that is inherently imperialist as it detaches the peasantry from the native environment, by transforming their place into a picturesque landscape.

The picturesque is then about the way an outsider wishes to see landscape, either as a colonising landlord or as a tourist in search of the picturesque. It, as we have discovered is about consumerism, i.e. consuming harmonious visions of the landscape. And because of this essential relationship between spectatorship and the land, the actual landscape is changed to suit the wishes of the picturesque connoisseurs. According to Reeves-Smyth, by the middle of the nineteenth century parkland occupied around 800,000 acres, or 4 per cent of Ireland, with over 7,000 houses featuring pleasure landscapes of ten acres or more.[38] The fixing of the viewing points is crucial to the way the landscaper could respond to the demands of these consumers of landscape.

This desire to see a certain vision of and on the landscape meant that the picturesque could evade ugly issues by hiding them from being viewed. One such issue was work and work activities. Since this landscape was designed to be a leisure garden, one of the essential principles of the project was to eliminate the appearance of work from the horizon. Repton advises this in the following:

> The pleasure of appropriation is gratified in viewing a landscape which cannot be injured by the malice or bad taste of a neighbouring intruder: thus an ugly barn, or a ploughed field, or any obtrusive object which disgraces the scenery of a park, looks as if it belonged to another, and therefore robs the mind of the pleasure derived from appropriation, or unity and continuity of unmixed property.[39]

A number of concrete strategies were developed to achieve this disappearing trick. Again, it was the tree that was the main instrument in this act of concealment as the tree clumps screened off the productive area of the estate. It was on this land that the tenants worked to pay a rack-rent to the landlord and it was this money which paid for these gardens of consumption.[40] Moreover, on a number of estates service tunnels and sunken roads were dug so that the supply of goods and services to the landlord's house might take place without disturbing the peace of the lawns.[41] Even the grazing 'picturesque' livestock on the parkland were kept at a visibly pleasing distance by the ha ha.[42] Therefore, this type of 'natural' garden and its inherent tendency to conceal will always be detached from the actuality of real nature and society's productive relationship to that nature.[43] Neil Smith argues that this is so because this ideological concept and physical reconstruction of nature has exorcised all forms of social activity from it, including work.[44] In doing so, the so-called natural picturesque garden has become dehistorisized. By excluding the concrete work of the Irish peasantry from the garden, the picturesque framework denies that class its social relationship to its native habitat and its subsequent historical relationship to that habitat. In the classic Saidian sense, the picturesque in a typically colonial way denies a history to the Other.[45] Their place has become somebody else's landscape. In filtering out work from the landscape, the framework has in a sense ideologically jumped from a state of nature to immediate consumption, without recognising the necessity of production. The object of nature becomes an object of consumption, without seem-

ingly having to go through the social activity of production. So when
the picturesque connoisseur came to appropriate a scene, through
whatever artistic means chosen, the portrayal of that scene may have
been an authentic representation of what was seen. The problem was
that the scene itself was ideologically biased, cocooned away from
the reality of the working countryside. We can now make sense of
the 'hidden' aesthetic aspects of the 'lovely background' to *The Quiet
Man*.

The dominant 'natural' backdrop to the movie is a highly idealised landscape, whose aesthetic appearance is determined by the
landscape gardening designs of the English Informal style of the
eighteenth century. It is a landscape which is thoroughly ladened
with symbolic icons, which evoke emotions associated with idyllic
characteristics of being a location which is safe, free and comfortable;
a place that is concerned with the pleasures of consumption rather
than production, a garden in which to grow roses rather than agricultural crops! Its essential ideological structure is therefore one of escape from the mundane reality of Irish everyday life. It is a theme
park of the visually exotic.[46] What is ironic is how Ford appropriated
the aesthetic of the English Informal garden of the eighteenth century
by filming in the grounds of Ashford Castle and in doing so engaged
in the ultimate act of a post-colonialist, making an English garden the
most globally recognised representation of Irish landscape.

Endnotes

[1] Keith Lamb and Patrick Bowe, *A History of Gardening in Ireland* (Dublin: National Botanical Gardens, 1995), p. 40.

[2] Luke Gibbons, 'Romanticism, Realism and Irish Cinema', *Cinema and Ireland*,
ed. by Kevin Rockett, Luke Gibbons and John Hill (London: Routledge, 1988), p.
203.

[3] Ibid., p. 224.

[4] Des Bell observes that 'there seems to be a clear line of historical development
leading from the late eighteenth century Romantic landscape tradition with its
painterly search for the sublime, to the picturesque knick knacks of the turn of
the century, via the contrived dioramas of the mid-century, and via the stage
designs and special effects of the melodrama in the last decades of the nineteenth

century, eventually to the advent of cinema in the early twentieth century. Film, once it had shaken itself free from the scientism that early photography had bequeathed to it, drew on the rich imagination of Romanticism to offer its audiences a "higher reality"'. (Des Bell, 'Framing Nature: First Steps into the Wilderness for a Sociology of the Landscape', *Irish Journal of Sociology*, 3 (1993) 14)

[5] Luke Gibbons, 'Topographies of Terror: Killarney and the Politics of the Sublime', *The South Atlantic Quarterly*, 95.1 (Winter, 1996) 25. Quoting Raymond Immerwahr, '"Romantic" and its Cognates in England, Germany and France before 1790', *Romanticism and its Cognates: The European History of the Word*, ed. by Hans Eichner (Manchester: Manchester University Press, 1972), p. 33.

[6] David Pepper, *The Roots of Modern Environmentalism* (London: Croom Helm, 1984), p. 77.

[7] Gibbons, 'Romanticism, Realism and Irish Cinema', p. 207.

[8] Ibid., p. 207.

[9] John Urry, 'The Consumption of Tourism', *Sociology*, 24 (1990) 31.

[10] Gibbons, 'Romanticism, Realism and Irish Cinema', p. 208.

[11] Ibid., p. 210.

[12] Ibid.

[13] In a previous article – 'Contested Terrain: Differing Interpretations of Co. Wicklow's Landscape', *Irish Journal of Sociology*, 3 (1993) – I argued that the insider perspective on landscape should be conceptualised as the native gaze and the outsider's perspective as picturesque.

[14] Ibid., pp. 23-55.

[15] John Barrell, *The Idea of Landscape and the Sense of Place: 1730-1840* (Cambridge: Cambridge University Press, 1972), p. 6.

[16] Éamon de Buitléar, *Ireland's Wild Countryside* (London: Tiger Books International, 1993), p. 86.

[17] David Bellamy, *Bellamy's Ireland: The Wild Boglands* (Dublin: Country House, 1986), p. 1.

[18] Gerry McGuinness, *The Quiet Man* (Dublin: GLI Limited, 1996), p. 24.

[19] Luke Gibbons, 'Romanticism, Realism and Irish Cinema', p. 162.

[20] Ibid., p. 200.

[21] Simon Pugh, *Garden-Nature-Language* (Manchester: Manchester University Press, 1988), p. 5.

22 Barrell, *The Idea of Landscape and the Sense of Place: 1730–1840*, p. 1.

23 D. Aldridge, 'How the Ship of Interpretation was Blown Off Course in the Tempest: Some Philosophical Thoughts', *Heritage Interpretation, Vol. 1*, ed. by D. Uzzell (London: Belhaven Press, 1989), p. 70.

24 The dualism of the beautiful and the sublime has had a long history of evolution of aesthetics (see M. Le Bris, *Romantics and Romanticism* (Geneva: Rizzoli, 1981), pp. 28–30). But it was not until the 1760s that the first British (and Irish) pictorial representation of the sublime was painted (see John Hutchinson, *James Arthur O'Connor* (Dublin: National Gallery of Ireland, 1985), p. 18). This coincided with the publication of Burke's treatise *A Philosophical Enquiry into the Origin of Our Ideas of the Sublime and Beautiful*.

25 Terrence Reeves-Smyth, 'Demesnes', *Atlas of the Irish Rural Landscape*, ed. by F.H.A. Aalen, Kevin Whelan and Matthew Stout (Cork: Cork University Press, 1997), p. 201.

26 Lynn Gallagher, 'Nature improved and raised by Art', *The Shaping of the Ulster Landscape* (Belfast: Ulster Folk Studies, 1989), p. 34.

27 Reeves-Smyth, 'Demesnes', p. 201.

28 Uvdale Price, quoted in M. Hadfield, *Landscape with Trees* (London: Country Life, 1967), pp. 133–34.

29 Barrell, *The Idea of Landscape and the Sense of Place: 1730–1840*, pp. 8–9.

30 Clifford, *A History of Garden Design*, p. 173.

31 The best-known picturesque connoisseurs of the nineteenth century were Mr. and Mrs. S.C. Hall. In the following they provide a description of the beautiful and the sublime with regard to the Crampton estate at Lough Bray: 'The wall that surrounds these grounds is not, in some places as high as the bank of peat (bog) within a few feet of it, and the contrast between the neglect, and desolation, and barrenness that reigns without, and the order, cultivation, and beauty within, is very striking, exhibiting the mastery which science and civilisation hold over nature even in her sternest and most rugged domain'. (Mr. and Mrs. S.C. Hall, *Hand-books for Ireland: Dublin and Wicklow* (London: Virtue, 1853), p. 104.)

32 M. Andrews, *The Search for the Picturesque: Landscape, Aesthetics and Tourism in Britain, 1760–1800* (Aldershot: Scholar Press, 1989), p. 45.

33 D. Lowe, *History of Bourgeois Perception* (Brighton, Sussex: Harvester Press, 1982), p. 15.

34 J.B. Hartley, 'Maps, Knowledge and Power', in *The Iconography of Landscape*, ed. by Denis Cosgrove and Stephen Daniels (Cambridge: Cambridge University Press, 1994), pp. 277–312.

35 Gallagher, 'Nature improved and raised by Art', p. 42.

[36] Edward Said, *Culture and Imperialism* (London: Chatto & Windus, 1993), p. 271.

[37] Eileen McCracken, *The Irish Woods since Tudor Times: Distribution and Exploitation* (Newton Abbot: David and Charles, 1971), p. 135.

[38] Terence Reeves-Smyth, 'The Natural History of Demesnes', *Nature in Ireland: A Scientific and Cultural History*, ed. by John Wilson Foster (Dublin: Lilliput Press, 1997), p. 551.

[39] Humphry Repton, quoted in S. Daniels, 'Humphry Repton and the Morality of Landscape', *Valued Environments*, ed. J. Gold and J. Burgess (London: George Allen & Unwin Publishers Ltd., 1982), p. 128.

[40] Eamonn Slater and Terence McDonough, 'Bulwark of Landlordism and Capitalism: The Dynamics of Feudalism in Nineteenth-century Ireland', *Research in Political Economy*, 14 (1994), 63-118.

[41] The most famous or infamous service tunnel was located on the Rockingham estate, Co. Roscommon. See Lamb and Bowe, *A History of Gardening in Ireland*, p. 46.

[42] The ha ha is a sunken fence, designed to act as a means of keeping cattle and sheep away from the house but not interrupting the view from the house.

[43] Karl Marx and Frederick Engels, *Karl Marx, Frederick Engels: Collected Works*, vol. 5 (London: Lawrence and Wishart, 1976), pp. 39–40.

[44] Neil Smith, *Uneven Development: Nature, Capital and the Production of Space* (London: Basil Blackwell, 1990), p. 16.

[45] Said, *Culture and Imperialism*, p. 269.

[46] Eamonn Slater, 'Reconstructing 'Nature' as a Picturesque Theme Park: The Colonial Case of Ireland'. *Early Popular Visual Culture*, 5 (2007) 3: 231–45.

12

Talking a Little Treason:
The Irish State and *The Quiet Man*

RODDY FLYNN

In former IDA (Industrial Development Authority) Chief Executive's Padraic White's *The Making of the Celtic Tiger*, he complains that attempts in the 1970s and 1980s to promote Ireland as a base for high technology firms from the US were hampered by the perception of Ireland as 'a romantic misty isle peopled by characters straight out of *The Quiet Man* and full of bog roads with stray donkeys'.[1] Although US Department of Commerce figures demonstrated that from the mid-1970s Ireland was the most profitable investment location within the EEC (European Economic Community, now European Union) for US firms, White notes that a 1982 IDA survey found that senior US business executives simply couldn't reconcile this with their view of Ireland as a 'tranquil, rural, backward country'.[2] Apparently it was 'hard to compete with repeated showings of *The Quiet Man* on American television'.[3]

The IDA actively set about countering this image in its marketing. Ironically, however, Luke Gibbons notes that the marketing was itself characterised by an 'ever more pronounced'[4] invocation of the past, using images of overseas company executives photographed in front of Newgrange and a modern logistics truck driving past the Rock of Cashel.[5] Clearly the IDA were not entirely uncomfortable with the traditional images of Ireland, provided they were in a position to manipulate and select which images were used and the manner in which they were used. *The Quiet Man* clearly did not pass this selection process.

There is a further irony in White's comments, of which he would have been entirely unaware: half a century earlier, the IDA, then integrated into the Department of Industry and Commerce, had been one of a number of state agencies at the heart of a concerted effort to ensure that the production of *The Quiet Man* – then a project regarded as 'advantageous to the national interest' – went as smoothly as possible. However, while Industry and Commerce unproblematically supported the production of the film, the Department of External Affairs adopted a more ambivalent attitude, especially after the film was released in 1952. What emerges from a study of Department of External Affairs documents from 1951 to 1953 in the National Archives is evidence of a much earlier attempt to manipulate and select images of Ireland and the Irish. Specifically, the picture of Ireland presented to the world by *The Quiet Man* raised concerns at an official level from the outset and the Department of External Affairs made strenuous efforts to 'police' that representation. This did not occur in a vacuum but, as this chapter will argue, as part of a much broader project to shape international perceptions of Ireland, which commenced soon after Ireland emerged from the isolation of World War II.

The publicity engendered by the production of *The Quiet Man* ensured that the Irish state would at least be aware of the production. However, the highly regulated nature of the still protectionist Irish economy in the early 1950s made it inevitable that any industrial activity of the scale of *The Quiet Man*[6] would have to co-operate fairly closely with various arms of the state to come to completion.

On 2 April 1951, Z.J. Rottman of Republic Pictures wrote to Patrick Hughes, the Irish Consul in San Francisco, advising him that the company was 'contemplating the production of a motion picture in Ireland this coming summer'. He went on:

The Picture is tentatively titled *The Quiet Man* to be produced
by Merian C. Cooper, directed by John Ford and to star John
Wayne and Barry FitzGerald, among others.

We contemplate sending from 50 to 75 people to Ireland,
all of whom will be actively engaged in the production of the
photoplay and will be employed directly by this corporation.

Present plans call for our personnel to be housed at the
Ashford Castle Hotel, Cong, C. Mayo, and at the Ballynahinch
Castle Hotel Connemara, County Galway.[7]

Rottman's letter was the first official contact between Republic Pictures and the Irish State. It would be followed by a flow of missives
from the company, plus various representatives of John Ford (including one L.W. Lukather and his representative in Ireland, Charles
Fitzsimmons) to the Irish Consulate in San Francisco and various
government departments in Ireland seeking to resolve problems (potential or actual) in producing the picture. The first letter simply
sought confirmation that US cast and crew would not be required to
produce visas to enter the country. Subsequent communications
would be more demanding.

The net effect of the approach through the Consul was to establish the Department of External Affairs (DEA) as the first point of
contact for the production: indeed, in an early indication of the perceived importance to the Irish state of the production, the Secretary
of the Department, Seán Noonan, became the interface for dealing
with the bulk of queries from the production.

Given that various External Affairs documents refer to the existence of a *departmental* view on the film, it raises the question of how
the two Ministers who held that post during the pre-production and
production of the film might have regarded the project. At the time
of Rottman's first letter to Patrick Hughes, the portfolio was held by
Seán MacBride, who had secured it on the basis of his leadership of
the Clann na Poblachta element of the Inter-party government which
held office from 1948 to 1951.[8] Although there is no archival material
available specifically expressing MacBride's approach towards *The
Quiet Man*, he had some well-publicised views about the film industry in general which might offer some clues as to his attitude. In 1945

MacBride had written an open letter to then Taoiseach, Eamon de Valera, pushing for the establishment of a permanent Irish film industry,[9] framing his call in cultural rather than economic terms. Describing film as 'by far the most important organ of popular thought and development',[10] MacBride argued that the time had come to use it proactively, rather than seeking to subjugate it through the crude mechanism of censorship. Stressing the importance of providing 'an alternative supply of films',[11] he continued that:

> Culturally and morally our mode of life and intellectual outlook is being undermined steadily by the stream of mediocre films which are fed to our people. Thus false values and artificiality are pumped into our youth night after night in every village and town in the country, without any alternative counteracting influence [...] Do not take me as condemning or wanting to exclude all foreign films; some are masterpieces. I merely want us to produce our own on a competitive basis as an alternative counteracting influence.[12]

As Minister for External Affairs, MacBride continued to advocate state support for an indigenous industry. Addressing the National Film Institute of Ireland in 1950, he outlined plans for a state-sponsored film industry, although he appears to have done little to bring these to fruition before the fall of his government in May 1951.

How these views might have disposed MacBride to the production of *The Quiet Man* is open to question. Technically this was another 'foreign film'. Against that, however, it was directed by John Ford who – as one of his biographers points out – was increasingly styling himself Seán Aloysius O'Fienne and who, when interviewed by a reporter from the *Connacht Tribune*, replied to some of the questions in Irish.[13] In a context where there was no domestic industry, it is conceivable that MacBride regarded *The Quiet Man* as the nearest thing on the horizon to an indigenous picture and worthy of support on that basis. Certainly, the official construction placed on the film by External Affairs after its release regarded it as Irish (see below).

In any case, even if MacBride had regarded it as a foreign film and, on high principle, had sought to block its filming in Ireland, he must have realised that the film would have gone on regardless. This point was made overt in a letter from Charles Fitzsimmons to the Department:

> 'The Quiet Man' could have been filmed in entirety in The United States of America. Mr. John Ford decided to shoot the exteriors in the countryside of his parents with the direct object of creating employment where he knew it would be welcome and of capturing some of the genuine beauty of Ireland for the screen.[14]

Given this, a pragmatist (and MacBride was certainly that when it suited him) would doubtless have concluded that it was better to 'facilitate a film company which was bringing in many dollars and employment here'.[15] Certainly there is ample evidence that his Department was at pains to facilitate the production. When L.W. Lukather sought assurances that camera equipment used by the production would not be subject to import duties and similarly that Customs Officers would not open exposed film at time of export, civil servant Kevin Rush – 'at the behest of the Minister for External Affairs' – immediately transmitted the request to the Revenue Comissioners:

> ... it was inferred [sic] that the opening of such film by Customs Officers for examination purposes had on a former occasion caused destruction of very valuable film, although it was not suggested that this had happened in Ireland.[16]

Rush noted that granting such assurances would obviously raise difficulties for the Commissioners given their standard practice, but asked that 'Mr Ford's' request be considered sympathetically 'in view of the fact that this Department considers it *advantageous to the national interest* to give whatever encouragement is possible to the enterprise' (italics added).

The Commissioners were suitably accommodating. In a letter to the Secretary of Industry and Commerce (copied to Seán Noonan at External Affairs), they offered no objection to the issue of a duty-free licence. Furthermore, although they could not guarantee not to examine goods presented for export or import, they noted that 'regard

will be had to causing minimum inconvenience in the unpacking of
the articles. Every possible facility will be allowed in dealing *with this
case*' [17] (italics added).

Even this – on the face of it reassuring response – raised alarm
bells with External Affairs, which immediately sought further assurances from the IDA (then run as an element of the Department of Industry and Commerce) to ensure that Revenue's strictures did not
unduly discommode Republic Pictures:

> I should be grateful if you could look into this matter insofar
> as it affects your Department and let me know what we may
> tell Mr Ford. The Secretary is anxious that we should facilitate
> the Co. [Republic] in every possible way in their request.[18]

By mid-May 1951, however, External Affairs was satisfied that the
Revenue Commissioners would place no insuperable obstacles in the
way of the import and export of the equipment and film. Production
problems requiring the department's assistance continued to arise,
however. On 23 May 1951, Seán Noonan wrote an 'urgent' letter to
the Secretary at the Department of Defence:

> A request has now been received from the film producing
> company for assistance in obtaining communications equip-
> ment on hire or loan. It appears it will be necessary to have a
> radio-telephonic communications system between Maam Val-
> ley, the site selected for 'shooting', and Ashford Castle Hotel,
> Cong, which will be used as a temporary headquarters for the
> undertaking.

Efforts to get such equipment from Pye and other firms having
proved unsuccessful, and 'in view of the short time remaining before
operations are due to commence, Republic pictures have asked
whether it might be possible for the Irish Army to assist them in this
difficulty'.[19] A response was immediately forthcoming: 'Military exi-
gencies'[20] (i.e. the fact that the relevant Army personnel and the
equipment requested were scheduled to be on training through June
1951) were cited as making it impossible to fulfil the request. Nonetheless, that External Affairs were willing to afford the production

access to such equipment is a further indication of their general eagerness to meet every need of the production. Further requests for Garda Síochána uniforms, a variety of Córas Iompair Éireann (CIE) uniforms and a special licence to purchase one stone of bread flour a day (a product then controlled as part of rationing) were accommodated by reference to the Departments of Transport, Justice, and Industry and Commerce respectively.[21] Again, although on paper trivial, it is – arguably – precisely the willingness of the Department of External Affairs to accommodate such small requests that points to an eagerness to facilitate the production of the film.

Having gone to such pains to assist the production, however, External Affairs's attitude towards it underwent a subtle shift once it was actually completed. Unusually, the department instructed embassies abroad (and in particular in the US) to assess/monitor local responses to the film. This would later become commonplace with regard to *indigenous* films commissioned by the Cultural Relations Committee. From the late 1950s, External Affairs required that embassies file monthly reports on not merely how often the stock of films they held were screened but also sought comments on how many people viewed them, how they were received and whether or not any particular comments were made about them. However there is little to suggest that hitherto *overseas productions* shot in Ireland were subject to such monitoring. Although *Man of Aran* was apparently a favourite of de Valera's, there is no evidence that his government was concerned with the reception of the film outside Ireland.

However the cultural politics of the era in which *The Quiet Man* was produced and released were quite different to those prevailing in the 1930s. Wartime isolation created, in the post-war era, a cross-party concern with how Ireland was perceived abroad and saw a number of measures introduced in an attempt to promote a more positive image of the country. These included de Valera's plan to broadcast Radio Éireann to an international audience via a short-wave transmitter. The 1948–51 Inter-party government killed off the short-wave station 'almost as soon as it came to power',[22] but similar thinking about the need to present to the world an Irish perspective on Ireland informed Seán MacBride's 1949 establishment of the Irish

News Agency[23](although, under MacBride, it was arguably rarely more than a propaganda instrument dedicated to raising the international profile of the evil of partition).[24] Considerations of how international understanding of Ireland on a broader level might be developed also underwrote the June 1947 decision (embodied in that year's Finance Act) to grant External Affairs £10,000 'for the development of cultural relations with other countries'[25] through – amongst other things – 'book, art, photographic and film exhibitions'.[26] Introducing the idea to the Dáil in 1947, Eamon de Valera noted that:

> ... our country in the past has not been sufficiently well known and understood abroad and the facts of the situation here have been frequently misrepresented: in fact they are frequently misrepresented even at the present time.[27]

In contrast to his administration's partisan dismantling of the short-wave radio station idea, MacBride brought de Valera's thinking on cultural relations to its logical conclusion, establishing an Advisory Committee on Cultural Relations in January 1949, tasked with enhancing Ireland's image and reputation overseas by undertaking or financially supporting Irish cultural projects of a high artistic standard. Applications for funding were to be assessed on their artistic and cultural merits but also on their appropriateness for the country for which a given event was proposed. It also became clear that the Committee took into account the potential of proposed projects to promote tourism and foreign direct investment.

Film was to be a key element in this and under MacBride the Advisory Committee on Cultural Relations (later the Cultural Relations Committee) became, *inter alia*, the most concrete support to indigenous film-making in the state up to that date. Between 1949 and 1951, the Committee spent more money (£5,651) on the production and acquisition of films on Irish subjects 'for distribution abroad'[28] than on any other single activity. In August 1949, during his first Dáil speech referring to the Committee, MacBride mentioned a long-term scheme to build up a library of short documentary films on Irish life and activity and to dispatch them to Irish embassies and consulates for dissemination wherever they were located. Even before Ford et al. arrived in Mayo, the Committee had commissioned the National Film Institute to make *W.B. Yeats – A Tribute*, and it would continue commissioning documentaries through the 1950s and 1960s. In short, under MacBride, External Affairs took a new interest in how Ireland was perceived abroad and made active efforts to police that perception.[29]

Nor did this alter significantly under Frank Aitken, who replaced MacBride in June 1951. Although Aitken called a halt to the scale of anti-partitionist propaganda emanating from his department, he appears to have shared the view of the importance of shaping overseas perceptions of Ireland. For example, writing with regard to the early 1960s (at which point Aitken was still Minister for External Affairs under Seán Lemass), J.J. Lee notes how 'skilful public relations' by Aitken's officials contributed to 'a national and international perception of the distinctiveness and importance of their contribution'.[30]

Thus under both MacBride and Aitken the representation of Ireland and the Irish offered by such a high profile Hollywood production as *The Quiet Man* was bound to catch the Department of External Affair's attention and it was these concerns that informed the department's approach to the film after its release. At its most optimistic, the department would express the hope that *The Quiet Man's* quasi indigenous status would make it suitable material for incorporation into their stock of filmic material depicting Ireland and available to be sent overseas for propaganda purposes. At a minimum, the department was concerned to limit any negative connotations attaching to Ireland which emerged from the film.

On 17 April 1952, Irish Ambassador Joseph Brennan wrote to Conor Cruise O'Brien at the Department of External Affairs to inform him that he had been to a preview of the film: 'The colour is beautiful. The scenery delightful. But the theme was not likely to be well received here.'[31] That Cruise O'Brien was the recipient of Brennan's communique is significant: as manager (appointed by MacBride) of the operations of the Irish News Agency, he was at the centre of efforts to police external perceptions of Ireland. Brennan asked O'Brien about the reaction to the film at home, but a perplexed O'Brien, who clearly hadn't seen the film, had to ask around the department as to whether or not in fact anyone had. Eventually the department ascertained from the local Republic Pictures office that, as yet, there had been no Dublin preview but that the company would inform the Department of External Affairs when one was to take place. Nonetheless, the ominous tone of Brennan's letter clearly piqued the department's curiosity.

However, when the Dublin screening did take place (in mid-May 1952), Republic Pictures failed to inform the Department of External Affairs who became aware of it only after the *Irish Independent* published a review based on the preview. They were unimpressed by the fact that they had not been informed – one note refers to Republic giving 'us the slip' and Cruise O'Brien instructed one of his officials to 'enquire as to why we were not kept informed by Republic of the preview [...] as promised'.[32] The tone of the *Irish Independent* review raised further concerns as to what impact the release of the film internationally would have on external perceptions of Ireland:

> Only an American [...] would have thought of a few [...]
> things that John Ford has included by way of embellishment
> in the film he made around Cong last summer.[33]

Although conceding that there could be 'no quarrel' with Ford's treatment of the scenery, the writer was less happy with the representation of the people:

> We are the wild Irish all right. Whiskey and porter flow like
> the Corrib in a flood, someone is always at hand to sing 'The
> Wild Colonial Boy' or 'Galway Bay' at any time of the night or
> morning, and if there is a fight in the village every able-bodied
> man joins in just for the fun of it.[34]

The review concluded: 'American audiences should like all of it; we will like *some of it* very much' (italics added).

The secretary of the Cultural Relations Committee wrote a steely letter to Republic Pictures at its 53 Middle Abbey Street office, inquiring as to why no warning of the preview had been given. However the letter also included the unusual addendum that:

… my Committee are most anxious to establish a library of suitable films on Ireland for lending to foreign institutions and organizations. Consequently we would be glad to be kept informed of any material available which might suit our purpose.[35]

T.V. Garland, Republic's Dublin manager, wrote back apologising for the failure to inform the Department of External Affairs, describing it as an 'oversight'.[36] However, it was the addendum in the original letter which suggests that the Cultural Relations Committee may have genuinely seen the production of *The Quiet Man* as potentially creating a representation of Ireland that might be sent around the world with the imprimatur of the Irish state. However, once intimations of the actual content of the film began to seep back to the department, it prompted active surveillance (as O'Brien's reference to 'giving us the slip' inadvertently suggests) of the film, with a view to ascertaining how its image of Ireland differed from an 'officially approved' version emerging from the work of the Irish News Agency and Cultural Relations Committee. The initial assumption was that the difference would be substantial: when Joseph Brennan in San Francisco read the *Irish Independent* review, he wrote expressing the view that the paper had let the picture off lightly:

If it were to be taken completely at its face value it would be accepted as a rollicking farce and no harm done, but I fear it will be regarded by the Irish-American element here as purporting to portray actual life in Ireland. We may then have protests.[37]

It appears to have been at this point that the department issued instructions that local responses to the film be collated (globally) with a view to ascertaining how it was being read outside Ireland. Given the major market for the film, the key concern was with the US. The embassy there collected press responses to the picture in the US (especially in Irish heartlands on the two coasts) and remitted them to Department of External Affairs in Dublin. These included reviews from *The New York Times, Newark Daily News, New York News, New*

York Herald Tribune, *San Francisco Chronicle*, *San Francisco Examiner*, *San Francisco News* and the *New York Daily Worker*.

Most of the reviews offered scant reason for concern, focusing as they did on representations of landscape ('Certainly Ireland lends itself to Technicolor. Scenically the comedy is a tour de force')[38] and the major fight sequence at the climax of the picture (the *New York News* splashed eleven images from the sequence, recounting virtually every blow). As Brennan's first missive to Cruise O'Brien in April 1952 (above) clearly indicated, the film's representation of Irish topography received the department's tacit approval.

However, one review expressed a perspective that, if widely held, might have raised real concerns: The *New York Daily Worker* (under the headline '"The Quiet Man" distorts Facts of Irish Life') complained that the picture created 'a totally false picture of Irish peasant life […] the film is based on an exploitation of the quaintness of rustic life, and on stereotyped Irish characterizations which give us no real picture of the people'. It went on:

> Particularly obnoxious is the last third of the film, in which great fun is derived from *The Quiet Man*'s mauling about of his wife, which is supposed to be part of restoring her faith in his courage.
>
> This vulgarly male-supremacist sequence is approvingly presented to the audience, presumably for emulation by the men.[39]

Concerns about protests from Irish-Americans prompted by such reviews were, however, negated by more positive reviews. At least one reviewer – the Dublin correspondent for the *Newark Daily News* – put forward a more nuanced take on the film which offered more reassurance to the department. The writer reported that although the initial reaction of the first-night Dublin audience was 'resentment and anger […] this feeling gave place to amusement and gales of laughter' as the audience began to understand 'the significance of the piece'. The writer agreed that the picture contained:

> … everything which until the Abbey Theatre came along and put them to rout, made up those plays about the irresponsible,

semi-civilised but lovable Irish, popular with English and other audiences, including the Irish, some 60 years ago.

However, the writer went on:

> In conceiving this [...] Mr. Ford had in mind the idea of satirising those old plays and of having a huge joke at the expense of those, outside of Ireland, who have no idea of the Irish or of the Irish mode of life [...] Unfortunately, there are many, even as near as across the Irish Sea, who today think that of the people of this country and, coming over as tourists, are agreeably surprised (or disappointed) to find the Irish as civilized and modern as they believe themselves to be.

He concluded by conceding that the reaction to the film in America, 'especially among those of Irish birth or descent, is a matter of speculation'. Invoking the *Playboy* riots of 1907, he warned that the 'Irish sense of humour must also prevail [...] so that it may be taken for what it actually is: an immense joke'.[40] The review thus acknowledged the concerns raised by the film but also assuaged them in language reminiscent of academic theorists writing about the film more than 30 years later.[41]

The availability of such antidotes to the more negative reviews, coupled with the fact that the vast bulk of reviews were overwhelmingly (if somewhat unthinkingly) positive, appears to have allayed the concerns of Irish diplomats within the US. On 2 September 1952 Brennan wrote to the department to the effect that the picture was 'getting by without trouble'.[42] Further reviews from Paris (passed on by the ambassador there) appeared to confirm this: in November 1952, the Irish ambassador to France wrote to the department citing 'enthusiastic' reviews in *France-Soir* and *Paris Presses Intransigeant*. Indeed, he notes that the film seemed 'likely to have a considerable box office success here'.[43]

Such responses led the Department of External Affairs to adopt the view that the film was best dealt with by portraying it as a fantasy version of Ireland. Thus although uncomfortable with the representation of the Irish characters, this was tolerable precisely because it could be dismissed as contrived ('totally false depiction of peasant life'). However, seeking to have it both ways, the department also suggested that the element subsequently identified as responsible for drawing tourists to visit Ireland – the depiction of the landscape – was real. This of course glossed over the fact that Ford took at least as many pains in framing/manipulating the landscape (even down to the use of painted studio sets) as he did to construct the representation of the people. Thus the depiction of the landscape in *The Quiet Man* is no less artificial than any other element in the film.

Nonetheless, the department took every opportunity to promulgate their Quiet Man-as-fantasy perspective. The template for the long-term Department of External Affairs approach to the film was established in February 1953, with the premiere of the film in Sweden. In November the Irish legation in Stockholm telegraphed the Department of External Affairs to state that the local distributors of the film – A. B. Svea Film – had sought the legation's cooperation in launching the film by hosting a reception after its premiere. However, clearly seeking the official imprimatur of the Irish state for the film, the distributors also suggested that the letters be written to the great and good of Swedish society inviting them to both the reception *and* the premiere. Critically, these invitations were to be issued in the name of the Irish ambassador. As a further incentive the distributors offered to pick up the tab for both the premiere and the subsequent reception. The telegraph concluded:

> Company [Svea Film] consider that resulting publicity would benefit not only film but also Swedish-Irish Society [a local cultural organization] and stimulate interest in Ireland [...] We are willing to cooperate if you see no objection. [44]

Remarkably no objection was forthcoming. Indeed the initial reply from the department noted that Frank Aitken regarded the film as 'excellent tourist publicity', recommended co-operation in launching the film, and remarked in passing that the Irish consul general in New York had already done the same thing.

The Swedish premiere duly occurred on 11 February 1953. In his account of the evening, the Ambassador (Minister Plenipotentiary) G. Ó Gallcobair stressed that:

> Before the film began I gave a short speech in Swedish and French to the effect that the film should not be regarded as a documentary on daily life in Ireland, that several national customs and characteristics had been exaggerated in the film but that a film producer, like a poet, was entitled to his licence.[45]

Nonetheless:

> While the film was produced by a wellknown [sic] American film company, it could be regarded as an Irish film; the producer was Irish parentage, two of the four principal actors were born and reared in Ireland and received their early training at the Abbey Theatre and that practically all the other actors were engaged by the producer in Ireland, where the film was shot. Furthermore the story of the film was based on a novel by a living Irish author, Mr. Maurice Walsh.[46]

In short, *The Quiet Man* was presented with the official approval of the Irish State, notwithstanding the 'difficulties' raised by its mode of representation. The touristic appeal of the film was further stressed in a letter written the same day by the ambassador to Bord Fáilte proposing to run a competition offering a trip to Ireland in co-operation with an unnamed Swedish newspaper and A.B. Svea Film. In an aside which made explicit how the embassy (and by extension the department) understood the film to be useful, the proposed competition would invite 'members of the public [...] to choose the most beautiful landscape in the film'.[47]

The *Quiet Man* crew arrived in Ireland at a key juncture in Irish film and cultural policy. Other major films had been shot in Ireland in the preceding decade but neither attracted anything like the same level of state interest. Laurence Olivier's production of *Henry V* in 1944, which used the Curragh for the climactic Agincourt scene, was aided by the state which made available members of the defence forces to play English and French soldiers. However, since the content of the film had little to with Ireland, there was no particular reason to follow its reception once released. Four years later Carol Reed filmed *Odd Man Out*, but since this was shot in Belfast and in studio locations in the UK, it fell outside the Irish state's jurisdiction. *The Quiet Man* was an Irish-themed film shot in Ireland.

However, the main reason for the state's interest was that the film arrived in a period when the state was, arguably for the first time, pursuing a concerted image control campaign. *The Quiet Man* threatened to undermine all that good work: compared to the global impact of a Hollywood film, the work of the Irish News Agency and the Cultural Relations Committee were drops in the ocean, a fact the Department of External Affairs must have been pragmatic enough to recognise.

The Department of Industry and Commerce – with an eye to the industrial development potential of film – had long concluded that it would be impossible to build an indigenous industry from scratch, given the cost of even low-budget production, the uneconomic scale of the Irish cinema market and US dominance of global distribution networks. *The Quiet Man* was a demonstration of the implications of this in cultural rather than in industrial terms. Unable to produce and distribute on a Hollywood scale indigenous films capable of offering alternate perspectives on Ireland, the department's best (only?) strategy was to attempt to control the content of and frame the subsequent interpretation of those films about Ireland which Hollywood did make.

Endnotes

[1] Ray MacSharry and Padraic White, *The Making of the Celtic Tiger* (Cork: Mercier Press, 2000), p. 239.

[2] Ibid., p. 239.

[3] Ibid.

[4] Luke Gibbons, 'Coming out of Hibernation: The Myth of Modernity in Irish Culture', *Across the Frontiers: Ireland in the 1990s*, ed. by Richard Kearney (Dublin: Wolfhound Press, 1988), pp. 205–18.

[5] Ibid., p. 215.

[6] Notwithstanding the fact that Ford regarded it as far too low, *The Quiet Man*'s $1.46 million budget made it by far the highest budgeted film shot in Ireland up to that point.

[7] Rottman to Hughes, 2 April 1951. National Archive 323/27/4 Republic Productions North Hollywood California Proposal to make a film *The Quiet Man* in Ireland summer 1951.

[8] The Inter-Party administration's period of office concluded on 30 May 1951, a week before *The Quiet Man* went into production. Nonetheless, MacBride was minister during the two-month long pre-production of the film.

[9] Given that MacBride's son Tiernan would become a leading light in the campaign to establish an Irish Film Board in the 1970s and 1980s, his father's interest is illuminating.

[10] MacBride letter addressed to national press, copied to de Valera, 26 November 1945 National Archive S 13914A.

[11] Ibid.

[12] Ibid. MacBride himself would demonstrate the power of film in the 1948 election campaign when he participated in what is generally regarded as the first Irish party political commercial, the Liam O'Leary-directed *Our Country*. Although in his posthumously published diaries MacBride is somewhat dismissive of the quality of the film ('a juvenile attempt') he acknowledged that it made 'quite an impact'. See Seán MacBride, *That Day's Struggle,* ed. by Caitriona Lawlor, (Dublin: Currach Press, 2005), p. 143.

[13] See Joseph McBride's discussion of *The Quiet Man* in his biography *Searching for John Ford: A Life* (London: Faber and Faber, 2003), pp. 509–19.

[14] Fitzsimmons to Kevin Rushe, 16 July 1951. National Archive 323/27/4 Republic Productions North Hollywood California Proposal to make a film *The Quiet Man* in Ireland summer 1951.

[15] See National Archive file P 38 John Ford and *The Quiet Man.*

[16] Kevin Rush (Department of External Affairs (DEA)) to C. Kennedy (Oifig na gCoimisinéirí Ioncaim (Office of Revenue Commissioners) 16 April 1951. National Archive 323/27/4 Republic Productions North Hollywood California Proposal to make a film *The Quiet Man* in Ireland summer 1951.

[17] Illegible signature but Revenue Commissioners to Secretary of External Affairs, 24 April 1951.

[18] Rush (DEA) to J.J. Duff (IDA in Department of Industry and Commerce), 2 May 1951. From Ibid.

[19] Noonan to Secretary Department of Defence, 23 May 1951. From Ibid.

[20] Secretary Defence to Secretary DEA, 30 May 1951. From Ibid.

[21] See National Archive file P 38 John Ford and *The Quiet Man.*

[22] John Horgan, *Irish Media* (London: Routledge, 2001), p. 55.

[23] See, for example, John Horgan, 'Government, Propaganda and the Irish News Agency', *Irish Communications Review*, 3 (1993) 31–43.

[24] See, for example, the discussion of the Irish News Agency in Donald Harman Akenson, *Conor: A Biography of Conor Cruise O'Brien* (Montreal and Kingston: McGill-Queens University Press, 1994), pp. 135–38.

[25] Eamon de Valera, *Dáil Debates Vol 106*, pp. 2295–96, 20 June 1947.

[26] Ibid.

[27] Ibid.

[28] Frank Aitken, *Dáil Debates, Vol. 127*, pp. 1034–1036, 21 November 1951.

[29] John Horgan makes a similar point with regard to the establishment of the Irish News Agency (under MacBride). See John Horgan, *Irish Media* (London: Routledge, 2001), pp. 58–61.

[30] J.J. Lee, *Ireland, 1912-1985* (Cambridge: Cambridge University Press, 1989), p. 370.

[31] Brennan to Cruise O'Brien, 17 April 1952. National Archive 323/27/4 Republic Productions North Hollywood California Proposal to make a film *The Quiet Man* in Ireland summer 1951.

[32] Handwritten note appended to cutting of the *Irish Independent* review from 19 May 1952. Included in National Archive 323/27/4 Republic Productions North Hollywood California Proposal to make a film *The Quiet Man* in Ireland summer 1951.

[33] Anonymous ('Our Film Critic'), 'John Ford Film: An Eye on the U.S. Market', *Irish Independent*, 1 May 1952, p. 8. 323/27/4 Republic Productions North Hollywood California Proposal to make a film *The Quiet Man* in Ireland summer 1951.

[34] Ibid.

[35] B. Durnan (sec Cómhar Cultúra Éireann at DEA) to PRO Republic Pictures International Corporation, Dublin. 4 May 1952. National Archive 323/27/4 Republic Productions North Hollywood California Proposal to make a film *The Quiet Man* in Ireland summer 1951.

[36] Garland to B. Durnin, 6 June 1952. National Archive 323/27/4 Republic Productions North Hollywood California Proposal to make a film *The Quiet Man* in Ireland summer 1951.

[37] Joseph D. Brennan, Washington Embassy to Brian Durnan, DEA, 2 July 1952. National Archive 323/27/4 Republic Productions North Hollywood California Proposal to make a film *The Quiet Man* in Ireland summer 1951.

[38] Hortense Morton, 'Quiet Man Really a Mad Irish Melee', *San Francisco Examiner*, 19 September 1952, p. 19.

[39] John Satchel, 'The Quiet Man distorts facts of Irish life', *New York Daily Worker*, 89/52 (not dated). Clipping included in National Archive 323/27/4 Republic Productions North Hollywood California Proposal to make a film *The Quiet Man* in Ireland summer 1951.

[40] J.J (?) 'Satire Gives Irish a Laugh'. *Newark Daily News*, 30 June 1952. Clipping included in National Archive 323/27/4 Republic Productions North Hollywood California Proposal to make a film *The Quiet Man* in Ireland summer 1951.

[41] See, for example, Luke Gibbons's take on the film in the seminal *Cinema and Ireland* (Luke Gibbons, 'Romanticism, Realism and Irish Cinema', *Cinema and Ireland*, ed. by Kevin Rockett, Luke Gibbons and John Hill (London: Croom Helm, 1987, pp. 194–257) where he identifies moments in the film which suggest a conscious and overt drawing of the audience's attention to the artificiality of the film on the part of Ford.

[42] Brennan to Durnin, 2 September 1952, National Archive 323/27/4 Republic Productions North Hollywood California Proposal to make a film *The Quiet Man* in Ireland summer 1951.

[43] Irish Ambassador to Secretary DEA, 13 November 1952. Interestingly, however, he also cited a review from the Paris correspondent of the English language *New York Herald Tribune* which was much more critical of the film, describing it as a caricature and complaining that Ford's treatment of the Irish climate was patently artificial: 'such things as the Irish mists and fogs are discarded and the sun shines with a Pasadena persistency'. (Thomas Quinn Curtis, 'Ireland and Hollywood – in Paris', *New York Herald Tribune*, 12 November 1952.) Clipping from National Archive 323/27/4 Republic Productions North Hollywood California Proposal to make a film *The Quiet Man* in Ireland summer 1951.

[44] Irish Legation to DEA, 21 November 1952. National Archive 323/27/4 Republic Productions North Hollywood California Proposal to make a film *The Quiet Man* in Ireland summer 1951.

[45] Ó Gallcobair to Sec DEA, 27 February 1953. National Archive 323/27/4 Republic Productions North Hollywood California Proposal to make a film *The Quiet Man* in Ireland summer 1951.

[46] Ibid.

[47] Gallagher to Irish Tourist Board, 27 March 1953 from National Archive DFA 300 Series 366/187 Public Competition in Sweden in connection with Showing of *The Quiet Man* Prize of Free Trip to Ireland.

13

The Quiet Man:
Ford, Mythology and Ireland[1]

JOHN HILL

Introduction (2009)

This essay was originally delivered at a conference in Coleraine in
1983 and intended for publication in *Cinema and Ireland*, which, at
that time, was planned as a more wide-ranging collection of essays
than it subsequently became. Partly because the film was discussed
by Luke Gibbons in the final version of the volume, it was agreed not
to use the essay in the finished book (which eventually appeared in
1987). A very short version of the argument was published as *'The
Quiet Man'* in the *International Dictionary of Films and Filmmakers*[2] but
otherwise the original essay has languished at the bottom of my fil-
ing cabinet for the last twenty years. Inevitably, it bears the marks of
the time at which it was written and, in publishing it so late in the
day, it may be of help to place it in context.

The article was conceived as a companion-piece to what became
my 'Images of Violence' essay in the co-authored work *Cinema and
Ireland*. The book itself was planned to overcome the critical neglect
of film in discussions of Irish culture and had two main aims. First, in
the chapters written by Kevin Rockett, it aimed to provide an account
of the then relatively unknown history of film production in Ireland.
However, insofar as most cinematic images of the Irish did not origi-
nate from Ireland, the book's second main purpose was to identify

the patterns of representing Ireland and the Irish that had been associated with British and American films.

In my essay on images of violence, I indicated the predominance
of two main sets of imagery: 'On the one hand, Ireland has been conceived as a simple, and generally blissful, rural idyll; on the other, as
a primarily dark and strife-torn maelstrom'.[3] Although I refer briefly
to *The Quiet Man*, the essay was primarily concerned with mapping
the second set of images and suggested – somewhat controversially –
how this continued to exert an influence upon contemporary films
(such as Neil Jordan's *Angel* (1982)). The piece on *The Quiet Man* was
therefore intended to complement my essay on violence through an
examination of the ways in which the film contributed to the ideological construction of Ireland as a rural idyll. Although the film had
been written about widely, it had, at that time, mainly been discussed
in a way that prioritised the authorial world-view of John Ford rather
than the film's relationship to more general patterns of representing
Ireland. It was this connection that the essay sought to bring out.

The critical interest in the films of John Ford had been fuelled by
the enthusiastic turn towards Hollywood in France in the 1950s and
in the US and Britain in the 1960s. This identification of popular cinema as a proper object of study largely rested upon the adoption of
the criteria of the 'legitimate' arts and a demonstration of the director
as the key creative personality – or author – involved in filmmaking.
My essay, and the *Cinema and Ireland* book more generally, shared the
conviction that popular cinema merited serious investigation. Indeed, the book's co-authored Introduction openly argued that one of
the shortcomings of Irish Studies had been its concentration on the
'serious' arts at the expense of popular culture. However, given the
critical convulsions of the late 1960s and early 1970s, the book – and
my essay on *The Quiet Man* – were also concerned to move beyond
the critical celebration of popular cinema as 'art' (or the expression of
a director's personal vision) in favour of an investigation of the social
and political role that popular films might be seen to play. To employ
Fredric Jameson's terminology of the time, films were to be understood as 'socially symbolic acts' involved in the construction and
elaboration of social and political meanings that it was the task of

criticism to unravel.[4] This seemed especially important in the case of the construction of cinematic 'Irishness', which had, up until then, rarely been the object of critical scrutiny. What gave this project an added urgency was the emergence of a 'new wave' of Irish filmmaking in the late 1970s and early 1980s that was seeking to overthrow the legacy of traditional representations of Ireland and provide more complex and questioning versions of 'Irishness'. In this respect, the critique of old patterns of representation was aligned with support for the emergence of new ways of representing Ireland on the cinema screen.

It is partly this spirit of iconoclasm that animated my account of *The Quiet Man* which wanted to take the film seriously but to identify nonetheless some of the ideological problems that it threw up in an Irish context. Despite the ostensibly right-wing character of Ford's films, the critical appropriation of Ford's work (and his westerns, in particular) by left-leaning critics in France and Britain had invested them with a 'progressive' aspect by virtue of the challenge that they posed to traditional notions of 'educated taste' and cultural value. However, whatever the attractions of Ford's mythology of the West for critics in Britain (and elsewhere), it was much less clear to me that the mythology of Ireland to be found in *The Quiet Man* could be held to be quite so 'progressive' in the Irish context.

The idea of 'progressiveness' had, of course, enjoyed considerable currency in critical debates during the 1970s. In their famous essay entitled 'Cinema/Ideology/Criticism (1)', first published in *Cahiers du cinéma* and then reprinted in translation in the British journal *Screen*, Jean-Louis Comolli and Jean Narboni had suggested, somewhat starkly, that although the majority of films were 'imbued through and through with the dominant ideology', there were nonetheless some films that appeared 'at first sight to belong firmly within the ideology [...] but which turn out to be so only in an ambiguous manner'.[5] The idea that some films might actually subvert the ideology that they ostensibly inhabit became an important one for film studies, which proceeded to engage in 'redemptive' readings of texts that might otherwise have been taken to be ideologically conservative. Significantly enough, the *Cahiers* editors themselves chose to apply this method to a John Ford film, *Young Mr Lincoln* (1939), which, through the course of a lengthy analysis, they identified as riven with ideological tensions and fissures.[6] However, in doing so, they also revealed a degree of uncertainty about the methodological procedures that they were adopting, claiming not only that their account of the film was 'authorised' by the text but that it was also the product of an 'active re-writing' of it.[7]

In a sense, it is this issue of 'progressiveness', and its identification, which hangs over the essay that follows. As I have indicated, one of the reasons the essay did not appear in *Cinema and Ireland* was that a discussion of the film was provided in the section written by Luke Gibbons. However, it is also the case that his own account of the film diverged in significant ways from my own. While there was much that was similar about our descriptions of the film, there was also a clear difference in the way that we summed up its ideological significance. Whereas my own account of the film stressed the ideologically conservative aspects of the film, Gibbons's reading emphasised the moments of formal self-consciousness and internal tension within the film that appeared to distance it from the very ideology that it might otherwise be regarded as sustaining. In this he has been followed by Martin McLoone, who suggests how the film is best read as a 'subversive comedy' that does not so much sustain a myth as undermine it 'from the inside'.[8]

While my own analysis does acknowledge the ways in which the film draws attention to its own 'imaginary' status, it tends to read this as providing a kind of 'alibi' for the film's mythologising, rather than a fundamental subversion of it. This, however, is not as well argued as it might be with the result that my enthusiasm for pinning down the film's ideological operations, and identifying them with broader cultural trends, inevitably leads to a degree of reductionism. However, while my own argument undoubtedly understates the ideological complexity of the film, I suspect that McLoone and Gibbons have also overstated its 'subversiveness'. My concerns here relate partly to the methodology of textual analysis and what readings the textual features of the film may be seen to 'permit'. For while my own essay underestimated the importance of certain features (such as the use of back projection or waving at the camera), subsequent writing on the film appears to have overestimated their formal disruptiveness and semiotic significance.[9] These concerns may also be related to the issue of context and the ways in which it is possible to locate contemporary accounts of the film in terms of historically available or activated modes of readership. McLoone's account of *The Quiet Man* in terms of 'postmodern irony', for example, is clearly seductive in the light of recent critical developments. However, it is much less certain that it would have been available at the time of the film's original release, and certainly did not manifest itself in contemporary reviews, which registered the film's indebtedness to pre-existing conventions – and stereotypes – but not the supposedly 'ironic' way in which they were inhabited.

Given such developments, the rationale for publishing this essay nearly twenty-five years after it was written has necessarily changed. At the time of its conception, the serious analysis of *The Quiet Man* in terms of its construction of 'Irishness' had scarcely begun. Since then it has become one of the most discussed films in the critical literature on Irish film. Given that I would have to write a completely different essay if I were to take this work as my starting-point, I have refrained from adding references to material published since the piece was written and, apart from some relatively minor changes, have left the essay unaltered. In this respect, it possesses some of the features of a historical document, indicating the concerns of the period in which it was written and demonstrating both the strengths and weaknesses of a particular kind of ideology critique. However, precisely because critical attitudes have altered so fundamentally in the intervening period, the argument it contains may also have the virtue of raising once again some of the issues at stake. When he was writing *Irish Film*, Martin McLoone expressed his regret that my essay had not been published because he would have liked to use it to argue against (which, without directly citing it, he partly does). In an odd way, the belated appearance of my essay permits a different kind of exchange to occur. For if it is the case that the writing on *The Quiet Man* has become increasingly 'knowing', then my own rather stern – 'take no prisoners' – account of the film all those years ago might help to revive discussion of the basis upon which contemporary readings of the film have constructed the film as 'subversive'. For while *The Quiet Man* is certainly a complex work, I retain my doubts as to whether or not the ideological operations of the film are quite as complicated as recent writing has suggested.

The Quiet Man is probably the best-known and most fondly remembered of all fiction movies to have been made about Ireland. Its director, John Ford, was himself a second generation Irishman whose father left Spiddal, Co. Galway, in 1872 and settled in Portland, Maine, apparently making a prosperous living as a saloon-keeper during prohibition and then entering into local politics. Ford's real name was Feeney and it has been claimed that he grew up able to speak both English and Irish.[10] It is perhaps not surprising then that, of all American film directors, it was Ford who most consistently turned to Ireland for inspiration. As early as 1926 he directed *The Shamrock Handicap*, about Irish horse-racing, while in 1965, nearing the end of his career, he shot a number of scenes for *Young Cassidy,* a film biography of Sean O'Casey. In between, Ireland and questions of Irishness proved a focal concern in films set both in Ireland – *The Informer* (1935), *The Plough and the Stars* (1936), *The Quiet Man* (1952), *The Rising of the Moon* (1957) – and elsewhere – *Mother Machree* (1928), *How Green Was My Valley* (1941) and *The Last Hurrah* (1953).[11] What has earned Ford a place in the history books, however, is not his Irish films (most of which figure low in the critics' pantheons) but his Westerns, particularly those that followed *Stagecoach* in 1939. Thus, while the Irish focus of Ford's work is clearly of interest in itself, it also gains added significance by virtue of the way in which it parallels and complements Ford's attitude to American experience and history more generally.

Colin McArthur[12] has defined the Western genre in terms of America talking to itself about its agrarian past, and it is undoubtedly the case that the attraction of the Western for Ford was its setting in a crucial period of American history when the West was being settled and communities established.[13] What, in particular, focused Ford's interest was the American Dream as it had inspired early pio-

neers and immigrants. This is a dream, described by Peter Wollen, as
that of an 'ideal moral community' – a community in which nature
and society, and the individual and the collectivity, achieve balance
and harmony.[14] The key film in this respect is probably *My Darling
Clementine* (1946). The settling of the West, and the apparent progress
from 'nature' to 'civilization', is mapped in terms of Wyatt Earp's
triumph over the anarchic forces represented by the Clintons (meeting their nemesis at the by now famous OK Corral). Earp's individualism, which is in a sense the other side of the Clinton's refusal to
bow to law and order, is itself partly tamed through his contact with
Eastern values as represented by the female school ma'am,
Clementine. This vision is pulled together in a central sequence in
which Earp joins a service of dedication in Tombstone's new church.
The church and the family are the cornerstone of Ford's vision of
community and the church's setting in once bare land, with the peaks
of Monument Valley visible in the distance, is central to the creation
of a new equilibrium between nature and civilization. However, it is
typically Fordian that in this scene the church is as yet unfinished
and the service is immediately followed by a dance. The authority
structures of the Fordian community are not formal and hierarchical,
but informal and democratic. The church is not the building but
rather the people in it, just as religion, according to Robin Wood, is
'essentially social rather than metaphysical'.[15] In this respect, the
dancing – with its combination of energy and convention – is as
much a ceremonial ritual as religion itself. As Earp takes partners
with Clementine, the thematic fusion of garden and desert, East and
West, individual and group is completed.

However, if this sequence represents the peak of Ford's American
idealism, it is also possible to detect a slow but sure disillusionment
with traditional Western values in his subsequent work. By adopting
a flashback structure and a claustrophobic studio-bound mise-en-
scène, *The Man Who Shot Liberty Valance* (1962) takes a sour and elegiac look at 'how the west was won' with all its attendant deceptions.
(It is in this film that we find the by now famous line, 'When the legend becomes fact, print the legend'). In *The Searchers* (1956) the cowboy hero (played by John Wayne) becomes little distinguishable from

the Indians he pursues as he scalps his Indian adversary, Scar. Finally, and most dramatically, in *Cheyenne Autumn* (1964) it is the Indians who now represent dignity and civilization while Wyatt Earp, the hero of *My Darling Clementine*, has become cowardly and ineffectual, too intent on playing poker to be concerned with defending Dodge City. However, what also occurs alongside this evidence of disillusionment is an increasing interest in Ford's work in other communities, where the values of the old West may be seen to survive. As Wollen indicates, 'a general movement [...] can be detected in Ford's work to equate the Irish, Indians and Polynesians as traditional communities, set in the past, counterposed to the march forward to the American future, as it has turned out in reality, but assimilating the values of the American future as it was once dreamed'.[16] Thus, in *Donovan's Reef* (1963), Ford counterposes the 'naturalness' of the Polynesian community of Halea-Kaloa to the cynically materialist values of Boston and the East. However, in this film, it is not the supposed 'civilization' of America that triumphs over 'nature'; rather it is Emelia, a perverse mutation of Clementine's girl from the East, who succumbs to the values of the island community. A similar process occurs, it will be argued, in *The Quiet Man* in which the values of the ideal moral community, which were formerly a feature of the American West, are now to be found in a different west, the west of Ireland.[17]

What *The Quiet Man* provides, therefore, is an image of the ideal community, in which the individual is balanced with society and society with nature and in which the modes of community regulation are both traditional and informal. However, just as the Western partly constructs a 'mythic' American past, so Ford's vision of Ireland is less situated in the past than in the imaginary. On his arrival, the American, Sean Thornton (John Wayne) finds himself bombarded by confused and contradictory directions (only resolved with the 'magical' appearance of Michaeleen Oge Flynn (Barry Fitzgerald)). It is therefore clear that his destination has no real geographical location; rather, it is an Ireland of the mind, out of time and unchanging. Roland Barthes has suggested that one of the key characteristics of modern myth is the removal, or denial, of history: 'Myth deprives the object of which it speaks of all history [...] all that is left for one is to enjoy the beautiful object without wondering where it comes from.'[18] While some critics have been content to do just this – McBride and Wilmington, for example, celebrate the film as 'Ford's most convincing and beautiful affirmation'[19] – this essay proposes to undertake what myth would like to forbid and investigate from 'where it comes'.

As previously suggested, it is helpful to understand the image of Ireland in *The Quiet Man* as a form of response to a disillusionment with modern America. The impetus for the narrative is provided by the return of an American, Sean Thornton, to his home of Innisfree ('I've come home and home I'm going to stay') who regards it as a lost Garden of Eden ('Innisfree has become another word for Heaven for me').[20] In contrast, his place of departure, Pittsburgh, is described as having furnaces so hot that 'a man forgets his fear of Hell'. Ireland is Heaven, America is Hell and already we find an interesting reversal of the earlier Fordian view of Ireland. In *The Informer* (1935), Ireland is dark and strife-torn with its wretched hero, Gypo, nurturing forlorn expectations of emigration to America. In *The Quiet Man*, the journey has been made and found wanting. The difference is worth bringing out. In *The Informer*, the choice of expressionist lighting, enclosed interiors and foregrounded objects and symbols establishes a fatal pattern from which Gypo's only escape is martyred blood-sacrifice. By contrast, *The Quiet Man*'s evenly lit and brightly coloured focus on landscape, captured in open compositions and fluid camerawork, firmly establishes Ireland on the side of life. It is now America that represents the repository of death. Not only has Thornton's mother died there but Thornton himself has faced his own symbolic execution. This is made evident in a stylistically aberrant flashback to America following Thornton's fall to the ground at his wedding on receiving a blow from Squire Danaher (Victor McLaglen). The subsequent intercutting of Thornton's gaze down on to his boxing-ring victim, positionally matched with Thornton on the floor at the wedding, suggests that Thornton is also staring at his own dead body. Thus his journey back to Ireland is not only an exile's return but also a form of resurrection.

In this respect, it is interesting to remember Warshow's remarks on the American gangster film as the 'no' to 'the great American "yes" stamped so big over our official culture'.[21] This 'no' may also be found in the American cinema's appeal to Celtic culture, not only in the case of Ireland but Scotland as well. A film such as *Brigadoon* (Vincente Minnelli, 1954), for example, may be seen to function as a piece of American self-flagellation in which the 'virtues' that America lacks are discovered in a curious Scottish village that awakens only for one day in every hundred years. Like *Brigadoon*, *The Quiet Man* creates its own version of a timeless Celtic paradise. The world into which Sean Thornton enters, following his transfer from train to Michaeleen's cart, is one that modern technology has largely by-passed (with no electricity and only one tractor apparent). Horses and carts and bicycles are the primary means of transport. A solitary car does make an appearance but it is from 'outside' (belonging to the visiting Bishop) and, as Anderson indicates, possesses a distinct 'pre-1914 air'.[22] It is a world virtually untouched by industrialisation and urbanisation and as such enjoying a harmony with nature missing from modern society. Livelihoods are of course earned by working the land and characters are intimately connected with their possession of it. Danaher, for example, presumes the Widow Tillane (Mildred Natwick) will not sell White O'Morn to Thornton because of its proximity to his own estate. It is as if land – 'mine lying next to yours' – sets up the natural expectation of lying together in bed. Moreover, there are few significant events and actions which are not in some way connected with nature.[23] As Sean and Mary Kate (Maureen O'Hara) embrace for the first time, the wind rushes through the cottage door. Refused permission to court Mary Kate, Sean's dejected departure from the Danaher home is accompanied by a sudden downfall of rain. A storm also breaks out when Sean and Mary Kate flee Michaleen and passionately embrace in a graveyard. The water motif recurs constantly: in the form of the streams which people cross, are knocked into, or in which they fish, the holy water Mary Kate gives to Sean, the water Michaeleen rejects in favour of whisky, and the inevitable buckets of water liberally employed throughout the fighting.

The linking of Mary Kate with nature – initially she is shown wandering barefoot over the green and forested hillside like some pastoral shepherdess – is of particular note. Colin McArthur has suggested in relation to films about Scotland (such as *Brigadoon, Whisky Galore* and *The Maggie*) how 'the outsider encounters an ethereally beautiful woman in some sense representing the spirit of Scotland'.[24] The similarity here is striking. The encounter, first of all, has a distinctly other-worldly feel to it. This is achieved initially through a dislocation of the spatial articulations normally characteristic of classical narrative cinema, such that the spatial relationship between Sean and Mary Kate is clear but not in relation to Michaeleen and Father Lonergan (Ward Bond). Thus, the first shot of the sheep and dog appears to position the couple on one side of the track; it is only eight shots later, when Michaeleen returns into frame, that it becomes clear that they are actually on the other side (and that the camera has cut nearly 180°).[25] As such, Sean and Mary Kate are clearly positioned in relation to each other but 'cut off' from the outside world. Moreover, the editing suggests that the first shot, which is initially empty of characters, does not correspond to anyone's point of view. It is only when a similar shot is established as Sean's point of view that we see Mary Kate, almost as if she had been wished there by him. In this way, Mary Kate's appearance is constructed within the terms of the look and her ethereal, fantasy-like quality is reinforced by the visual splendour of her entrance, the change in music on the soundtrack and the subsequent conversation between Sean and Michaeleen ('Is that real?' (Sean). 'Ah nonsense, it is only a mirage brought on by your terrible thirst' (Michaeleen)). In a sense, she becomes the wish fulfilment of Sean's desire to return to Ireland, at one with nature and embodying the 'spirit of Ireland'.

This association of the feminine and Ireland is reinforced by Sean's initial views of his family cottage, White O'Morn, and the village of Innisfree. Again, these are both situated in terms of his fantasy, his point of view, but at the same time are linked by the soundtrack to his dead mother's voice (whereby his point of view is aligned with his mother's descriptions of the places he is seeing). In psychoanalytic terms, Sean's desire to return to Ireland may be characterised as a desire to return to the womb. Unlike the oedipal trajectory of a Ford film such as *Rio Grande* (1950), in which a son rebels against his mother to win the respect of his father, Sean's journey is more regressive, involving a desire to recapture the pre-oedipal unity of mother and son. This is not, however, simply a personal trajectory insofar as the mother (and the feminine more generally) may be seen to embody nature and, by corollary, Ireland itself. Indeed, MacCana has noted that 'in Irish tradition it would be hard to exaggerate the importance of (the) idea of the land and its sovereignty conceived in the form of a woman',[26] while Ní Brolcháin has indicated how 'the image of Ireland as a woman took a tenacious hold on the imagination of the Irish, and survives until the present day'.[27] Breatnach also draws attention to the recurrence of the 'puella senilis' in which the chief aspects of youth and age are united.[28] This point is developed by Ní Brolcháin who traces the continuing appeal of the representation from such an early myth as 'Echtra Mac n Echach' (The Adventures of the Sons of Eochaid) through to Yeats's play, 'Cathleen Ni Hoolihan', in both of which an old hag is transformed into a beautiful young girl.[29] In this respect, *The Quiet Man* could be said to draw upon a well-established pattern. Mary Kate is in effect both a 'mother' to the Danaher household and Sean's object of sexual desire. By virtue of her association with Ireland, she also, in effect, becomes the metamorphosis of Sean's own mother. In this way, one of the mechanisms of Barthes' 'privation of history' becomes clearer: history is collapsed into nature and nature into woman (natural, eternal, perennially capable of rejuvenation and as such embodying the 'spirit of Ireland').

However, Sean's return to Ireland is not only predicated upon a reconnection with natural forces but also a successful integration into Innisfree's community structures. Again, his relationship with Mary Kate is crucial, not just because of her attachment to nature but also because of her links to traditional forms of community regulation. Thus, while Sean and Mary Kate's initial encounter is clearly privileged within the film's structure, it is also signalled as incomplete in the way that it occurs: the couple are spatially 'cut off' from the community and their exchange of point-of-view shots lacks the symmetry conventionally associated with the representation of the 'romantic couple'. In this respect, Sean's fantasy must in part give way to social convention and it is these conventions that help to explain Mary Kate's refusal to consummate her marriage and her subsequent departure for Dublin in retaliation for Sean's refusal to fight for her dowry. This is worth emphasising in the light of recent feminist film criticism which has attempted to read these acts as a 'progressive' assertion of female independence. Janey Place, for example, has gone as far as to describe the film as 'one of the most revolutionary films of the American cinema'.[30]

However, a more plausible interpretation of the dowry's importance is that, far from involving an assertion of female economic independence, it signifies the regulation of sexual desire within traditional forms, and thus allows the substitution of one form of economic servitude for another. It is precisely because Sean refuses to accept the traditional ways of handling sexuality in the community, to bow to its rules, that Mary Kate refuses to submit to him despite her obvious love. In this respect, there is a variation on the theme in the film's treatment of Danaher and the Widow Tillane. Danaher likewise keeps overstepping the codes of the community in his courtship of the Widow Tillane (blabbing in pubs, jumping the gun at Sean and Mary Kate's wedding) which again prevents a successful union despite their mutual affection. Such a union will be achieved only once he agrees to join the Widow in the courtship cart driven by Michaeleen and hence submit to the traditional way of expressing romantic interest ('the proprieties' as Michaeleen puts it). In both cases, the women and their differing sexualities have to find an appropriate expression within community structures. If Mary Kate is initially over-sexed in her relationship with Sean, so the Widow Tillane is under-sexed in hers. Thus both excessive sexuality and repressed sexuality are equally unvalued outside of marriage and family, and change is required of both in a way that is paralleled in other Ford movies such as *Donovan's Reef* (1963) and *Mogambo* (1953) (Tillane, Emily and Linda Nordley, on the one hand; Mary Kate, Miss Lafleur and Eloise Kelly, on the other).

As a result, the union of Sean and Mary Kate finally occurs when Sean participates in the donnybrook.[31] How this takes place is revealing of both the inner structures of Ford's vision of community, as well as the whole mythological/ideological operation of the film. Althusser has defined ideology as an 'imaginary relation between [men] and their real conditions of existence [...] a relation that expresses a will [...] a hope or a nostalgia rather than describing a reality'.[32] It is precisely this imaginary resolution of real conflicts and tensions through a mix of nostalgia and hope that characterises the ending of *The Quiet Man*.

The donnybrook is central to the resolution of conflict because it is at once traditional, informal and democratic in nature. Thus, the fight between Sean and Danaher and the dragging home of Mary Kate earlier are not separated from the group context. Indeed, in the case of the latter, the camera consistently holds on the crowd after Sean and Mary Kate have left the frame. Personal problems are thus translated into collective concerns, but through a means which rejects centralised legal and judicial structures.[33] This disrespect for formal authority is clearly exemplified when Michaeleen halts the fight to tell Sean and Danaher to follow the Marquis of Queensberry rules (just as Feeney (Jack McGowran) had rather sternly called for 'parliamentary procedure' in the pub earlier). Both men agree before Danaher immediately kicks Sean in the face. The inappropriateness of formal authority is likewise reinforced by the refusal of both the priest and the police to put a stop to the fighting. Father Lonergan admits it is his duty to put an end to it but carries on with his excited shadow-boxing; the police call for reinforcements only to receive instructions on betting from the Inspector.

As such, the donnybrook might be characterised as an example of 'functional conflict'[34] – conflict that takes place within the clearly defined parameters of traditional and populist community values and that ultimately works in the interest of social cohesion. It is a type of conflict that characterises many of Ford's films from *Rio Grande*, where a brawl is allowed to continue under the guise of a 'soldier's fight', through to *Donovan's Reef*, where Mike Mazurki's ineffectual policeman allows John Wayne and Lee Marvin their traditional scrap. Likewise in *Young Cassidy*, the hurley players drop their earlier differences with Cassidy and his brother to join them in a jolly punch-up with the Royal Irish Constabulary. At another level, however, it could also be argued that the ritualisation of conflict in this way involves little more than a (temporary) symbolic resolution of continuing material problems.[35] For what *The Quiet Man* appears to do is raise genuine problems of class, sexual and sectarian difference only to 'magically' resolve them through symbolic ritual, a 'cheat' that the film itself acknowledges by having a near dying man, taking his last rites, magically come to life again with the onset of the fighting.

First of all, the donnybrook may be seen to resolve the sexual tensions between Sean and Mary Kate but in a way that disguises the basic inequity involved. As has been suggested, Mary Kate, in demanding her dowry, is not so much asserting her independence as upholding community tradition. However, this is a tradition that primarily allocates to women a role of domestic subservience. What, for example, is strikingly absent from most discussions of the film is the shockingly humiliating way in which Sean drags Mary Kate back from the train, causing her to lose her shoe, pulling her along the ground, kicking her and then throwing her at her brother's feet. (Anderson cheerfully describes this as 'fairy-tale')[36]. It may be Sean's revenge for having to walk five miles home earlier in the film but his treatment of Mary Kate is hardly a fair equivalent, just as his throwing away of the stick given to him by an older woman along the way could hardly be said to represent the enlightened attitude to marriage some critics have suggested. Indeed, whatever the claims made for Mary Kate's representation, it seems to differ little from the attitude to women described by Peter Wollen: 'Women, for Ford, are a fundamentally lower order than men. Originally headstrong, they have to be humiliated before they learn their proper place and become devoted wives.'[37] Thus, once community tradition has been satisfied by Sean's acquisition of the dowry and participation in the donnybrook, Mary Kate is only too happy to acquiesce in her domestic subordination ('I'll be going on home now. I'll have the supper ready for you'). The effect of the fighting on Mrs Playfair (Eileen Crowe) is similar. She bets on the outcome and loses while her husband (Arthur Shields) makes a bet with the Bishop and wins. That this has a deeper symbolic significance is evident from the way she then turns on her heel with the comment: 'If you'll excuse me, I'll get your tea Snuffy'. This message is reinforced following Sean and Danaher's return to White O'Morn. Just as Mary Kate had stood rear of frame serving the men in the Danaher household, so she now does the same in Sean's. Dialogue reinforces the parallel. Danaher enters the house muttering, 'God bless all in this house', just as Michaeleen had previously done when he and Sean had visited Danaher. Sean's exact repetition of what Danaher had said then, 'Sit down, sit down, that's what chairs are for', also makes it evident that Mary Kate has merely substituted domestic service in one household for that of another. The repression implicit in this conclusion is underlined by the very last shot. Sean and Mary Kate turn towards the cottage, with the implicit suggestion of prospective love-making. They then proceed to use the stepping stones across the stream while remaining completely dry. Given that we have never seen these stones used before (and that we *have* seen Mary Kate dash through the stream in a state of impassioned agitation) and given that their earlier sexual desire was consistently visualised in terms of water (wading through the stream, embracing in the graveyard) the implication seems to be one of constraint. Mary Kate is thus not just returned to domestic drudgery, but her sexuality is constrained as well.

A similar overcoming of tensions may be seen to take place in the case of religion. As with many of Ford's films, the action is infused with a religiosity such that events appear to combine a metaphysical and social significance. The marking of Sean's courtship of Mary Kate in terms of holy water and a graveyard is hardly accidental. Moreover, the agents of religion are central to the film's unfolding. Not only does Father Lonergan act as narrator, he is central to the unfolding of the plot (the deception of Danaher, the counselling of Mary Kate). Nevertheless, the village is not completely Catholic and the Protestant minister, Playfair, has his role to play too (primarily as confidant to the non-Protestant Sean). But once again the potential for social division that sectarian difference possesses is resolved through the healing balm of the donnybrook. Under threat of removal because of falling congregations, Playfair is reprieved by virtue of the village's Catholics. Instructed by Father Lonergan to 'cheer like Protestants', Playfair and the Bishop are successfully incorporated into a tension-free village community.

The film's concluding celebration of community also succeeds in overcoming economic and class divisions. It is apparent that the community of Innisfree is divided between those who own the land (the Squire, the Widow) and those who work it, and that these are divisions that inspire resentment. The accordion player complains to the Squire in the pub that 'you've too much land as it is', while the IRA's continuing interest, albeit in part jokey, in 'treason' is primarily directed at Danaher. Thus, they enjoy the prospect of him breaking his neck during the horse race and scoff at his comment about their involvement in settling the dispute over the dowry ('So, the IRA's in this too?' 'If it were, not a scorched stone of your fine house would be standing.'). However, once again the donnybrook heals all wounds as such resentments are suppressed and the villagers, including the IRA, join together to cheer on the Squire and Widow Tillane as they pass through the village on Michaleen's horse and trap.

Now, having said all this, it might be contended that, taken in context, it is all really rather innocuous. The film is, after all, a comedy, a playful *jeu d'esprit*, certainly intelligible, even enjoyable, in the light of the almost inevitable romanticising hue of Irish-American nostalgia. More positively, it might be contended that it is a filmmaker's privilege to pose desire over reality and that the film exhibits a 'utopian sensibility' that could be regarded as welcome and, even, progressive.[38] This might be so were it not the case that the film's sensibility less challenges the prevailing constructions of 'Irishness' than reinforces them. In his discussion of Anglo-Irish literature, Daniel Corkery identifies what he calls 'the three great forces [...] working for long in the Irish national being' as 'Religious Consciousness', 'Nationalism' and 'The Land'.[39] Although *The Quiet Man* is hardly the kind of work that Corkery had in mind, the film's representation of Ireland largely conforms to this limited (and limiting) conception of Irish identity. As has been seen, 'Irishness' in *The Quiet Man* is primarily associated with the land and nature, the rural rather than the urban, the agricultural rather than the industrial. The film is also infused with a religious consciousness that knits together the metaphysical and the social and ultimately rests upon the subsumption of Protestantism into Catholicism. It is also significant that when Mary Kate goes to Father Lonergan for advice about her marriage she asks if she may speak in Irish. As such, the Irish language comes to signify the authentic voice of Ireland, the only form in which the truly important matters (of the heart) may be discussed. In common with traditional discourses of nationalism, therefore, *The Quiet Man* ultimately works to suppress class, sectarian, gender and regional divisions in favour of the essential unity of the nation/community. Indeed, in the case of gender, it is not only that sexual conflicts are suppressed but that the very identity of the nation itself becomes gendered (as woman, the feminine). It should now be apparent why the film's symbolic resolution of material conflicts scarcely constitutes a triumph for utopian desire. It is not only that the film looks to the past rather than to the future but that it both draws upon and mobilises an ideologically restrictive version of 'Irish' identity at odds with the complexities of Irish society (and potentially obstructive to social change). Not, of course, that John Ford would see it this way: 'I come from a family of peasants. They came here and got an education. They served this country well. I love America. I am not political.'[40]

Endnotes

[1] This is a revised version of a paper initially given at an Irish Association for American Studies conference, The New University of Ulster, in February 1983. My thanks to Seán Connolly and Caoimhín Mac Giolla Leith for their help with references.

[2] Nicholas Thomas (ed.), *International Dictionary of Films and Filmmakers – 1: Films* (Chicago and London: St. James Press, 1990), pp. 732–33.

[3] John Hill, 'Images of Violence' in Kevin Rockett, Luke Gibbons and John Hill, *Cinema and Ireland* (London: Croom Helm, 1987), p. 147.

[4] Fredric Jameson, *The Political Unconscious: Narrative as a Socially Symbolic Act* (London: Methuen, 1981), p. 20.

⁵ Jean-Louis Comolli and Jean Narboni, 'Cinema/Ideology/Criticism (1)', *The Screen Reader 1* (London: SEFT, 1977), pp. 3, 7.

⁶ The Editors of Cahiers du cinèma, 'John Ford's *Young Mr Lincoln*', *The Screen Reader 1*, pp. 113–52. In her discussion of the kind of redemptive reading encouraged by this analysis, Charlotte Brunsdon suggests how the 'loved object, Hollywood cinema [...] could be retrieved if its textual (here standing for ideological) coherence could be demonstrated to be only apparent' in *Screen Tastes: Soap Opera to Satellite Dishes* (London: Routledge, 1997), p. 118.

⁷ This was a point I had pursued in my discussion of the *Cahiers* approach in "Ideology, Economy and the British Cinema', in M. Barrett et al. (eds.), *Ideology and Cultural Production* (London: Croom Helm, 1979), pp. 112-34.

⁸ Martin McLoone, *Irish Film: The Emergence of a Contemporary Cinema* (London: British Film Institute, 2000), p. 58.

⁹ I have suggested elsewhere (in relation to the films of Michael Powell), how an (exaggerated) emphasis upon formal self-consciousness and stylistic excess has been a key aspect of the redemptive reading of popular films. See Kelly Davidson and John Hill, '"Under Control": *Black Narcissus* and the Imagining of India', *Film Studies*, 6, (2005), p. 11.

¹⁰ For further biographical details, see Andrew Sinclair, *John Ford: A Biography* (New York: The Dial Press/James Wade, 1979).

¹¹ Victor McLaglen also gave an 'Oirish' presence to many of Ford's Westerns: most notably as Sergeant Quincannon in *She Wore a Yellow Ribbon* (1949) and *Rio Grande* (1950).

¹² Colin McArthur, *Underworld USA* (London: Secker and Warburg, 1972), p. 18.

¹³ In consistently referring to John Ford, I am not implying that he can be located as the conscious, originating source of all the meanings I am discussing. Recent film criticism has been concerned to distinguish Ford, the man, from Ford, the structure, system, or sub-code, as revealed through analysis. Clearly the two are related but the pattern revealed by analysis does not depend on the conscious awareness of the man (and, indeed would not expect to). While this essay indicates the value of locating *The Quiet Man* in relation to the 'Fordian system', it also goes on to suggest that it is insufficient in itself and that the film must also be placed in the wider context of 'inter-textual' ideologies (related to the nation, gender and religion). For a discussion of the conceptual and methodological issues raised by John Ford in relation to 'auteurism', see Peter Wollen, *Signs and Meanings in the Cinema* (London: Secker and Warburg, 1972) and John Caughie, 'Teaching through Authorship', *Screen Education*, 17 (Autumn 1975), pp. 3–13.

[14] Peter Wollen (pseudo. Lee Russell), 'John Ford', *New Left Review*, Jan/Feb., 1965, p. 69.

[15] Robin Wood, 'John Ford', in Richard Roud (ed.), *Cinema: A Critical Dictionary*, Vol. 1 (London: Secker and Warburg, 1980), p. 375.

[16] Wollen, *Signs and Meanings in the Cinema*, p. 101.

[17] Gibbons has drawn a parallel between the representation of the West in American and Irish culture in terms of their modernisation and hostility to centralised law and order (Luke Gibbons, 'Synge, Country and Western: The Myth of the West in Irish and American Culture', Paper presented to the Sociological Conference of Ireland, Limerick, 1981). However, by drawing on the work of Synge (*The Aran Islands, The Playboy of the Western World*) he also wants to distinguish the two in their attitudes to sexuality: identifying the American west, on the one hand, with a suppression of sensuality and the Irish west, on the other, with an escape from the puritan ethic. While this is undoubtedly true in the case of Synge, it is less so in the case of *The Quiet Man*, in which, it will be argued, the project is to regulate sexuality rather than to give it free rein.

[18] Roland Barthes, *Mythologies* (Frogmore, St Albans: Paladin, 1973), p. 151.

[19] Joseph McBride and Michael Wilmington, *John Ford* (London: Secker & Warburg, 1974), p.124.

[20] There is an obvious reference here to Yeats's poem 'The Lake Isle of Innisfree': 'I will arise and go now, and go to Innisfree [...] And I shall have some peace there, for peace comes dropping slow' (*The Collected Poems of W.B. Yeats* (London: Macmillan, 1977), p. 44).

[21] Robert Warshow, *The Immediate Experience: Movies, Comics, Theatre and Other Aspects of Popular Culture* (Cambridge, Mass: Harvard University Press, 1974), p. 136.

[22] Lindsay Anderson, *About John Ford* (London: Plexus Publishing, 1981), p. 132.

[23] For a useful discussion of natural imagery in *The Quiet Man*, see Marilyn Campbell, 'The Quiet Man', *Wide Angle*, 2.4 (1978), pp. 44-51. Campbell also makes some suggestive connections between the film and the conventions of Shakespearean and Greek New Comedy. However, the generalising thrust of such comparisons inevitably works against her being able to provide any specific socio-historical context to her conclusion that: 'Comedy is the perfect form of cultural propaganda' (p. 51).

[24] *Visions: Cinema*. Channel 4, tx. 3 March 1983.

[25] The 180° rule is employed in classic narrative cinema as a means of preserving spatial continuity. A cut of more than 180° would involve a switch to the opposite side of the action and would effectively reverse screen direction such that characters would appear to have changed position. The logic of the 180° rule is described by Thompson and Bordwell as follows: 'This minimises the spatial

disorientation over cuts; if the spectator's position vis-à-vis the action is always clear, he or she will be able to follow the action in a continuous flow without pausing to search the screen for clues as to the new spatial relations of the shot' (Kristin Thompson and David Bordwell, 'Space and Narrative in the Films of Ozu', *Screen*, 17.2 (1976), p. 42). The disorientating effect of the 180° cut in *The Quiet Man* is minimised by cutting to a space empty of characters but, as I indicate, it does effectively mislead the spectator with respect to 'the new spatial relations of the shot'.

[26] Proinsias MacCana, 'Women in Irish Mythology', *The Crane Bag*, 4.1 (1980), p. 7.

[27] Muireann Ní Bhrolcháin, 'Women in Early Irish Myths and Sagas', *The Crane Bag*, 4.1 (1980), p. 16.

[28] R.A. Breatnach, 'The Lady and the King', *Studies*, 42 (1953), pp. 328–35.

[29] Ní Brolcháin, 'Women in Early Irish Myths and Sagas', pp. 13–15.

[30] Janey Place, *The Non-Western Films of John Ford* (Secaucus, NJ: Citadel Press, 1979), p. 196. The basis for this extraordinary claim seems to derive from a notion of the film being in some way 'materialist' (as in historical materialism): 'The most revolutionary element of his (Sean's) journey is its economic foundation: it requires him to give up romantic illusions and understand the economic basis of Mary Kate's (and thereby his) relation to herself, her environment, and her husband' (p. 197). However, Sean's 'understanding' (if such it is) seems less to derive from economic insight than a submission to the community's traditional value-system. As such, the film does not uncover material relations but provides an 'ideal' solution to material conflicts which remain (as I shall argue later). French puts a different emphasis on the film's 'progressive' qualities, arguing that the film's representation of Mary Kate combines the two female archetypes of 'goddess' and 'shrew' such that 'a *real* woman' emerges (Brandon French, *On the Verge of Revolt: Women in American Films of the Fifties* (New York: Frederick Ungar Publishing, 1974), p. 16). Apart from the assumption that film can provide 'real women' (as opposed to constructing representations within discourse), the essay's emphasis on 'psychic integrity' seems to lose all sense of the traditional and communal nature of the characters' relationship. The fusion of the two female types, however, is suggestive in relation to my argument regarding the fusion of Sean's mother and Mary Kate in the film.

[31] The term donnybrook derives from the annual fair traditionally held at Donnybrook (now a suburb of Dublin) from the thirteenth to the nineteenth century and at which, at least latterly, fighting was to become a commonplace occurrence.

[32] Louis Althusser, *For Marx* (London: New Left Books, 1977), p. 234.

[33] Wollen (*Signs and Meanings in the Cinema*, p. 101) draws suggestively, in his discussion of Ford, on Weber's distinction between rational-legal, traditional and

charismatic authority (Max Weber, *The Theory of Social and Economic Organization* (New York: Free Press, 1947), p. 328). Authority in *The Quiet Man* is clearly local rather than centralised, traditional rather than 'rational-legal'.

[34] For a presentation of the functionalist theory of conflict, see Lewis Coser, *The Functions of Social Conflict* (Glencoe, Illinois: The Free Press, 1956). While functionalism emphasises the contribution of conflict to social cohesion, the suggestion here is that this is temporary and can only be contained, not resolved, within the limits of the social system.

[35] Margaret A. Coulson and David S. Riddell employ the example of Zulu women who wear men's clothes for one day of the year, in a fleeting symbolic triumph over male domination, in their discussion of the ritualisation of conflict in *Approaching Sociology: A Critical Introduction* (London: Routledge & Kegan Paul, 1970), pp. 56–81, 100.

[36] Lindsay Anderson, *About John Ford*, p. 132.

[37] Peter Wollen (pseudo. Lee Russell), 'John Ford', p. 72. Wollen also notes the role of women in saloons who act as a type of counterpoint to the wives and mothers generally sanctified in his films. However, even these tend either to be redeemed through marriage (Dallas in *Stagecoach*, Miss Lafleur in *Donovan's Reef*) or ennobled through death (Chihuahua in *My Darling Clementine*, Lucy Lee in *The Sun Shines Bright* (1953)). Sacrificial death seems almost the only avenue tolerated by Ford for those women who remain outside home and marriage. This is perhaps most evident in two of Ford's strongest female characterisations: Dr. Cartwright (Anne Bancroft) in *Seven Women* and Mary Stuart (Katharine Hepburn) in *Mary of Scotland*. Cartwright makes the 'ultimate sacrifice' for the children and missionaries before committing suicide while Mary is executed.

[38] For a discussion of the 'utopian sensibility' in popular culture, in part derived from the Frankfurt School's ideas of art embodying and preserving the utopian and critical dimension of human experience, see Richard Dyer, 'Entertainment and Utopia', *Movie*, 24 (1977), pp. 2–13.

[39] Daniel Corkery, *Synge and Anglo-Irish Literature* (Dublin and Cork: Cork University Press, 1931), p.19.

[40] Sinclair, *John Ford*, p. 3.

IV

Gender, Ethnicity and Mary Kate

14

Feminist Icon or Prisoner of Patriarchy? An Exploration of Mary Kate's Character in *The Quiet Man*

DÍÓG O'CONNELL

The Quiet Man is a film evoking diverse and confused responses. Its enduring popularity is testament to its loyal following along a spectator spectrum from liberal to conservative who enjoy and celebrate it in equal parts despite it appearing to be laden with paddy-whackery and drooling offence. For the female viewer, the scenes of domestic violence are regressive if interpreted literally, yet they often invoke laughter leading to unease, in turn prompting questions about one's apparent strongly held views and allegiances. Does this reaction suggest a hidden and suppressed comfort with conservative and regressive approaches to gender relations, making it somehow acceptable when couched in nostalgia? If so, it is deeply unsettling as a thought and response, particularly when directed at the *feminist* viewer. Confining intellectual analysis of the film to John Ford as an auteur or *The Quiet Man* as an Irish western with the frontier transposed to the west of Ireland is one way of evading the more uncomfortable dimensions of the film, those that implicate the audience with seemingly regressive, discriminatory and chauvinistic politics. This chapter is an attempt, therefore, to face the demons, avoid the evasion and explore those narrative aspects that are unsettling and difficult to process along ideological lines. By assessing the narrative function of scenes such as when Sean Thornton is presented with 'a stick to beat the lady with' or when he is portrayed 'dragging Mary Kate across the fields for five miles', light is shed on the multiplicity of contradictory meanings within and responses to the film. In examining this film in such a way, its enduring legacy in an Ireland that has long since cut the cord with de Valera's protectionist approach to all aspects of Irishness will be explored. One method in revealing the way these contradictions function and sustain themselves is through a narrative analysis.

The main narrative tension in *The Quiet Man*, it will be argued, centres on contradiction. This aspect of the film has been explored by Luke Gibbons (2002), Des MacHale (1999) and Brandon French (1978) among others. Luke Gibbons writes that 'if there is anything more stereotypical than the characters in *The Quiet Man*, it is the responses of critics who take the film entirely at face value and see in it only the surface simplicity that Sean Thornton himself mistakes for the real Ireland'.[1] This statement opens up many issues and dualities within the film, not least whether or not there is any possibility that Mary Kate can be seen in a progressive light and that those of us who enjoy her character are not setting the clock back in terms of the role, place or achievements of women in society. Like Gibbons, whose view of the film is that 'everything we see in it is framed in such a way — whether by the camera, the narrative structure, the mise-en-scène, the set design or the script — as to raise questions over what exactly it is we are seeing and where reality ends and imagination begins',[2] it can be suggested that the contradictions and duality of representations of gender within the film equally demands the questioning of automatic responses to the construction of male/female relations within the text and assumptions made about meaning.

This chapter seeks to explore the character of Mary Kate (played by Maureen O'Hara) and examine to what extent she can be regarded as either a 'feminist icon' or a 'prisoner of patriarchy' as one way of figuring out this contradiction, between the rational and irrational, the intuitive and the intellectual, in responding to Ford's *The Quiet Man*. Using a formalist approach to narrative scrutiny, the character formation of Mary Kate is uncovered, revealing a highly contentious and contradictory portrayal of this female character. Does Mary Kate enslave herself to her new husband, thus continuing the status quo? Or does she seek to rid herself of the shackles of domineering and suppressive practices within male/female relations? In doing so, does she further the feminist cause (in a pre-feminist way)? These are among the questions posed here and examined within a framework of narratology. This chapter argues that focalization as a narratological tool can contribute to an analysis of how the characters function, on many levels, within the text, suggesting that monolithic readings and responses are redundant in multi-layered texts such as those created by John Ford. The challenge lies in revealing structural elements contributing to the overall nuanced complexity.

Focalization is a useful narratological tool in film analysis by revealing how characters function in 'telling' the story, in the broadest sense. According to Edward Branigan, this is achieved simply by living in their world, that is the story world, and speaking to other characters and acting out sequences of action. As a tool of narratology, focalization allows not the exploration of representations but instead the close scrutiny of how the character, as an agent defined by actions, functions within the story world, or in this instance, how Mary Kate operates within the story world of *The Quiet Man*. A device particularly useful in removing the barriers put up by extra-textual factors, it facilitates a scrutiny of narrative and its structural form. Rather than simply commenting on the structure or form of a specific film (which is a valid and useful exercise in and of itself), this technique reveals content, suggests explanations for meaning and consequently can be used as an interpretive tool. In this case, because Mary Kate presents such a contradictory and contentious approach to female characterisation, using tools of narratology (which identifies a character as an agent within a causal scheme) raises issues about the character's awareness of events in her world, that is, the story world constructed. This method presents key insights into the world of a specific film and in this case goes some way in explaining Mary Kate's character. It accommodates the conflicting and often uncomfortable responses to her character for women, particularly since the emergence of the second wave of feminism and, more recently, post-feminism.

But how do we get into the mind of the character in a medium that relies on action and the unfolding of a story through 'showing, not telling?' The principal obligation of narrative structure, it could be argued, is to reveal character through action. Thus for the narratologist, focalization as a tool of analysis presents a useful way into the thoughts of the character. In Branigan's words, 'Focalization [...] involves a character neither speaking (narrating, reporting, communicating) [...] but rather actually experiencing something through seeing or hearing it [...] [and can] extend to more complex experiencing of objects: thinking, remembering, interpreting, wondering, fearing, believing, desiring, understanding'.[3] In Branigan's schema of eight levels of narration, which includes the narrative in its historical context, as fiction, constructed as a story world, the eighth level functions by revealing and accessing perception and a character's thought within the narrative. At this level, also known as internal focalization, light can be shed on the interior thoughts of the character or what they 'see and hear', as opposed to 'say and do'. In theoretical terms this level ranges and accounts for simple perception (the point of view shot) to impressions (usually depicted through hazy or soft focused shots), to deeper thoughts, such as dreams and memories.[4]

While narratology is a useful analytical tool for revealing structure and story construction, it is not the only branch of theoretical enquiry involved in understanding character formation and function on screen. Feminist theory has long been concerned with the gaze and particularly the male gaze within classical Hollywood cinema. What focalization can reveal is whether a character controls the gaze and point of view or is the object of the gaze. How does the audience experience events within a film – is it by accessing the characters' thoughts through internal focalization or by events portrayed and action executed in an externally focalized way? Is Mary Kate an object of the film's gaze or does she control the narrative view? Is she subjected to the gaze of Sean Thornton or does she direct the narrative progression with her point of view? The first encounter scene between Thornton and Mary Kate sets the parameters of the gaze. In the scene followed by Father Lonergan's voice-over, the audience is shown Sean Thornton seeing and looking at Mary Kate for the first time followed by her looking back, across the fields, as she herds the sheep. She looks again, followed by him, followed by her looking again, again and again. In this sequence she is visually dominant, not an unusual position for the female lead in a classical film, but she is not controlled by Thornton's gaze. Although he presents the first look, from then on there is an exchange as both reveal their interest and curiosity. This sequence sets the tone of the film, particularly with regard to the relationship, by combining an exchange of looks rather than positioning one character as controlling and the other subjected to the gaze or the look. Out of earshot Thornton says, 'Is she real?' and although she doesn't hear, Mary Kate responds with another look. In narrative construction, it could be argued that the framing and focalization within this sequence, while revealing what the characters see and hear, set the parameters for how the relationship will unfold, and thus is pivotal to understanding Mary Kate's character. Rather than suggesting dominance or subjugation, it implies parity and balance, giving the impression that the role for Mary Kate in the narrative is more complex than a surface reading would indicate. It could be argued that Mary Kate's function within the film is neither one of object nor subject, but combines both. As revealed later in the film, when she can, Mary Kate makes things happen rather than simply waiting for events to come her way.

Is Mary Kate, therefore, a feminist icon or does she remain a prisoner of patriarchy despite her attempts to break free? Returning to the contradictions and dualities of characterisation within the text, it could be suggested that these inconsistencies are not so much confused portrayals, but rather an appropriation of the common devices by John Ford of employing opposites as a narrative device to present variations on a position. Indeed, in the portrayal of Mary Kate within the public domain, she is shackled to a dowry system that puts a financial value on women. But in her private sphere, the dowry is key to her independence within marriage and the maintenance of her identity: 'it's my fortune', she says, 'and my mother's before me [...] I'm no married woman without it. I'm a servant girl like I've always been without my dowry. I want my dream.' But if it is truly her dream, why does she acquiesce in the destruction of it when Thornton throws it into the furnace? Does she set a test for him as a way of proving his love, or does she simply want the traditions of her culture honoured? This is where the meaning gets confused and contradictory, giving rise to many different explanations. James MacKillop suggests the tradition is being repudiated and rejected by destroying the money,[5] a view Luke Gibbons challenges by suggesting that the dowry system is rejected for its financial element but not for its symbolic connection with the past.[6] Another interpretation or reading might propose that Mary Kate, although recognising the significance of the dowry, refuses to be bought, rejects a price being put on her and for this reason the money must be destroyed. Yet she still wants to maintain her identity within marriage, as separate and distinct from her new husband, suggesting an independent and progressive character. This identity is symbolically embodied in her possessions that have a value, which cannot be counted in monetary terms, yet are hers alone.

Despite her independence of spirit, Mary Kate lives in a society that positions women in a particular way. Although she does not protest outwardly to the term spinster, she indicates that she clearly doesn't like it, revealed through narrative focalization. The public displays of Thornton kicking Mary Kate's behind and honking the horn at her, in which she conspires, are scenes that ought not to sit easily with the female viewer. However, like many aspects of this film, these scenes do not invoke outrage. Are female viewers complying tacitly when they fail to disapprove of such objectifications of women through these scenes? How can these scenes be explained or rationalised for the feminist viewer? Linking to the playing out of opposites, it could be argued that just as the fight scene is a charade, a spectacle for public consumption, so too are these scenes. In fact, the scene between Mary Kate and Thornton whereby she moves to hit him, he ducks, she misses and spins around, presenting her behind to him which he then kicks, is a scene audiences are more familiar with from the circus, performed by clowns. Bakhtinian-like, the meaning of the sequence is manipulated such that the events are not quite what they seem. Far from endorsing the treatment of women as sex objects, these public displays are undermined when juxtaposed with what happens in the private sphere between Sean and Mary Kate, described by Brandon French as 'a sophisticated reversal'. French says that in many ways the film 'encourages conventional expectations and then confounds them'.[7] For example, there is an expectation in narrative terms that Thornton will rape Mary Kate when he breaks down the door and throws her on the bed after they have been married. However, as Brandon French points out, such is the public expectation of sex in marriage that Mary Kate asks him not to 'shame' her by telling his friends that she refused him on their wedding night. When she does reveal that the marriage is not consummated, she does so through Irish and to the priest, and as expected he is suitably shocked. 'Níor lig me m'fhear chéile isteach i mo leaba', she says — by confessing to the priest she is conforming to her community's norms, the notion that the wife has bedroom duties within marriage.

Brandon French points out that through convention and accepted views of sex in marriage, whereby sex is often portrayed as a reward, one would expect the marriage to be consummated once Thornton fought and won Mary Kate's dowry[8] — she owes him now! However, Ford's treatment of sex within marriage plays on his idiosyncratic approach to opposites, of public and private, as the narrative works out a position that embodies a combination of conservative and progressive values. Thus the difficulty in responding to the film is an absence of fixed positions whereby one can either embrace or repudiate what is being suggested. On the one hand, the public portrayal and allusions to sex are indeed regressive, but the private (and arguably what matters to the characters Mary Kate and Sean) is much more complex and equal. French says: 'Sex alone does not solve the couple's problem. Nor is it held out until the end of the movie as the ultimate reward for problem solving.'[9] In this film, Ford plays with the public and private by way of exploring and examining perceived cultural norms and actual personal realities.

This enlightened treatment of sexuality promotes, as few American films have, the superiority of a mature and liberated love relationship by juxtaposing some of our conventional expectations about sex (justifiable rape, sex as a reward and a problem-solver) with a few unconventional fulfilments (husband forbearance, sex as mutual compassion, and passion as an expression of overall concord).[10]

Analysing Mary Kate's character, French sees Ford using it to explore a combination of the extremes of the 'goddess and the shrew' which eventually 'cancel each other and clear the stage for the introduction of a real woman who is neither'.[11] Mary Kate's battle for her dowry is about status in her marriage. By conspiring in the destruction of the material reward for her battle, she defies all conventions. She has established the ground rules for the relationship, which are neither about domination nor submission but rather recognition and equality, even if it appears on the surface to reinstate the status quo. In this way, Ford plays with the conservative and the traditional, but ultimately endorses the progressive.

The final scene of the film is revealing, particularly in terms of focalization. The crowds are gathered to cheer the arrival of Reverend Playfair and everybody joins in to give the impression of a vibrant Protestant population in Innisfree, both Catholics and Protestants. Once the Reverend has passed through, the crowd continues to cheer as Danaher and the Widow Tillane start their courtship under the watchful eye of Michaeleen. However, the illusion is broken and the seamlessness of narrative coherence shattered with the montage sequence of the various characters in the film, cheering almost in slow motion, evoking memories of *Battleship Potemkin* (1925) and Sergei Eisenstein's approach to montage, as the pace is slowed down. This sequence, dreamlike in a focalized way, suggests a meaning beyond surface reading. Catholic and Protestant are united together in presenting a charade, and the male/female relationship is established on an equal footing. Mary Kate turns to Sean and whispers something in his ear and the two head off arm in arm, not quite into the sunset, but towards their marital home. Is this John Ford's final comment on unity, of Catholic/Protestant and man/woman — a progressive and positive message articulated through a scene that breaks through the narrative seam?

So to what extent is Mary Kate a feminist icon or a prisoner of patriarchy? Luke Gibbons suggests that the film acts by contesting tradition, especially as it affects the subjugation of women. He suggests that viewers may have a problem with the way Sean treats Mary Kate but states that 'such responses fail to register the intricate narrative undoing of this "custom" (the dowry) at the end of the film'.[12] Gibbons points out that it is this reversal which leads Brandon French to conclude that it is not only the 'outsider' Sean but also the 'insider' Mary Kate who questions an unthinking conformity to tradition. Mary Kate's break with tradition is symbolised in the scene in which she tosses away the stick an old woman had given Sean to keep Mary Kate in line. According to Brandon French, 'Mary Kate rejects the notion of her husband's mastery, to which the older women have obviously acquiesced'.[13]

But is the narrative sufficiently redeemed through the ending? Does a progressive narrative end have the effect of cancelling all that has gone before? Is it a reversal of the tacked-on ending that brought about the expected, reassuring sense of closure in classical films attempting alternative portrayals of women in the preceding sections of the narrative (1940s' *film noir* in particular)? It is at this level that the film's characterisation is most problematic. While Mary Kate clearly is not a prisoner of patriarchy as she rejects many of the expectations of women laid down by such systems, it is difficult to argue that she is a feminist icon. In some respects she is both. Although she stands up to the men around her and patriarchal expectations at one level, she does so more for personal than for political reasons. This is facilitated by who she is, rather than what she thinks. The character created by John Ford is a hot-headed redhead, demonstrating and exhibiting demands that must be met, according to how she sees her world. She continues to serve the men in marriage – her new husband now reconciled with her brother – but she does so on *her* terms. Is she thus staging her quiet, personal revolution?

It could be argued that this film neither presents a story that can be appropriated for feminist ends, nor one simply boxed as another misrepresentation of women. Instead, this film might be re-imagined within the shadows of what has emerged as post-feminism. Although post-feminism is often associated with 'backlash' and is sometimes deemed anti-feminist, in more recent times it has been appropriated to explain the complexities and nuances of feminist theories and practices. A useful framework for examining contemporary popular culture, particularly aspects engaged with women's lives now, it is a different project to that of second-wave feminism. In the twenty-first century the objective and expression of feminism is more often personal and less political, and, as Ann Braithwaite suggests, with the emphasis on *fun*.[14] While the personal became the political for second wave feminism, post-feminism turns the political objective into the personal aim. Yet in the process concerned with the individual, the fight becomes a collective objective as many more women take it on. Like many women of previous generations, the silent, individual and private struggle, although often unacknowledged, is as effective as the organised collective response. All women benefit because of the belligerence of a few!

It is within this context that an explanation can be offered for the enduring legacy of *The Quiet Man* and explain intuitive responses to the film that on a rational basis one should reject. The instinctive reaction generated by the narrative is to laugh at the scenes whereby Mary Kate is maltreated by the men around her but political awareness suggests that this response is problematic. However, if an explanation is sought in the arena of post-feminism, it might imply that Mary Kate is having the last laugh and ultimately challenging those forces that are trying to keep her down, ironically without them knowing it. Her struggle is highly individualistic, yet contributes in a small but personal way and inevitably reverberates at some level, as is the case with the unrecorded private histories of women everywhere. Like many women the world over, she writes the rules for her own life, in this instance involving a combination of dependence and independence, rebellion and conformity, tradition and progression, and thus suggests that the characterisation in this film is more complex than a surface reading might suggest.

Endnotes

---

[1] Luke Gibbons, *The Quiet Man* (Cork: Cork University Press, 2002), p. 18.

[2] Ibid., p. 19.

[3] Edward Branigan, *Narrative Comprehension and Film* (London: Routledge, 1998), p. 101.

[4] Ibid., p. 103.

[5] James MacKillop 'The *Quiet Man* Speaks', *Contemporary Irish Cinema: From The Quiet Man to Dancing at Lughnasa*, ed. by James MacKillop (Syracuse: Syracuse University Press, 1999), pp. 175–76.

[6] Gibbons, *The Quiet Man*, pp. 72–3.

[7] Brandon French, *On the Verge of Revolt: Women in American Films of the Fifties* (New York: Frederick Ungar Publishing, 1978), p. 18.

[8] Ibid., pp. 18–19.

[9] Ibid.

[10] Ibid., p. 19.

[11] Ibid., p. 16.

[12] Gibbons, *The Quiet Man*, pp. 18–19.

[13] French, *On the Verge of Revolt: Women in American Films of the Fifties* (1978), p. 18.

[14] Ann Braithwaite, 'Politics of/and Backlash', *Journal of International Women's Studies*, 5.5 (June 2004): 24.

15

Before She Was Mary Kate:
Maureen O'Hara's Contradictory Career

RUTH BARTON

Maureen O'Hara's screen reputation now rests primarily on her collaborations with John Ford and John Wayne, and most popularly on her role as Mary Kate Danaher in *The Quiet Man*. So canonical has this performance become that when Chris Columbus cast the ageing star in *Only the Lonely* (USA, 1991), audiences were left to infer the film's premise – that this is what her life might have been like if Mary Kate had had one son and gone to live in Chicago.

That the figure of Mary Kate Danaher is a problematic representation for feminist critics is discussed elsewhere in this volume. What I want to concentrate on here is that peculiar combination of dominance and subordination that to me is the key to O'Hara's characterisation in *The Quiet Man* and which, I would like to argue, she brought with her to that role from her earliest screen performances. O'Hara published her autobiography, *'Tis Herself*, in 2004 and I also want to draw on this to explore the actor's own blurring of the distinctions between her on-screen and off-screen personae. This is not to assert the primacy of the individual's own interpretation of her life story but to explore the intertextuality of biography and performance.

According to her biography, O'Hara comes from a middle-class, educated urban background that instilled in her from birth a sense of her own worth and groomed her for a career on the Abbey stage. Although she glosses over this, she was, in fact, discovered after winning the Dawn Beauty contest organised by a new Irish women's magazine, *Woman's Life*, although she did briefly attend the Abbey School of Acting.

A somewhat reproving article published in *Woman's Life*, shortly after the then Maureen Fitzsimons had returned from London following her small role as a secretary in *Kicking the Moon Around* (Walter Forde, 1938), found the starlet in giggly mood, happily tucking into unsuitable foods in Arnotts' café:

> As we parted, I couldn't help feeling that this young star with the passion for doughnuts was looking forward to returning to England, not so much because of the fame and fortune awaiting her in films, but because of a naïve longing to occupy again that 'gorgeous dressing-room with its "sunshiny walls" and the carpet with the "deep, deep pile"'.[1]

The magazine's tone soon changed. In 1938, Maureen Fitzsimons was offered a contract in Hollywood and the *Woman's Life* reporter was just behind her as they flagged a series of forthcoming interviews:

> Her story is one that must thrill every woman in the country. A five-figure contract [...] the friendship and admiration of the world's most famous people [...] a thrilling career and the promise of stardom [...] these are the glamorous and exciting things that have come to Maureen Fitzsimons in the short space of four months.[2]

The *Woman's Life* interviewer flew to London in a state of enormous anticipation; reviewing in her memory Maureen Fitzsimons winning the beauty contest and her swift take-up by London and now Hollywood, she wonders if the simple Irish girl will have been spoilt by fame. To her relief, Maureen is simply more beautiful but otherwise unchanged. On set, the interviewer watches Laughton deliver his lines and then turn and wave to Maureen: 'Think of it!' she gasped to readers, 'Maureen Fitzsimons on waving terms with Charles Laughton! Is it really true? Or do you think it's all a dream?'[3]

The set was for *Jamaica Inn* (Alfred Hitchcock, 1939), the film that was to make O'Hara's name, literally as it was also the moment when Laughton decided that she should no longer be called Fitz-simons. More than that, it established for her a screen persona and a career path that was to remain consistent up to and beyond her appearance in *The Quiet Man*. It was Laughton who cast O'Hara as Mary Yellan, the recently orphaned young Irish woman (in the novel she is English), who has come to live in the Jamaica Inn with Joss Merlyn (Leslie Banks) and his wife, her Aunt Patience (Marie Ney). Laughton is described by O'Hara in her autobiography as a benevolent father figure, yet, in this and in their second film together, *The Hunchback of Notre Dame* (William Dieterle, USA, 1939), this benevolence is tinged with a grotesquery that insinuates its way through Laughton's performance and is expressed in a kind of leering sexual longing.

Maureen O'Hara plays Mary Yellan with a lissomness of movement that accompanied her through her screen career and militated against the camera's drive to constrain her. We can see this right from her first appearance in *Jamaica Inn* – an introductory sequence establishes Laughton's position and character, with his Squire Pengallan holding forth on the theme of beauty to the assembled dinner guests. The squire's toast is accompanied by his fetishistic handling of a porcelain figurine. Beauty, he ruminates, is dead and lives on only in his horse, his 'exquisite Nancy', which is duly led into the dining hall by a manservant. The action cuts to the coach and horses riding through the moor at night, bearing a full cargo of passengers. The first shot of O'Hara is of her face framed by dark curls, a bonnet and the cinema screen. Her expression is of childlike wholesomeness and innocence, her skin gleaming white against the dark, gothic background of the exterior set and the interior of the coach. This very tight shot is held for a couple of seconds, encouraging the audience's gaze to linger on and hold O'Hara/Mary Yellan within the frame. The shot is repeated when Squire Pengallan first sees Mary Yellan after she has appeared in the hall of the manor. On the announcement of her arrival, Pengallan wagers Ringwood (A. Bromley Davenport) that she will be ugly. Hearing the squire's voice, she turns and again her face fills the screen.

On seeing the young woman, Pengallan exclaims, 'My dear, you're a beauty!' and tosses a purse of coins to Ringwood. He then slowly circles her, unwrapping her cloak as he moves while quoting the poetry of Byron. This scene is only outdone by a later one where Pengallan, now deranged, binds and gags Mary before carrying her off to the ship in which he will escape to St Malo.

On each of these three occasions, where O'Hara is apparently trapped by the camera, she seems a perfect exemplar of Laura Mulvey's classic analysis of the objectification of the female within mainstream narrative cinema. Moreover, although not an icy blonde, she conforms to a Hitchcockian type, a strong woman who is the target of the director's, as Mulvey argues, sadistic voyeurism. On each of these three occasions, also, O'Hara as Mary Yellan breaks the hold of the frame, rupturing that moment of intense contemplation to assert her own will. She lashes out (verbally) at the coach driver for not stopping at Jamaica Inn; in her first encounter with Pengallan, she demands a horse to take her to her aunt's home and, finally, on board ship, knowing that the squire is insane, she prevents the military from shooting him.

O'Hara's role in *Jamaica Inn* alternates between moments of narrative dominance and disadvantage. After the scene in the squire's manor, Mary and Pengallan ride together to Jamaica Inn, where Mary will rescue Trehearne (Robert Newton), a secret agent disguised as a bandit, from death by hanging, be rescued in turn by him after she allows their escape boat to become unmoored during a spat, save Joss and Patience from the police, be captured (again), save a ship from wrecking, be kidnapped by Pengallan, witness the deaths of Joss, Patience and finally Pengallan's plunge to his own end, before, it is suggested, being romantically paired with Trehearne at the narrative's end. This less than convincing denouement is overshadowed by the hysterical energies of the previous scenes with Laughton.

The critical success of *Jamaica Inn* encouraged Laughton and Pommer to decamp to America, taking their protégée with them. The Hollywood of 1939 into which O'Hara arrived was one that was cer-

tainly accustomed to seeing women playing dominant roles, such as
those commandeered by Bette Davis at Warner Bros. It was also a
cinema on the cusp of change, newly committed to a politics of ethnic integration and wartime inclusiveness. From now on, women
were to dedicate themselves equally to the national cause and to
home life.

This, according to her memoirs, O'Hara did. Yet, as a number of
reviews of her book remarked, it seems extraordinary to a contemporary reader that such a strong-willed woman should have allowed
the various men in both her personal and professional life to domi-
nate her in the way they did. Firstly she married a man, George Han-
ley Brown, whom she barely knew, simply because he pressurised
her into it; then, after her divorce, she married Will Price, a chronic
alcoholic and womaniser who struck her when she was pregnant
with her only child, Bronwyn, and whose sexual leanings were ambiguous. Staying with Price for over ten years, she also had a relationship that John Ford ended, and a social relationship with Ford
that, she suggests, was founded on his fantasies of her. Once she had
scotched these, he sent her lewd letters and stymied her ambitions
with other directors, as well as snooping around her home and inter-
fering with other family matters, including her own brother Jimmy's
fledgling acting career.

All this is better understood against a background of a studio
system that enjoyed complete control over its contract artists, and
of a patriarchal society that fetishised the strong female while simultaneously working to undermine her. The practice, pioneered
by feminist theory, of reading against the grain of the text to provide a counter-history of strong female performances has opened
up a space to celebrate such performances rather than bemoaning
their limitations. Yet, to date, O'Hara has never been the beneficiary
of such recuperative 'herstories'. Perhaps it is because of her patri-
cian attitude, perhaps because of her often unconvincing love-
making, or perhaps because the roles in which she excelled, as pirate
queen, belong to a much neglected genre, that of the swashbuckler.
Maybe too, her friendship with ultra-conservative John Wayne
counted against her.

Only one of O'Hara's films, *Dance, Girl, Dance* (Dorothy Arzner, USA, 1940) has been retrieved by feminist history, and that more on account of its dialogue and the reputation of its auteur/director than for the performance of its co-star. Although she moved between numerous genres, she was at her most popular when playing the pirate queen or similar swashbuckling parts.[4] O'Hara's fame in this genre was established in her first outing with Tyrone Power, *The Black Swan* (Henry King, USA, 1942). She followed this with similar roles in *The Spanish Main* (Frank Borzage, USA, 1945), *Sinbad the Sailor* (Richard Wallace, USA, 1945), *Bagdad* (Charles Lamont, USA, 1949), *Tripoli* (Will Price, USA, 1950), *At Sword's Point* (Lewis Allen, USA, 1952), *Flame of Araby* (Charles Lamont, USA, 1952), and *Against All Flags* (George Sherman, 1952). Any analysis of these films must firstly acknowledge that they reify every sin of Orientalism in the book. They exhibit a will to control and create representations of a manifestly different world that exists, as Said has lucidly argued, in an uneven power relationship with Western, particularly American-European culture. They assume that this world cannot represent itself and they reinforce accumulating stereotypes of the 'mysterious Orient'. They create an imaginative geography of regions that do not exist in real time but in some kind of perpetual present in the past; they infantilise and exoticise native characters, regarding them with equal measures of fear and desire. That they are evidently fantasies should not entirely excuse them.

These films were released contiguously with Universal Studios' cycle of John Hall/Maria Montez productions from 1942-1945, although O'Hara's screen persona contrasts with that of Maria Montez in a number of ways, primarily as a consequence of her greater agency and physicality. O'Hara, of course, was also unmistakably white, unlike Montez, who was Spanish. Throughout her career, O'Hara played a range of roles that required her to pass as 'other'. In *The Hunchback of Notre Dame*, she was Esmeralda the gypsy; in *They Met in Argentina* (Leslie Goodwins, Jack Hively, USA, 1941), she was the half-Irish, half-Argentinian Lolita O'Shea; in the swashbucklers, she regularly played non-Caucasian parts, including Contessa Francesca in *The Spanish Main*, Shireen in *Sinbad the*

Sailor, Princess Marjan in *Bagdad* and Princess Tanya in *Flame of Araby*. As these titles indicate, O'Hara was most often cast as an upper-class character or member of the royalty.

We may surmise that there were a number of related grounds for this practice. The first was fear of miscegenation; at a deeper, symbolic level, the films drew on a history of representation that portrayed the East as feminine territory, ripe for invasion/rape by the conquering male power. Further, the costuming of oriental women, whether veiled or scantily clad, with their promise of nakedness/cover, threatened to lure on the adventurer in the man. The practice of casting a white actor as the oriental female allowed for an element of disavowal to enter this potent ethnic collision, with viewers invited to (mis)recognise the exotic princess' origins.

O'Hara's Irish-Catholic background further allowed the studio to wrap itself in a cloak of moral rectitude, one quite at odds with the images on screen: 'She is her own Hays office. She balked at taking a bath in a tub for a movie scene because "my folks in Dublin would think I had turned out all bad". She has kept a strict promise to her mother never to pose for leg art. She is strict about the negligees she wears for the movies'.[5]

Articles accompanying the release of *Sinbad the Sailor* danced a tightrope between titillation and moral rectitude; the *Hollywood Citizen News* turned to RKO's technical advisor on the production, Dr Paul Singh from Punjab Province, India to advise their female readers on the lessons they might learn from the film's style, one which reminded them of the 1945 'diaper drape':

> 'Women should never, never walk around completely undressed in front of their husbands', Dr. Singh declared. 'That's the quickest way in the world to lose him. He'll look for somebody who keeps part of her figure in mystery'.
>
> He eyed luscious Maureen O'Hara, whose curves were poured into a lowcut gold brocade bra and clinging silk pantaloons. As the princess in 'Sinbad', which takes place in 800 A.D., she wasn't wearing much.

> 'But enough', Dr. Singh added hastily, 'Just enough to be
> tantalizing. Much more so than a woman who parades around
> completely undressed.'[6]

Joseph Breen was less convinced. After reading an article in the *Herald Express* (4 February 1946) that reported that 'Maureen O'Hara's wardrobe for *Sinbad the Sailor* will make her costume in *The Spanish Main* seem Puritanical', he swiftly wrote to RKO: 'You will recall the difficulty we had with the costumes of this same lady in your production, *The Spanish Main*. I hope that our experience with that picture will not be repeated.'[7]

I would like to argue that Maureen O'Hara traversed the binaries of West/East, active/passive, masculine/feminine in a manner that was ultimately containable within a discourse committed to upholding those very binaries. In film after film, she participated in a masquerade of gender and ethnic identities that opened up a space for female as much as male viewing pleasure. Moreover, she was romantically paired with exotic lovers who were more often feminised than masterly and whose revolt against the patriarchal despot she shared. Think of the teaming of O'Hara with Tyrone Power in *The Black Swan*; both (she as the daughter of Lord Denby [George Zucco], deposed governor of Jamaica; he as the tool of Captain Morgan's [Laird Cregar] political manoeuvrings) are rebels in a system of power that offers them either staid conformity or reckless adventuring. Here, the female viewer is invited not just to wonder at the costumes, the sumptuousness of the mise-en-scène and the naked male torsos, but to partake vicariously in the heroine's display of athletic prowess. O'Hara does not just dance (and sing); she rides horseback, initiates kidnappings, fences and slaps in the face men who displease her. In *The Black Swan*, she appears to swoon under Waring's insistent attentions, only to clock him over the head with a stone when he leans forward to kiss her. Verging on the dominatrix, she is inevitably brought to heel by the film's ending and subjected to a token punishment for her transgressions, before being rewarded with a man with whom she can ride off to greater adventures. In *Bagdad*, O'Hara's Princess Marjan arrives in the palace of the Pasha Ali

Nadim (Vincent Price) to avenge her father's death at the hands of
the Black Robes, led, she believes, by Prince Hassan (Paul Christian).
The latter displays a languid, cosmopolitan masculinity and speaks
in an accent that the English-educated Princess mistakes for French
but is revealed to be Viennese. In an almost indecipherable plot,
Princess Marjan, accompanied by her loyal servant, Mohammed Jad
(Jeff Corey), discovers that the Pasha is in league with her father's
assassins and gallops off after the Black Robes. Disguised as a gypsy,
she attempts to put a spoke in the Pasha's plan for domination of the
Arab world. Before she can pull this off, she is unmasked and her
accomplices brutally tortured in front of her eyes. Only the last moment intervention of Hassan saves her from a lingering death at the
stake and provides for their happy union. *At Sword's Point* saw
O'Hara masquerade briefly as male, posing in tight-fitting hose and
wielding a finely pointed sword.

It's a shame that these films have become so forgotten because I
believe that they provide a key to reading Maureen O'Hara's performance in *The Quiet Man*. They reflect her own peculiarly unstable
star persona, simultaneously victim and victor, at once exhilaratingly
active and dispiritingly submissive. It is this performance history that
she brought with her to Ford's film, where again she challenges the
viewer to reconsider the normative framework of 'womanly' behaviour.

Rescuing Maureen O'Hara for feminism is, without doubt, problematic, particularly when her early fame was derived from a genre
known within the studios as 'tits and sand' films. Yet, I would like to
suggest that it is this very combination of play and punishment,
those dominatrix qualities that she brought with her to *The Quiet
Man*, and that marked her precarious off-screen working relationship
with Ford, that make her Mary Kate so fascinatingly complex.

Endnotes

[1] *Woman's Life*, 11 December 1937, pp. 16, 37.

[2] *Woman's Life*, 19 February 1938, p. 6.

[3] *Woman's Life*, 6 February 1938, p. 14.

[4] Too popular, it seems, for Richard Rodgers who personally vetoed her from being cast as the lead in *The King and I* (Walter Lang, USA, 1956), pronouncing that he would have 'No Pirate Queens!'. My thanks to James MacKillop for this information.

[5] Production Notes for *The Black Swan* (Maureen O'Hara file, Academy of Motion Picture Arts and Sciences (AMPAS)).

[6] V. MacPherson, '"Tip from a Harem Expert: Be Tantalizing, Ladies!"', *Hollywood Citizen News*, 26 March 1946 (Maureen O'Hara File, AMPAS).

[7] RKO Production Files, Box P154, UCLA.

16

Tisn't Pity at All That She is a Whore – Irish Ethnicity and the Female Body in John Ford's *The Quiet Man*[1]

Conor Groome

1. The Anatomy of a Whore

American scholar Arthur F. Kinny, writing on John Ford's best known work, summarises that it is:

> [a] powerfully haunting masterpiece [...] about two young people who are deeply in love yet forbidden to marry: they are caught remorselessly, between an older order of unbending orthodox belief and a newer world of emergent individualism and emancipated faith in human nature.[2]

Kinny, however, is not referring to *The Quiet Man*, nor indeed to the John Martin Feeny born in Cape Elizabeth, Maine in 1895. His topic here is actually the Caroline playwright John Ford and his 1633 work entitled, *Tis Pity, She's a Whore*. The play tells the story of Giovanni and Annabella, lovers condemned for their passion because they are brother and sister. Characteristically for the Renaissance Ford and not unlike *The Quiet Man* the play culminates in a surfeit of violence. Among the bodies piled high on stage, it is Annabella's that is most scorned and unfairly treated. Having already blinded herself in atonement for her incest, she is then killed by her very lover, who will himself be stabbed to death in the final act. Not before, however, he has removed his sister's heart, accusing her of being inconstant and then paraded the organ on the tip of a dagger before a banquet. His is one of three bodies lying dead on stage as the Cardinal, a guest at the feast, speaks the final lines of the play:

> We shall have time
> To talk at large of all; but never yet
> Incest and murder have so strangely met.
> Of one so young, so rich in nature's store,
> Who could not say, 'TIS PITY SHE'S A WHORE [3]

Ford Scholar Lisa Hopkins observes:

> The audience, however, are likely to feel that the blame for events cannot be so easily offloaded onto Annabella alone, and that just as Giovanni has anatomised his sister's body, so the play has anatomised the society it shows us – but even when we have seen its heart, a mystery remains. [4]

2. 'Put the Blame on Mame' [5]

The mystery is a familiar one. Why, in the midst of all this slaughter and inequity is the blame placed squarely, as Gilda would have it, 'on mame, boys'? Why, is the most transgressed and ill-treated body defined as the locus of all blame? Indeed, the body of Annabella, one could argue, is given a final insult. It is reduced in summation, to its performance of a single function – the sexual act – and then, reduced further by having this single act contextualised as illegal, marginalised and sinful. Luckily, no such bloody end occurs for the heroine of *The Quiet Man*. However, Mary Kate Danaher could well be tarred with a similar brush. Given her bodily movements, her identification with the elements and her general independence, in any other film by John Ford, she could have been a whore. However, the unique ethnic situation of the Irish allows Mary Kate Danaher to take on the role of heroine proper and eventually be triumphant, with her body and integrity intact.

The female body is the central cipher to the oeuvre of John Ford. It stands on both sides of the ancient dialectic between goddess and whore. It is also symbolic of the tension pervading his work – particularly his Westerns – between civilisation and wilderness. This dialectic is most clearly seen in Ford's *My Darling Clementine* (1946). On one side there is the Mexican saloon girl, Chihuahua (Linda Darnell); ethnic, wild and possessing an earthy sexuality. Clementine Carter (Cathy Downs) is the foil, playing the restrained, white school-marm. For Charles Ramiriz Berg, writing on Latino stereotypes in American movies, Chihuahua is the 'archetypal example' of 'the harlot'. Like her male equivalent, 'the bandit', she is 'a secondary character, lusty and hot-tempered [...] [W]ithout a man she is left in the wind', so she turns to whichever male is closest. She is, in her movements, always seductive, free and unfettered. Whether actually singing in the saloon or not, she is at all times performing for the male gaze, attracting it.[6]

Equally, the way that men treat her implicitly recognises the definition she cannot escape by virtue of her ethnicity and its sexual stereotyping. When WASP hero Wyatt Earp (Henry Fonda) catches her helping a 'tinhorn' to cheat at cards, his reaction is to 'cool her down' by throwing her into a horse trough. This dunking suggests her indigenous heat; her fiery temperament is at fault and the situation is best dealt with by fighting one element with its opposite. The comedic dousing with which this possible saloon stand-off ends, while being thoroughly characteristic of Ford, also leaves Chihuahua in an infantilised state – the butt-end of a childish prank. Earp can never take a Latina seriously. She is pigeon-holed by her ethnicity and her inherent inferiority to the Anglo mainstream. He even threatens to run her back to the reservation, showing that all 'ethnics' – Indians and Mexicans, alike – when they get out of line can be bunched together indiscriminately. Chihuahua is inescapably always out of line and never to be afforded the respect afforded ladies such as Clementine. Also, she has slipped further toward the margins because she is a whore.

As Chihuahua threatens Marshal Wyatt Earp that her boyfriend, Doc Halliday (Victor Mature), 'will twist that star around your heart', he wisely keeps his eyes front. Rocking rhythmically in his chair, he lets the tempest behind him blow itself out. She childishly stamps her foot at the fact that her passionate outburst has been ignored. And, a short while later, Wyatt's brother, Virgil, bares the brunt of Chihuahua's heat. Already shown to be a healthy fellow who 'just put away a whole skillet of ham and eggs', Virgil can't help but whinny at her free-moving body. In its presence, he becomes de-evolved to a simpler state.

3. Anatomy of a Goddess

Virgil Earp neighing at her like a stallion is acceptable because she is a wild and untamed product of the frontier. Again, the presence of such earthy sexuality requires cooling down. This time, Virgil has his heat tempered when Chihuahua throws a jug of milk in his face. Again, it is a piece of trademark Fordian humour, and at the expense of the Latina's fallen nature. The animalistic sexual display can be appreciated only when juxtaposed to Wyatt and Virgil's reaction to Clementine's arrival in the film. First to spot her is the Marshal as she alights from the stagecoach, after which she stands still; an incongruous form among the dusty commotion of the scene. It is a definite and particular female form; corseted, with hair pinned up and a skirt – controlled by concealed hoops – that floats, in contrast to Chihuahua's bustle. Moreover, her hands are kept down and towards her lap in a prayerful pose throughout the scene, unlike the Latina, whose first close-up presented her, bare-shouldered, with one arm above her head, her elbow leaning on a post. Chihuahua's other hand rested on her hip as she helped the gambler cheat Wyatt. If her brassy entrance heralded trouble, Clementine's entrance augers the opposite. Her movements – poised, undemonstrative and entirely Anglo-Victorian – have a calming effect on the whole town and awaken latent civility in the Earp brothers. As she enters the hotel, former would-be-stallion Virgil is ordering in a loud voice 'a stack of buckwheat cakes, plenty of molasses, a steak, blood rare, a couple of hunks of bacon, if ya got it and a big pot of…', but he trails off and becomes quiet, partly in reaction to her beauty and also in deference to a 'real lady' entering the room.[7]

Clementine's subdued and softly spoken entrance is a clarion cry for the coming of 'civilisation'. Earp's threat to send the gregarious Latina body farther away 'to the reservation' and therefore towards the disappearing frontier is here given more significance. With the arrival of Clem, one female form is replaced with another. Chihuahua's wild ways ultimately lead to her own destruction when she is shot during a gun battle brought about by her own sexual duplicity. Clementine has come west seeking a lost soul in the form of Doc, only to find that he had become wedded to the body of Chihuahua and, therefore, symbolically corrupted by all that her body represented. Doc too is now wild. In an effort to save her, he tries to regain his old self by operating on her bullet-wound, but she dies despite his efforts. Her body, therefore, becomes a locus of failure on two counts: firstly the initial inappropriate attraction that the Anglo-doctor succumbed to, and secondly his failure to 'cure' her. Like the seventeenth-century Ford's Annabella, her body is twice penetrated. While Annabella is stabbed by a knife, Chihuahua's sins are punished with a bullet. Both bodies then fall under a scalpel – and both are left with the burden of blame upon them. In contrast to the play, the townsfolk in *My Darling Clementine* take pity on Chihuahua's damaged body. Cluckish matron, Mrs Nelson (Jane Darwell), says she's going to take her home and care for her, if that is alright with the Marshal. Doc and Wyatt exchange a glance, before he says, indulgently, 'sure'. Only in this most reduced and infantilised state is Chihuahua accepted – with pity – into the Anglo mainstream. Her role in the lawlessness of the town seems forgotten; she couldn't help herself; 'tis pity she's a whore'.

Clementine's body is never transgressed and indeed her space is almost never entered. From the outset she is observed from a reverential distance and only in the highly ritualistic church dance sequence does any spatial intimacy occur between her and Wyatt. The most salient expression of how hers is the body of the goddess – the absolute foil to Chihuahua – comes in the final few shots, and in the immediate afterlife of Ford's film. As Ford shot it, Wyatt – before riding away – shakes Clementine's hand, thus showing a deference that test audiences in 1946 found unsatisfactory. The studio inserted a brief moment, shot on a sound stage, into the final edit where he kisses her on the cheek. She is still left looking after him – somewhat forlornly – as he disappears back into the wilderness. But Ford was furious at this addition of spatial intimacy, preferring to leave Clem's body immaculate.[8]

4. 'Tis Herself, She Is, To Be Sure

Contrast this treatment of the female body with the iconic scene in the cemetery from *The Quiet Man*. As Maureen O'Hara describes it in her own words, from her autobiography, '*Tis Herself: A Memoir*:

> The rain drenches us and his white shirt clings to his body and becomes translucent. In that moment we are truly together in each other's arms, and we kiss. It is sensual, passionate and more than any other scene we ever did together displays the on-screen eroticism of the Wayne and O'Hara combination.[9]

Such behaviour should bode ill for Mary Kate Danaher and her body's condition by the end of *The Quiet Man*, but yet it escapes censure. Officially, the Irish film censor demanded the removal of nudge-nudge references to Mary Kate and Sean's marital bed before a certificate could be issued. Two years later the kisses between Grace Kelly and James Stewart in *Rear Window* (Alfred Hitchcock, 1954) were all removed despite the fact that they are each an effort by Kelly's character to persuade the male lead to marry her. The passion, sensuality and 'on-screen eroticism' of Mary Kate's body were acceptable even to those most eager to make cuts. How does she get away with it?

As Kinny saw *Tis Pity, She's a Whore* as a dialectic between 'an older order of orthodox[y]' and an 'emergent individualism', so too is *The Quiet Man* a clash of locally received ritual and its subversion for personal desire. The above-mentioned kiss is even more transgressive when one considers that it seals Mary Kate's decision – made with very little persuasion from Sean – to ignore the established courtship progression: 'First there it'd be the threshing parties, then there'd be the walking out together…'

This kiss is not the first with which Mary Kate shows bodily independence. In the cottage, after she has pointed out with 'a wallop' that Sean has 'no leave to be kissing her', she steals a second kiss from him before departing. Much has been made of Mary Kate's fiscal individualism as a female character and the dowry, as her insistence on financial independence. She was not alone in the cinema of the time as a woman struggling for monetary security on her own terms, nor indeed, as a female character winning a partner of her own choosing. Jane Wyman encounters as much familial interference and societal orthodoxy in her path to Rock Hudson's arms in *All That Heaven Allows* (Douglas Sirk, 1955), and, predating *The Quiet Man* by some six years, *Mildred Pierce* (Michael Curtiz, 1946) saw Joan Crawford balancing the roles of *femme fatale* and domestic goddess in order to keep her daughter (Anne Blyth) in the kind of life to which she had grown accustomed.

Such 'Women's Pictures', contemporaneous with *The Quiet Man*, according to Kathleen Anne McHugh, 'distribute appropriate places and roles among women whose differences of race, class, and sexuality are visually and narratively related to their appearance'[10] and by so doing also define the women's 'suitability to star in the dramas of domestic life'. The '*other* women'

> ... are relegated to the public obscurity of service jobs or labor, while the white women must inhabit the familiarised and domesticated place of woman as wife, mother, sister, and Woman; her place secures everyone else's.[11]

Because Mary Kate is Irish, she traverses the gender and racial demarcations made here. She moves freely from being *other* to the norm, from the margins to the centre, from being white to being ethnic and still finishes up as the suitable and unquestioned star.

This freedom of movement is achieved by her close identification with the Irish landscape – seen in *The Quiet Man* for the first time in Technicolor – and with the elemental forces that fill it. In *My Darling Clementine*, the element of water was repeatedly used to cool down sexual fire. But, it is clear to anyone watching O'Hara's face pressed against Wayne's sodden chest, her fingers gripping the moist nylon of his sleeves, that the rain actually fans the flames.[12] If Ramirez Berg sees Chihuahua's weakness as being 'without a man she is left in the wind', for Mary Kate, being tempestuous is a strength, if not the elemental essence of herself. Indeed, it is the full force of a gale that provides the backdrop, and atmosphere, for Mary Kate's first kiss with Sean Thornton. This scene – in the cottage – is the perfect expression of her dual nature. One moment she is frightened by her own reflection, suggesting an infantilised, almost animalistic demi-woman, then when Sean says with mock surprise 'so, you can talk', her reply demonstrates the verbal dexterity the Irish are equally known for: 'I can, I will and I do'.[13] She has the last 'say' in this exchange, before returning to her natural setting, running with the elements through her own wild landscape. Even when she attempts to enter civilised discourse by 'putting her bonnet up', it is left fluttering in the breeze.

Mary Kate's movements are never tempered by the forces of respectability for long. When the official courtship begins, she is attempting to strike a Clementine-esque posture as she walks sedately with her fingers clasped at her waist. Beside her walks Sean in his bowler hat, under the eye of the chaperone. Soon enough, her wild side yet again appears; the tempest is released and Thornton receives another 'wallop'. The charade of Anglo decorum is joyously shattered when they break away from Michaeleen Oge Flynn's (Barry Fitzgerald) less than vigilant stewardship. It is Mary Kate who leads Sean farther and farther into the landscape. The fetters are thrown off; Sean discards his hat and Mary Kate removes her nylons before they run across a stream. However, she insists that he avert his gaze, showing that she might be the kind of girl who takes off her stockings, but she is not the kind that would have a man watch her remove them.

That which should be Mary Kate and Sean's successful entry into civilised discourse – their marriage ceremony – is not shown on screen. Tellingly, it is replaced by a shot of the couple in full nuptial regalia, looking terrified. A flash signals this as their wedding photo and the camera makes a quick backward track. Ford tended not to move his camera, believing that it disconcerted the audience. This stylistic deviation expresses the couple's discomfort in formal constraints.

The Quiet Man is not the first film by John Ford in which O'Hara had looked less than comfortable in a wedding dress. In *How Green Was My Valley* (John Ford, 1941), she played Angharad, the only daughter of a Welsh mining family.[14] For most of this film, she is very similar to Mary Kate; free-moving, independent and willing to speak out against the received narrow notions of propriety in her community. Like Mary Kate, she desires to be married and quite openly pursues the man she loves, Rev. Gruffydd, until he rejects her in favour of a life solely dedicated to his ministry. Her marriage that soon follows – to the pit owner's son – is treated as a defeat by means of the facial expression that O'Hara wears beneath her veil and also in the reaction of the valley to the event. The bells toll with solemnity rather than chime, and as she leaves the church, her father must ask the townsmen 'Is there to be no singing for my daughter's wedding?'

As soon as Angharad puts on her wedding dress, she is physically defeated in her movement and emotion. Later, after some years abroad with her husband, she returns as the starched lady of the house. This position has stripped her of bodily expression to such an extent that when her younger brother, Hew (Roddy McDowell), runs to embrace her, she stiffly keeps him at a distance. The film's title and structure make it an exercise in remembrance, set in a time before the slag from the pit covered the green hillsides. As all aspects of the valley are dominated by the coalmine and ravaged by it, so too is its personification: Angharad. The final sequence of the film, after the death of the family's benign patriarch, lapses back to shots of the characters when the valley was still green and the family was whole and alive. The immigrant brothers stand, reunited at sunset, in a field of high grass and Angharad is shown as she was before her marriage – hair down – waving and smiling.

Mary Kate also waves to us at the end of *The Quiet Man*. It is – in contrast to the wave of Angharad in *How Green Was My Valley* – a wave of triumph and precedes the infamous disposal of the stick. She then coquettishly leads Sean into the cottage, with its emerald green door, running ahead and looking back at him. While Ford had to lapse into fantasy-remembrance to give something approaching an upbeat ending to *How Green Was My Valley*, *The Quiet Man* expresses a lush future. Emerald green turns out to be actually 'more durable' as Mary Kate – unlike the slag-covered hillside – remains uncorrupted, free and earthy until the end. Most importantly, Mary Kate's body remains undefeated as represented by the discarded stick and more so by her unfettered and unapologetically sexy movements right up to the final shot. Given this ultimate victory by Mary Kate and the elements and landscape she represents,

'Of one so young, so rich in nature's store ... '
tisn't pity at all that she is a whore.

Endnotes

[1] I am greatly indebted to the students who, over five years, have taken part in the seminar *John Ford: Irish, American, Film-maker* at NUI Galway. Without their good, bad and seldom indifferent opinions on *The Quiet Man*, this chapter would not exist. Also, many thanks are due to Dr Adrian Frazier and Dáithí O'Connor, who helped me greatly in its completion.

[2] Arthur F. Kinny, *Renaissance Drama, an Anthology of Plays and Entertainments* (London: Blackwell, 2002), p. 833.

[3] John Ford, *Tis Pity She's a Whore*, Act V, sc. Vi, 164–68. *Kinny, Renaissance Drama, an Anthology of Plays and Entertainments*, p. 841.

[4] Lisa Hopkins, Sheffield Hallam University, 'Tis Pity That She's a Whore', *The Literary Encyclopedia*, 12 December 2002.

[5] Rita Hayward's eponymous character, in *Gilda* (Charles Vidor, 1946), performs a song, the lyrics of which ironically suggest that disasters – many elemental, such as the great fire of San Francisco – should all be blamed on women.

[6] Charles Ramirez Berg, *Latino Images in Film, Stereotypes, Subversion, Resistance* (Austin, Texas: University of Texas Press, 2002), pp. 70–71.

[7] This contrasts to how he earlier boasted about gustation. Here, Virgil perhaps disavows the deadly sin of gluttony in the presence of a decent, God-fearing woman.

[8] See Joseph McBride, *Searching for John Ford: A Life* (London: Faber & Faber, 2003), pp. 436–37.

[9] Maureen O'Hara (with John Nicoletti), *'Tis Herself: A Memoir* (New York: Simon & Schuster, 2004), p. 166.

[10] Kathleen Anne McHugh, *American Domesticity: From How-To Manual to Hollywood Melodrama* (Oxford: Oxford University Press, 1999), p. 146.

[11] Ibid. My italics.

[12] Interestingly, Ireland was soon to be denied the equally iconic image of Burt Lancaster and Deborah Kerr's watery kisses in *From Here to Eternity* (Fred Zinneman, 1953), when the entire scene was cut by the Irish censor. See Kevin Rockett, *Irish Film Censorship: A Cultural Journey from Silent Cinema to Internet Pornography* (Dublin: Four Courts Press, 2004), pp. 136–40.

[13] Novelist Molly McCloskey cites a Bord Fáilte study that found tourists' expectations of the 'Irish Experience' to include encountering 'ethnically specific verbal dexterity'. *The Irish Times*, 16 July 2005, 'Weekend', p. 7.

[14] I am here indebted to Richard C. Allen of the University of Sunderland, who suggested re-examining *How Green Was My Valley* in this context.

V

Final Reflections

17

The Quiet Man as Cult Movie

DES MACHALE

Let me begin by noting that my background is as a mathematician, a field of study much older and very different from film and one with seemingly inhuman standards of logic, precision and accuracy. And yet mathematicians love to analyse, judge and dissect, so I have been drawn into the world of film commentary and criticism as a result of my obsession with one movie – John Ford's *The Quiet Man*, shot on location in the West of Ireland in 1951. I was brought up about twenty-five miles from Cong which served as both Innisfree and Castletown and I was five years old at the time of the shooting. I vaguely remember that something very important and exciting was happening at the time as hundreds of local people descended on the locations every day to observe and indeed take part in the action. Individual encounters with John Wayne, Maureen O'Hara, Barry Fitzgerald, Victor McLaglen and John Ford himself became part of Mayo and Galway folklore. Alas, I was too young to really understand what momentous happenings were afoot and never saw any of the shooting myself, though I have since met many people who did.

I grew up in the pre-television era (just!) and ever since I would describe myself as a 'bacon and cabbage' filmgoer with a special love of films of Irish interest. The Sunday matinee (costing the ludicrous sum of four old pence) at the now sadly defunct County Cinema in Castlebar became one of the highlights of the week for me and a whole generation like me. The programme usually consisted of a black and white gangster movie or a cowboy film in glorious Technicolour and there was always a serial to make sure you returned the next week. Later, when I was a university student in Galway, a Saturday night visit to the Estoria or Savoy cinemas was a real treat as a break from serious study.

I first saw *The Quiet Man* in the summer of 1953 while on holiday with my family in Inniscrone, County Sligo, not far from W.B. Yeats's Isle of Innisfree. There was little else to do at night, so we all went to see the movie every night for nearly a week in a very primitive cinema – a 16mm print projected onto what was probably a large bed sheet. Even then, *The Quiet Man* had a hypnotic repetitive effect on people and as a little boy I remember falling in love with Maureen O'Hara and her gorgeous red hair. But the character that had the most impact on me was Jack MacGowran's Feeney and I particularly liked the way he licked his pencil stub before entering a name in Red Will Danaher's dreaded book. The 'hay fight' was another highlight re-enacted by myself and my three brothers many times in the years to follow. Indeed, a friend of mine, John Gibbons, who operated a mobile film service all over the West of Ireland, showing films like *The Quiet Man* to packed audiences in village halls often in aid of parish funds, told me that as part of his contract with the local parish priest, the hay fight scene had to be rewound and shown at least three times to satisfy local demand! My more conservative parents, however, while clearly enjoying the action and the scenery, were upset by the spectacle of a man dragging his wife across the countryside and felt that this reflected very badly on the mores of the West of Ireland where they had been brought up.

Having outlined my background, I want to now turn to a consideration of *The Quiet Man* as a cult movie. But, firstly, what is a cult movie? By any count there aren't many cult movies and there seems to be broad agreement as to which ones deserve the classification – *Gone with the Wind* (1939) undoubtedly is one, as is *Casablanca* (1942). *Citizen Kane* (1941) is another but, funnily enough, none of those three appears on my list of top one hundred movies that I like to watch again and again. The wonderful *Wicker Man* (1973), however, is a cult movie of

which I am fanatically fond; the same goes for *The Thirty Nine Steps* –
all three versions of which I watch endlessly (four if you count *North
by Northwest* (1959)). But whether one likes all these films or not, it is
difficult to argue against their merits or to deny their cult following.
There are films like *The Rocky Horror Picture Show* (1975) whose cult
status mystifies me, but I suppose this is a classic case of *de gustibus
non est disputandum*. Finally, there are individual cult movies given almost cult status by very small groups of people – my next-door
neighbour, Dermot Jones, sane in almost every other respect, has a fanatical devotion to the film *Shane* (1953) and hero-worships Alan Ladd.

I have on my bookshelves several books listing movies widely
held to be cult and *The Quiet Man* is listed in virtually all of them.[1]
Others frequently listed that appeal to me are *Duck Soup* (1933), *Bad
Day at Blackrock* (1955), *The Blues Brothers* (1980), *Get Carter* (1971),
Invasion of the Body Snatchers (1956), and *The Terminator* (1984).

What then are the commonly accepted criteria for a film to be
classed as a cult movie? They appear to include the following:

1. The film must have a large and persistent following of devoted
    fans.

2. These fans must be fanatical in their devotion to their chosen film,
    often exhibiting a profound tunnel vision with regard to all other
    movies which are regarded as unimportant and inferior.

3. Every actor, every bit player, every technician, every location and
    every camera angle is identified and remembered.

4. Every line of dialogue is memorized exactly and frequently re-
    peated aloud during showings in the cinema or on television and
    indeed in everyday conversation.

5. Film memorabilia are frequently acquired at astronomical prices.

6. Fan clubs are set up (now much easier using the internet) where
    cult followers can interact, ask questions, exchange information
    and deepen their devotion even further.

7. In extreme cases, books are written and conferences are organised
    to cater for the fans' never-ending hunger for further details.

8. Cult followers develop an intense and personal affection for their cult movie. This causes them to ignore or even to be totally unaware of any flaws or shortcomings it may have.

All these criteria apply to cult followers of *The Quiet Man* and I have coined the term 'Quiet Maniacs' to describe them. In my experience, they tend by and large to be menopausal males of Irish-American or Irish ancestry, many of whom have developed hot flushes for Maureen O'Hara. Wives and younger family members are in turn infected with the bug through endless viewings on television and location trips to Cong, Lettergesh and Ballyglunin. All involved genuinely come to believe that *The Quiet Man* is the greatest movie ever made to the exclusion of all others. Every detail of the movie has been analysed, every line of dialogue transcribed, every performer identified and every location and camera angle pinpointed. I myself have watched each of the 184,320 frames individually and seen many things Ford was probably unaware of, such as a fly landing on Maureen O'Hara's face and Michaeleen Oge Flynn accidentally spitting on the traitorous Feeney.

Original posters from *The Quiet Man* change hands for thousands of dollars on the internet and the Railway Hotel in Westport has posters in French, Polish, Swedish, Romanian and many other languages. Gerry Collins in Cong runs a 'White O'Morn' replica and a *Quiet Man* museum and there is another replica cottage in Maam Cross. There are *Quiet Man* theme pubs all over the world – in Rome, New York, Paris and many other cities. Cohan's Bar has been a Mecca for tourists for over fifty years. There are at least six books devoted to the movie, as well as guided tours of the locations and a thriving fan club which holds annual conferences.

In the light of all this activity, we must ask the obvious question: why? What is it about this particular movie that has captured the interest and affection of so many millions of people over the last fifty-five years and indeed the scorn of not a few critics and commentators at the same time? Cult movies are rarely without merit and I would like to list some of the reasons that I think are responsible for *The*

Quiet Man's cult status. Individually these reasons may not be conclusive but collectively I think they are overwhelming:

1. The Irish Factor

Maureen O'Hara is on record as saying that Ireland was the real star of *The Quiet Man*.[2] This was the first colour feature film made in Ireland and the first to show to the world (and Ireland itself!) the country's devastating greenness and beauty. Ford used every opportunity, thinly disguised as plot, to show fields, mountains, rivers, streams, trees, horses, sheep, and thatched cottages as they had never been seen before. This was the Irish emigrants' dream world – the Irish *Brigadoon*. In the United States alone there are said to be forty million people of Irish descent, and *The Quiet Man* quickly became their movie of choice, not just on Saint Patrick's Day, with corned beef, cabbage and green beer, but at Christmas and throughout the year. This was the dream world of every Irish-American's imagination seen through the eyes of a returned emigrant; this was really an image of home. At a deeper level, *The Quiet Man* represented a return to the womb (as represented by Sean Thornton's sleeping bag) for which every emigrant's descendant secretly yearned, where safety from the cares of industrial and strife-ridden America could be found.

2. The Wayne Factor

Nowadays, we tend to forget that 'Duke' Wayne had strong Irish ancestry on both sides – Morrisons from the Glens of Antrim on his father's side and Browns from County Cork on his mother's side. Some scoff at Wayne as an actor – arguing that he played just one part and that was always himself. Yet Wayne was the highest grossing star and most popular film actor in the 1940s, the 1950s and even into the 1960s, a feat equalled only by Clint Eastwood for three decades in recent times. Wayne had a personal cult following even before he made *The Quiet Man* and won a belated Oscar for his role in *True Grit* (1969).

3. The O'Hara Factor

Maureen O'Hara is a woman of immense beauty, whose red hair was just made for the Technicolor *Quiet Man*. Early on, she achieved cult status in Ireland as the local girl who made good and never lost her Irish accent. The intense chemistry between O'Hara and Wayne, first seen in *Rio Grande*, continued right down to the slapstick *McLintock!* and reached its peak in *The Quiet Man*. Maureen O'Hara, or Maureen Fitzsimons-Blair as she prefers to be known nowadays, still commands enormous affection internationally. Sadly, she has never even been nominated for an Academy Award, despite many worthy performances.

4. The Supporting Cast

The Quiet Man's supporting cast included Barry Fitzgerald and Victor McLaglen, Oscar winners, scene stealers and character actors of immense experience and versatility. Many of the other players were members of the Ford stock company – Shields, MacGowran, Natwick, McClory, Bond and Fitzsimons.

5. Music

Vic Young, nominated nineteen times for an Oscar, never achieved the award in his lifetime, but ironically was awarded a postumous statuette. His orchestration of the Irish music chosen by Ford was masterly – 'The Rakes of Mallow', 'The Kerry Dances', 'Moore's Melodies' and 'Galway Bay' – and there are solid grounds for classifying *The Quiet Man* as an Irish musical. But Young's crowning glory was his arrangement of Richard Farrelly's *Isle of Innisfree* inspired by the poem by W.B. Yeats. This sublimely beautiful melody dominates the movie and is a major factor in its cult status.

6. The Nugent Factor

The screenplay of *The Quiet Man* was the culmination of the work of several people, from the original story of Maurice Walsh, through Richard Llewellyn and Laurence Stallings, to the final version by Frank Nugent, with the addition of humour and local knowledge from Ford himself. This gave the film a very wide international appeal – and not just in the English-speaking world. There are versions in French, German, Italian, Spanish and several other languages. Basing the screenplay on a version of *The Taming of the Shrew* theme was an excellent basis for international cult status.

7. Local Enthusiasm

Ford raided Dublin's Abbey Theatre for 'Irish Players' to lend colour and authenticity to the production and these actors were all highly experienced and knew what was expected of them. But he also plucked from obscurity local men such as Paddy O'Donnell (the railway porter) and Kevin Lawless (the train fireman) because he liked how they looked in reality – of course, he firmly believed that all the Irish are natural actors. The hundreds of willing local extras also blended seamlessly into the scenarios.

8. The Visual Impact

Winton Hoch and Archie Stout deservedly won the Oscar for best colour cinematography for their work on *The Quiet Man*. The colour and scenery are little short of stunning, and Ford had wisely entrusted the choice of locations to Lord Killanin and Charles Fitzsimons. Never has green been seen to better advantage and part of *The Quiet Man's* cult attraction is that many, many people from all over the world have come to Ireland over the last fifty years just to see if it is as green as depicted on the screen. They are rarely disappointed.

9. The Ford Factor

Finally, and most importantly, there is the matter of the world's greatest movie director returning to the land of his ancestors to pay tribute to his Irish heritage. Towards the end of his glittering career, Ford achieved his lifelong ambition of paying homage to his ancestral country using all the cinematic skills that had brought him four Academy Awards as best director (plus two for documentaries). His direction of the scenic sequences and the close-up compositions are extraordinary.

I believe that it is Ford's coordination and overall fatherly control of all the factors I have mentioned that constitute the basis of *The Quiet Man* as a cult movie. And yet there is an additional magic factor there – a gestalt principle ensuring that the movie is much more than the sum of its component parts. Innisfree is perhaps fairyland, a dream world in the West of Ireland where impossible things happen and the cult followers are happy to re-enact that dream *ad infinitum*.

Like all good cult followers we will gloss over the imperfections of *The Quiet Man* – some poor lighting in the studio scenes, several breaks in the continuity of the storyline, heavy-handed humour mostly involving water-carriers, and inappropriate and even incestuous casting. Like little blemishes on the faces of those we love, they serve only to increase our affection.

Endnotes

[1] For example, Karl French and Philip French, *Cult Movies* (London: Pavilion 1999) and Danny Peary, *Cult Movies* (New York: Gramarcy Books, 1981).

[2] Maureen O'Hara, *'Tis Herself: A Memoir* (New York and London: Simon & Schuster Ltd, 2005), p. 157.

18

The Quiet Man: Myth, Commodity and Fetish

ROD STONEMAN

'When something is popular it is often for the wrong reasons.'
– Jean-Luc Godard

1. Rus in Urbe (The Country in the Town)

The images and sequences of John Ford's 1952 film have become iconic, frozen, literally anachronistic. For a film of that epoch its continued popularity in different domains is unusual and significant and it is a timely to return to the film and its reception in order to make some sense of the phenomena that surround it. The essays in this volume indicate that academic fascination is undiminished. As a result of the specific gratifications possible in association with the film, it has also perpetuated a very non-academic cult following. Abroad, particularly among the Irish-American diaspora, it continues to draw enthusiastic interest. A fundamental feature in the intensity of the pleasure it generates in all these domains seems to stem from the distance of the film and its system of imaginary referents to contemporary representation or experience.

The meanings of this film may often be projections, in the psycho-analytical sense of that word; interpretations or certainly associated connotations that are heavily determined by the viewer, rather than the text. Visual art may present an image which combines many

different meanings at once and we are familiar, through psycho-
analysis, with things not meaning what they ostensibly say they
mean as their implications are displaced and relocated through the
workings of the unconscious. It is precisely because images of a fan-
tasised Irish rural culture come from so far away, geographically and
temporally, that they have such potency for others in contemporary
contexts. Modern fascinations manufacture an imaginary poetic place
that has been expelled from the centre and relocated at the periphery
– it can be seen as one of the displacements which, as Roland Barthes
wrote, 'constitute the mythic fabric of a mass-consumption society'.[1]
The specific perspective of expatriation is determined by a desire to
confirm and fix projected images of historical fantasy and this is con-
sonant with current ideological frameworks that reset the world as
centred, static.[2] Ideas of a more dynamic concept of experience[3] are
set aside in the remoteness of the rural which allows for the reconstruction of the imaginary community of the past, in a space which is
resistant to notions of change.

The search for an idyll, a happy and unencumbered innocence,
that can be contemplated in the distance, inhabits those permeable
categories of documentary as well as fiction. While working in a British television station, Channel 4, in the 1980s and early 1990s, I no-
ticed the disproportionate succession of careful, crafted documentaries about remote islands. The section I worked in, the Independent
Film and Video Department, contributed some of them;[4] there were
programmes about the Shetland Islands, Barra, Iona and also the
Isles of Scilly. Small islands,[5] the opposite of lakes, are normally only
able to provide tenuous, small-scale rural inhabitation at this point in
history, and their distant green landscapes seem intensified by the
surrounding sea.

The persistence and popularity of these sets of imagery can be interpreted in terms of metropolitan desires for the Other.[6] At a point
when the majority of the human population has come to live in cities,[7] perhaps it is not strange for urban dwellers to develop a thirst
for representations of its opposite, the rural. After all, the 'exotic' is
not only characterised by the clichéd characteristics of sand and palm

trees found on the beaches of Polynesia or the desert oasis, but by its distance from everyday reality.[8]

From books like Hemingway's *The Old Man and the Sea*[9] to Flaherty's film *Man of Aran* (1934), the frame of a remote location is crucial for the scale of human drama. The enactment of resonant, timeless human performance by 'noble savages' takes place within a necessarily dislocated backdrop; these narratives would be small and soapy in a city café.[10] In this case a mythic rural setting enables the familiar story-telling structure: exposition – jeopardy – redemption, to deliver the projection of sexual power and pleasure as its resolution.

The perceived light and colour of the countryside is defined by its contrast with the darkness and drabness of the city, which is reiterated in the everyday as we move through cityscapes which are themselves permeated with the images of cities. An initial realisation of this was apparent in the first years of twentieth century, in the early modernist disconcertion with the metropolis:

> Unreal city,
> Under the brown fog of a winter dawn,
> A crowd flowed over London Bridge, so many,
> I had not thought death had undone so many.[11]

The non-individuated masses in T.S. Eliot's 1922 'The Waste Land' prefigure the flow of proletarians who trudge through Fritz Lang's *Metropolis* (Germany, 1926). It is from the context of the urban that metropolitan desire constructs an image of the tranquil idyll encountered in representation, to be inhabited briefly, or passed through as tourism.

A precondition of its repositioning and usage – indeed the very projections that sustain its pleasures – are possible because the film is far enough from engagement with the present. In an epoch where the countryside is internationally being transformed into a recreational amenity, *The Quiet Man* offers a signifying ensemble which offers the rural idyll and a recently constructed version of its values (an Irish variation thereof) providing that timeless moment that offers a refuge from the continuous calamity of our epoch.[12]

2. Et in Arcadia Ego (I, too, am in the Country)

While I was working in Bord Scannán na hÉireann/the Irish Film Board from 1993 to 2003, the shadowy image of *The Quiet Man* fell across the exponentially increased range of production enabled in that decade. The project of new Irish filmmaking was underwritten by the compelling logic of direct and separate speech, indigenous autonomy in cinema, one could say 'ourselves alone'.[13] There are often subtle cultural and political distinctions between what is seen and said from 'inside' vis-à-vis what can be seen or represented from 'outside' an imagined community. Those differences are apparent in Irish self-images made in situ and those from the diaspora, particularly in the US. A basis of all anti-colonial movements starts from the construction of self-identified subjects. This is also an important realisation in post-1968 social politics motivating 'communities of interest' from sexual politics to racial groupings, exemplified in a slogan like 'Nothing about us without us'. The whole notion of national film agencies is predicated on speech by, with, or from an identified community in a unified place.[14] However, the identification of place and subjects who might speak directly from that place does not necessarily imply any preconception limiting or directing what could or should be said.

Like other national cinemas in Europe, in Ireland there has been a consistent conscious attempt to promote identifiably authorial visions. A policy of radical pluralism – announced in the initial programmatic statements of the new film agency[15] – was the vehicle for the maintenance of adequate diversity within that identification. The apparently unsourced quotation in the annual report, 'Let a thousand flowers bloom and a thousand schools of thought contend',[16] was a clear proposition for the newly reconstituted Film Board's approach. It also drew upon a description of heterogeneity from other, more classical texts: 'There should be a very wide diversity of styles and of subjects: the rural and urban, the contemporary and the ancient, the high brow and the low brow, the "tragical-comical-historical-pastoral, scene individable or poem unlimited" – in Polonius's words from Shakespeare's *Hamlet*'. The new agency aimed to maximise the range produced within the newly funded possibilities of Irish Cinema: 'We should see films from the traditional communities of agrarian Ireland to the Cork or Belfast working class, the different generations, cultures and classes that make up this island...'[17]

Whether through a quotation from Shakespeare or a horticultural dictum from a Chinese communist, the intertexts pointed towards a mobilisation of heterogeneous forms of filmmaking to articulate the modern and plural identities available in modern-day Ireland. Many of these may combine elements of gender / sexuality / youth cultures which can properly be called post-national or semi-national. Although it had its provenance in an analysis of nationalism, Benedict Anderson's conception of 'imagined communities' (of interest)[18] extends towards complex identity formation in the modern era. All individuals inhabit overlapping categories of identity which traverse and intersect with their perceptions, presentations and self-realisations. A national film agency needs to recognise the hybridity that is inevitably at work in contemporary society and support it.

This conception of the development of Irish national/cultural identity cuts across the operation of a representational system which is pleased to utilise *The Quiet Man* to efface or even obliterate the series of other more complex interactions or co-ordinates. The strategy of radical pluralism is antithetical to this – if one begins to understand culture as the site of a complex combination of materialisations, there can be no exclusive centre, no conception of a 'real' Ireland from which things emanate.

From the start in 1993 the reconstituted Film Board set itself against 'paddy whackery', the inauthenticity[19] of the exaggerated and frozen image of historical, rural Ireland, and largely it avoided supporting films which perpetuated the continued circulation of a mythologised version of Irish society. *The Quiet Man* continues to be the key reference for modern replications of the myth; writing the introduction to a volume celebrating 10 years of the second Film Board in 2003, I proposed that there is an inverse connection between new Irish cinema and 'that wider range of films from *The Quiet Man* (1952) and *Ryan's Daughter* (1970) to *Waking Ned Devine* (1998) that are sometimes perceived as Irish, although the telltale signs of paddy-wackery may be taken as clear evidence to the contrary'.[20]

There was immediate remonstration from Hilton Edwards when Ford's film was first released in 1953: 'I cannot for the life of me see that it has any relation to the Ireland I or anyone else can have seen or known'.[21] This characteristic overstatement denies the basis on which myth takes certain elements, negotiates and transforms them; the relationship is not entirely unrelated or arbitrary, but selective. Over fifty years later the same anachronistic myths are still perpetuated in relatively recent films such as *Waking Ned Devine* (Kirk Jones, 1998) or *The Boys from County Clare* (John Irvin, 2003). A commercially successful medium budget film, *Waking Ned Devine* was conceived as a non-specific rural tale originally set in Cornwall in the south-west of England. It was rewritten for Ireland at the last moment and shot on the Isle of Man, for tax purposes.[22]

Of course these obsolescent narratives are not the result of some carefully and consciously planned cultural conspiracy, rather a commercial opportunity offered by the persistence of outdated assumptions. The bad faith involved is not disputed by dominant opinion as there are still economic motives to market Ireland through the 'myth and stereotype (and the tourist brand image) which conjures up an unchanging land where time stands still'.[23] When BSÉ fell under a redesignated and amalgamated government department, Arts, Sport and Tourism, we seized upon the significant proportion of American tourists who claimed that the image of Ireland on film was a leading motive for visiting Ireland.[24] We built a case opportunistically for increasing government support for BSÉ whilst suspecting that the 'film' that influenced American tourists and provided us with such useful statistics was a certain single feature made in 1952 by John Ford and not any combination of contemporary productions.

Generally the critical mass of the Board's funding went towards projects that engaged with modernity and change, tending towards forms of film that connected with the experience of modern-day Ireland. This took forms mostly situated outside of current representation of the rural; but not exclusively – *Korea* (Cathal Black, 1995), *Dancing at Lughnasa* (Pat O'Connor, 1998) and *Country* (Kevin Liddy, 2000) returned to the recent history of the rural origins of the modern.[25] From this viewpoint, versions of paddywackery were inevitably rejected with disdain as distorted and anachronistic manifestations of the past, intrusive and lacking integrity.

An exponential increase in Irish filmmaking developed in and through that fast-moving moment of Ireland's modernisation and economic transformation. Its provenance is inevitably linked to the dynamic of social change. Even if we do not wish to talk of simple economic determination, we need to understand the interactions of cultural texts and historical material transformations. The specific factors that have played through the seismic changes in the island of Ireland include:

- The strength of the historical in contemporary culture (and therefore contestations and revisionist versions of that history).

- A recent colonial experience and therefore pervasive post-colonial negotiation and adjustment.

- The relationship with the Irish diaspora.

- The continued and proximate presence of a recent rural cultural context.

- The speed of transformation.

- The scale of Ireland as a nation state.

These impinge on the production of new films and the continued circulation and interpretation of a text like *The Quiet Man*.

A side-effect of the national conflict was a strengthening of the role of the Catholic church in Northern Ireland (in Poland in the 1980s, Solidarity's struggle with the communist government arguably also strengthened the church as a hub of resistance). *The Quiet Man* includes murmurs of the Republican sentiments, apparent in Michaeleen Oge's oxymoronic desire to 'join me comrades and talk a little treason'. But apparently more liberal and modern ideologies project the non-sectarian moment in the film when the mainly Catholic community rallies round to defend the retention of the kindly Church of Ireland vicar. This is an enhanced and necessarily benign retrospection from the ecumenical present; although it was apparently based on a nineteenth century incident that Ford may have read about.[26]

The film constitutes a permeable space for such liminal historical references from other times and places. This is how it functions in Stephen Spielberg's romantic movement through the intertextual quotation of the film in *ET The Extra-Terrestrial* (USA, 1982) – a kiss is transmitted (via an alien route) from Ford's film to a schoolroom in the United States.

3. Videri Quam Esse (To Seem Rather Than to Be)

Although many aspects of the provenance of our pleasures are indefinable, it seems that the specific combination of a gender dynamic in the frame of a mythic rural past perpetuates the continuing fascination and longevity of this particular film. Desire is realised at the far end of a pleasurable narrative process: a love story with a feisty red-haired woman leads to contestation between men, then resolution and redemption. Aspects of its form, its narrative construction, its magnificent saturated colour pictorial appearance and Vic Young's powerful music also strengthen these elements to allow *The Quiet Man* to stand out from the ensemble of available films. For a section of its audience these elements also lead to the film's persistence and allow it to become the subject of a cult fascination.[27] The devotees are only a small proportion of the film's viewers, but their activities constitute a remarkable and revealing phenomenon all the same.

The seemingly diverse objects of cult interests share the same relationship: the constitution of an aim or a domain of obsessive behaviour to ensure the possession and control of knowledge within it. There is fascination and immersion, passion and mania, a proliferation of ancillary activity. Obsession and possession are twinned because the forms of pleasure are based on excessive detail and repetition: an absorption with surface rather than depth, recording information rather than analysing it. It enacts a celebratory enthralment born of proximity rather than critical distance. Inside the cult there are extreme examples of multiple viewings, including those who talk of having viewed *The Quiet Man* over one hundred times. Fetishistic relations often manifest displacement and containment, distance and denial and this connects the investment in excess by self-described 'quiet maniacs' with those who take a 'sensible' interest in the film more widely.[28] As Roland

Barthes wrote about photography, 'It allows me to accede to an infra-knowledge; it supplies me with a collection of partial objects and can flatter a certain fetishism of mine: for this "me" which likes this knowledge, which nourishes a kind of amorous preference for it.'[29]

Cult status is not often linked to the commercial success of a film, although *The Sound of Music* (Robert Wise, USA, 1965) indicates it can be. John Huston's 1954 *Beat the Devil* was initially a box office failure, although subsequently and gradually it accumulated a degree of cult success. A fan club of Cambridge University students formed a special society to organise annual screenings. It was re-released in 1967 specifically for niche audiences; 'only phonies like it' Bogart quipped. '*Beat the Devil* was ahead of its time, its off-the-wall humour left viewers bewildered and confused. A few critics hailed it as a little masterpiece – they were all European' was Huston's own laconic verdict.[30]

Other examples of cult movies, such as *The Rocky Horror Picture Show* (Jim Sharman, USA, 1975) or *Withnail and I* (Bruce Robinson, England, 1987), *El Topo* (Alejandro Jodorowsky, Mexico, 1971) or *Pink Flamingos* (John Waters, USA, 1972), have generated cult followings which all exhibit something of the same patterns of image and information ownership. It is difficult to determine the factors that predispose any particular film to particular audience responses when one considers such diversity; cult status is not linked to a particular configuration within a movie, but more to the potential for a specific relationship with a section of the audience. The significations of style and distance are important; it is impossible to think of cult attention within the codes of realism and films made from a proximate reality to the spectator. The fascination with a single film or television series[31] (and cultists rarely spread their attentions to several films) paradoxically involves both an exaggerated respect for the film and an enhanced passivity.

Cult attention often involves discovering the ignored and celebrating the obscure. A highly devoted, but relatively small group of fans celebrate a perverse counter taste – 'so bad it's good'. The relation with a specific film takes place in a protected space because it is enclosed and containable. Sometimes, as in the case of *The Rocky Horror Picture*

Show, it can be associated with camp[32] and sometimes a participatory dimension can develop, such as the mimetic costume enactment with *Rocky Horror*, sing-a-long with the reissued *The Sound of Music*, and the organised groups meeting and drinking in carefully orchestrated synchrony during screenings of *Withnail and I*. Like other forms of cinephilia, socially cultist pleasure also confirms the individual in the differentiated and exclusive group.

The subterranean world of film cults is relevant to understanding some of the dimensions of other more 'legitimate' appreciations. It raises questions about the disingenuous motives and hidden determinations that lead academics to embark on intensive analysis about particular texts.[33] Perhaps these may manifest a milder version of the same cultist preoccupations and motives. Even if there is a semblance of clinical distance in a well-judged turn of footnoted discourse, the way in which the over-determinations behind the selective fascinations of the academy with specific texts are effaced indicates that they are analogous to other types of viewers. The question of the 'quality' of the disputed text can be seen as a displacement which conceals and blocks understanding of the particular forms of activity around the film. The deployment of an old paradigm, rationality – modernity – progress, is a continuing imperative in the project to bring analytical reason to the domain of the non-rational, although that starting point should also acknowledge its own limitations and contradictions.

Of course cinema is a very subsidiary element in a complex image system which works to stabilise subjectivities and social formations, but it is part of the domain of the dominant illusions, falsities and selectivities that sustains our culture and our society. We live within complex interacting, circular systems which are international in scope and reach.

We should endeavour to introduce greater degrees of argumentation and analysis to the various gratifications of this text. How does a film circulate and make meaning? How does this film relate to the contemporary cultural politics of Ireland and to new film production? How does the origin of films affect their authenticity and integrity? How is 'about' linked to 'from' or 'by'? This debate about national cinemas and the differences of indigenous filmmaking is essential to an understanding of the ways in which direct speech from within a culture can offer some resistance to the incursions of global monoculture.

These incisions may break open some of the elements of *The Quiet Man*'s significations and functions, but that does not necessarily undermine or diminish those pleasures of the text. *Au contraire...*

Endnotes

[1] Roland Barthes, 'Mythology Today', *The Rustle of Language* (Berkeley, Calif: University of California Press, 1989), p. 67.

[2] Francis Fukuyama, in *The End of History and the Last Man* (London: Penguin Books, 1992) which expands on his 1989 essay 'The End of History', tries to arrest historical process as he expresses himself in triumphalist form; but recurrent financial crises indicate that applying the notion of stasis to late capitalism is premature.

[3] Thinkers as diverse as Hegel or Heraclitus construct a more dynamic model for interaction and change, indicating the way in which the disjunctures of understanding and experience may have progressive potential.

[4] *Shepherds of Berneray* (Jack Shea, 1981); *The Last Post Run* (Caroline Tisdall, 1984); *The Work They Say is Mine* (Rosie Gibson, 1986).

[5] The Irish word 'Innisfree' means island of heather and contains the English word for open or emancipated.

[6] As Sean Ryder suggests in his contribution to this volume, it is an encounter with an alien 'other' while remaining safely at home.

[7] The level of the world's urbanisation depends on the definition used for urban centres, but has been calculated at 47 per cent in 2000 and 55 per cent now (David Satterthwaite, 'Will Most People Live in Cities?' *British Medical Journal*, 321 (November 2000): 1143–45), although urbanisation in Ireland remains behind the rest of Europe.

[8] *Saturday Night and Sunday Morning* (Karel Reisz, 1960), known for its grey Midlands realism in English terms, apparently found a cult of fascinated followers on an American mid-western university summer school in the 1990s.

[9] Ernest Hemingway, *The Old Man and the Sea* (New York: Charles Scribner's Sons, 1952).

[10] Although the idea of remoteness seems to figure in popular comedies – *Father Ted* on Craggy Island and *Fawlty Towers* from Torquay – it doesn't seem to have the same function in that genre.

[11] T.S. Eliot, 'The Waste Land', I: Burial of the Dead, *Selected Poems* (London: Faber and Faber, 1969), p. 53, lines 60–64.

[12] 'The "state of emergency" in which we live is not the exception but the rule.' Walter Benjamin, 'Theses on the Philosophy of History VIII', *Illuminations* ed. Hannah Arendt (London: Fontana, 1973), p. 259.

[13] *Ourselves Alone?* (Donald Taylor Black, 1995), a documentary made with Kevin Rockett about new Irish cinema, its title punning on the Republican slogan and political party while adding a question mark.

[14] The crucial criterion for funding at Bord Scannán na hÉireann/the Irish Film Board was 'normally resident in Ireland', thus embracing a multi-cultural version of Irish society.

[15] When I arrived at Bord Scannán na hÉireann/the Irish Film Board in 1993 from the formative experience of Channel 4 in the early 1980s, it seemed that the commitment to dynamic diversity, a conscious form of radical pluralism, was also appropriate as the underlying approach to funding for a national film agency as for a new television station.

[16] In fact, my mis-memory of the original quotation and a desire for even greater diversity served to have multiplied Mao Tse Tung's original numbers by ten.

[17] *Review/Athbhreithniu* (Galway: Irish Film Board, 1993), p. 3.

[18] Benedict Anderson, *Imagined Communities* (London: Verso, 1991).

[19] Perhaps inauthenticity is better understood as a lack of integrity, which avoids a notion of the essential or original constituting the authentic.

[20] Rod Stoneman, 'Icons of the Imagination', *Ten Years After*, ed. Kevin Rockett (Galway: Irish Film Board, 2003), p. vii.

[21] James MacKillop, 'The Quiet Man Speaks', *Contemporary Irish Cinema* (New York: Syracuse University Press, 1999), p. 169.

[22] Despite the revisionist appreciation outlined by Michael Gillespie in this volume!

[23] R.F. Foster, *Luck and the Irish: A Brief History of Change 1970–2000* (London: Allen Lane, 2007), p. 3.

[24] Fáilte Ireland indicates that 12 per cent of American and 14 per cent of EU visitors to Ireland cite 'Films/Movies' as an important source of information for choosing to holiday in Ireland (The Irish Film Board Production Catalogue 2005 / 2006, p. 37). According to Tourism Ireland, 10 per cent of all tourists visiting Ireland for the first time do so as a result of seeing 'Ireland' on screen, 'Creating a Sustainable Irish Film and Television Sector' A Review of Section 481 film relief, IFB Submission to Indecon, 29 June 2007.

[25] More recently (and since I left the Film Board) a perceptive exploration of the present-day rural has been undertaken by Lenny Abrahamson and Mark O'Halloran in *Garage* (2007).

[26] The incident is outlined by Des MacHale in 'The Ecumenical Priest', Chapter 9, *A Quiet Man Miscellany* (Cork: Cork University Press, 2009).

[27] In Des MacHale's contribution to this volume, the cult phenomena is sketched by a participant, who is also a meticulous scholar of the film (and of mathematics).

[28] 'I thought of fetishism as a psychological and social structure that disavowed knowledge in favour of belief.' Laura Mulvey, 'Preface', *Fetishism and Curiosity* (London: BFI, 1996), p. xi.

[29] Roland Barthes, *Camera Lucida* (New York: Hill and Wang, 1981), p. 30.

[30] John Huston, *An Open Book* (London: Macmillan, 1981), p. 248.

[31] Television series like *Star Trek* (USA, 1966–89) or *The Prisoner* (UK, 1968–69) also exemplify this.

[32] 'The ultimate camp statement: it's good because it's awful.' Susan Sontag, 'Notes on Camp', *Against Interpretation* (New York: Picador, 1966).

[33] This reached a high point with Roland Barthes' *S/Z*, *Cahiers du cinéma* on John Ford's *Young Mr Lincoln* (USA, 1939), *Screen* 13, 3 and Stephen Heath on Welles' *Touch of Evil* (USA, 1958), 'Film and System: Terms of Analysis', *Screen* 16, 1.

Index